PEACE & CONFLICT SERIES

RON MILAM, SERIES EDITOR

ALSO IN THIS SERIES:

Admirals Under Fire: The U.S. Navy and the Vietnam War, by Edward J. Marolda

The Air War in Vietnam, by Michael E. Weaver

Capturing Skunk Alpha: A Barrio Sailor's Journey in Vietnam, by Raúl Herrera

Charging a Tyrant: The Arraignment of Saddam Hussein, by Greg Slavonic

Conscientious Objectors at War: The Vietnam War's Forgotten Medics, by Gary Kulik

Crooked Bamboo: A Memoir from Inside the Diem Regime, by Nguyen Thai; edited by Justin Simundson

Girls Don't: A Woman's War in Vietnam, by Inette Miller

Memorial Days: Việt Nam Stories, 1973–2022,

by Wayne Karlin

Rain in Our Hearts: Alpha Company in the Vietnam War, by James Allen Logue and Gary D. Ford

The White Pebble: Madame Nhu's Memoirs, by Trần Lệ Xuân; edited by Tuong Vu

Keyes Beech on Iwo Jima, February 1945. Courtesy of National Photo Archives, no. 127-N-110066.

THE BEAUTIFUL SIMPLICITY OF WAR

A REPORTER'S JOURNEY FROM IWO JIMA TO VIETNAM

JONATHAN WEBB

TEXAS TECH UNIVERSITY PRESS

This book is typeset in Adobe Caslon Pro. The paper used in this book meets the minimum requirements of ANSI/NISO Z39.48-1992 (R1997). ♾

Every attempt has been made to trace and acknowledge the owners of photographs that appear in this book. Any information that would help to rectify oversights would be appreciated.

Designed by Hannah Gaskamp
Cover design by Hannah Gaskamp

Library of Congress Cataloging-in-Publication Data

Names: Webb, Jonathan, author. Title: The Beautiful Simplicity of War: A Reporter's Journey from Iwo Jima to Vietnam / Jonathan Webb.
Description: Lubbock, Texas: Texas Tech University Press, [2026] | Series: Peace and Conflict | Includes bibliographical references and index. | Summary: "Traces the life of Pulitzer Prize–winning correspondent Keyes Beech, a Tennessee farm boy who became one of the most influential war reporters in US history"—Provided by publisher.
Identifiers: LCCN 2026026877 (print) | LCCN 2026026878 (ebook) | ISBN 978-1-68283-319-3 paperback | ISBN 978-1-68283-320-9 ebook
Subjects: LCSH: Beech, W. Keyes | War correspondents—United States | Journalists—United States | Journalism—United States—History—20th century | LCGFT: Biographies
Classification: LCC PN4874.B3637 W43 2026 (print) | LCC PN4874.B3637 (ebook)
LC record available at https://lccn.loc.gov/2026026877
LC ebook record available at https://lccn.loc.gov/2026026878

Texas Tech University Press
Box 41037
Lubbock, Texas 79409-1037 USA
800.832.4042
ttup@ttu.edu
www.ttupress.org

For Vivian, who knows all about dead Australian journalists

Was it worth it? Of course not. But it never occurred to us then that it wasn't. It was a different America and we were different Americans. Life was simple and there were no self-doubts. We were good and clean and brave. And of course it was a "just war."

—KEYES BEECH REFLECTING ON IWO JIMA IN FEBRUARY 1970

Contents

Illustrations

Acknowledgments

My thanks to Walter and Barnaby Beech for their generosity in sharing their memories of their father and their family photographs.

I depended for much of the material in this book on the invaluable Newspapers.com. However, neither the *Chicago Daily News* nor the *St. Petersburg Evening Independent* had been digitized at the time of writing. For these papers I accessed the microfilm records located at the main branch of the Chicago Public Library and the St. Petersburg Public Library. I am deeply grateful to these institutions, both of which appeared to be operating under financial duress, despite which the librarians—and notably the security staff in Chicago—showed consideration for a lone researcher. The same goes for staff at the Syracuse University Archives and, in spades, for the extraordinarily knowledgeable staff at the National Archives and Records Administration (NARA), who led me to the typescript pages of Beech's dispatches from Tarawa and Iwo Jima and produced original negatives of Beech from the photo archives.

I have enjoyed working with Travis Snyder and the people at Texas Tech University Press. I am similarly grateful to the anonymous reviewers of the draft manuscript, whose comments helped make the book better. Its remaining imperfections, of course, are down to me.

Preface

A REPORTER AT WAR

Keyes Beech was nine when he shot his brother.

In other circumstances the incident would have marked him out for a life of delinquency and crime. But Keyes was born before World War I in Tennessee, in the town that gave birth to the Ku Klux Klan, at a time when roads were tracks and horses not cars were the chief form of transport. This was a rough but close-knit community in which the ability to take care of yourself was not just expected but required. Even a boy was sometimes sent out to shoot dinner. It's not surprising, then, that Keyes, the youngest son of a sharecropping farmer, grew up lean, hard, and sinewy, with an independent cast of mind. Being the youngest, with a much bigger brother, may have sharpened his competitiveness. According to family legend, the older brother, William Walter, cut the trimming from a bugle the younger boy was given one Christmas, precipitating a fight that was broken when Walter pushed Keyes to the floor and stepped outside. Keyes, unwilling to see his brother's aggression go unpunished, fetched his .22 caliber rifle. From the open door, his shoulder against the doorframe, he first aimed at Walter's back, reconsidered, smiled slightly, and shot him in the buttocks.

Their mother died when Keyes was still young and the family decamped to Florida, but Tennessee had marked him. He would always be something of a country boy and fiercely self-reliant. He dropped out of school when he was sixteen to take a job as a copyboy with a St. Petersburg newspaper. His rise through the ranks there was steady: from the sports and society pages to the city desk and the state capital. From there, now married and still ambitious, he took a more senior job in Akron, Ohio, where he became known for his sharp, funny feature articles. And then war changed the course of his life. Over the years that followed, he was a Marine correspondent who saw the flag raised on Iwo Jima, the scourge of MacArthur's rule in postwar Japan, and one of the toughest reporters to cover the nearly catastrophic first year of the war in Korea. He was in China to witness the collapse of the Nationalists and in Indochina to describe the end of French colonial rule at Dien Bien Phu. The dispatches he wrote for the Chicago Daily News Foreign Service were picked up by some seventy newspapers across the United States. He was a Pulitzer Prize winner and a Harvard University Nieman Fellow. *Newsweek* said he epitomized Hollywood's conception of a foreign correspondent—rough-hewn, hard-living, sardonic, and smart. He was an indefatigable traveler, a fearless reporter, and a commentator whose views were his alone. He was a natural leader, well liked by his colleagues, always on the lookout for the next challenge. By the end of his career, he was the acknowledged dean of old Asia hands.

In his way he embodied an ideal of America, nurtured in the Depression, inspired by the prewar recovery, hardened in World War II, made cosmopolitan after it through his travels in the Pacific and Asia. He believed in the Marines. He believed that America was preeminent among nations, set apart by its industrial might, by its ingenious people, and above all by its democratic institutions. He acknowledged—and sometimes satirized—his nation's mistakes and weaknesses, but he also saw how consistently they were overcome. He believed that there was nothing America couldn't achieve if once it decided the objective was worth it. He believed that America was invincible.

And then came Vietnam.

It looked at first like any other war the United States had been involved in. When Franklin Roosevelt led America in the fight against fascism, his and the country's resolve was implacable. When Harry Truman sent troops to fight the Communists in Korea, Beech didn't doubt that he was doing the right thing. Now another Asian nation was threatened by Communists, and America supported the regime that opposed them. This was what America did: it stood for liberty against tyranny. True, there were complications. There was reason to think that Ho Chi Minh, the Communist leader, headed a righteous cause, seeking to liberate his people from foreign oppressors. He had defeated the French, who for years had colonized the region. Now the United States was stepping in where the French had been to back a regime that was itself oppressive and corrupt. This was awkward.

The awkwardness was felt in Washington, where opponents emerged almost as soon as the war began. Reservations were evident even in the White House. John F. Kennedy wondered if the problem could be resolved by irregular means, using the CIA or special forces. When that didn't work, he sought to limit the commitment to advice and material support. Lyndon Johnson, following Kennedy, prosecuted the war both vigorously and reluctantly: he wanted it won so he could focus on his domestic programs. He gave the military what it asked for, counting on it to deliver a win that he could present to the country and move on. It didn't deliver, and it was he who moved on. By the time Richard Nixon took over, Vietnam was a war that few wanted and perhaps fewer expected to win.

Conflicted views of the war were reflected by the men and women who covered it. Even before most Americans were aware that there was a war underway in 1961 and '62—before most could place Vietnam on a map—a small group of reporters based in Saigon was butting heads with the American advisory mission. They believed in the cause but complained that the South Vietnamese regime was corrupt, that American officials were incompetent, and that the war against the Communist insurgents was being lost. Some of these reporters became famous: David Halberstam of *The New York Times* and wire-service reporters Malcolm Browne, Neil Sheehan, and Peter Arnett all went on to have distinguished careers. But at the time they drew fire from some of their older colleagues. Their decision to focus their reporting as much on politics as on the actual fighting was markedly different from the way earlier wars had been covered. Their critics, almost none of whom were based in Saigon, and almost all having had experience in earlier conflicts, denounced the younger cohort for their defeatism. The critics' condemnations, and the resident reporters' retorts, were passionate and sometimes viciously personal.

Beech was one of the outsiders, a visiting correspondent based in Tokyo who dropped in periodically to assess the war's progress. He did not join in the vituperation that some of his peers directed at the Saigon-based reporters. He went into the field with them and listened to what they said. When the contentiousness came to a head, he stood apart by defending them. But he didn't agree with them either. He had been a Marine correspondent whose job it was to celebrate the Corps' achievements. His dispatches had been subject to official vetting, and he had no problem with that. Nor did his readers: they were on the same side. He had been a civilian correspondent in Korea, where he sometimes wrote articles critical of the way the war was conducted—but there was never any doubt about which side he was on.

And when he visited Vietnam he brought with him the same attitude. He thought—he felt in his bones—that if America was involved, America would triumph. His faith was affirmed when the Marines landed in Vietnam, and he moved there to be on hand for the first big battles that were fought in the late summer and autumn of '65. His faith remained strong despite successive changes of government in Saigon and the lack of demonstrable progress in the field as President Johnson committed more troops—ultimately half a million—to the campaign. Increasing numbers of observers saw the war as futile and immoral. The reporters who had been condemned for the way they reported the war now felt themselves vindicated. Malcolm Browne, for one, argued that not only was America losing but that it was probably right that it lose, that America shouldn't have been in Vietnam in the first place. Beech bitterly disagreed. But his faith in the project faltered when the Tet Offensive offered proof of the enemy's continued resourcefulness and determination. He was disturbed by demonstrations against the war that he witnessed on trips to the US mainland. He was deeply shaken by the My Lai massacre. When he said that America would defeat the Communists, he started adding a caveat: America would win, but only if its will wasn't undermined by dissension at home.

At some point Beech understood that the war would end badly. The seed was planted in the aftermath of the Tet Offensive when a general he had known as a colonel in the Pacific and whose exploits he had followed in Korea voiced despair. But it was the Cambodia incursion that affected him most deeply. The wanton bloodletting set in motion by contending warlords, the deposed head of state and his feckless usurper, threw him. So many innocents penned in camps waiting to be murdered. So many corpses in the Mekong River that he gave up counting. Beech admitted later that the carnage in Cambodia broke through his built-up tolerance for war's horror. He was disgusted, finally, by the manner of the US withdrawal from Vietnam, the abandonment of its ally, the humiliation of the frantic scenes at the US Embassy—the unseemly scramble to climb the embassy wall and the fight for a place on the last helicopter. He was never more eloquent than when he described those final days. And never so deeply affronted.

After the war the press controversy took another turn. The press, or more broadly the media at large, was said to be responsible for having lost the war. Among those making the accusation were some of the same critics who had complained of the way the younger cohort covered the war in its earliest stages. Members of that cadre, notably Halberstam and Sheehan, gave back as good as they got in books that anatomized the war's conduct. But the original debate had undergone a metamorphosis. No longer was the emphasis on whether politics or the battlefield was properly reported. The idea now was that the war had been covered too closely. The public had heard, read, and seen too much. This contention suited the military, anxious to deflect blame for what had happened. It suited the politicians.

Some years after the war, Beech would add his voice to those of the critics. But this represented a shift in his attitude. He was sometimes critical of his colleagues during the war, especially those who insulted the Marines, but it was only when he retired that bitterness undermined his judgment. It was then that he joined those looking for a scapegoat, saying the media, not the military, was responsible for the loss.

He had been a happy warrior. He had seen America gear up for war in the 1940s, its awesome industrial might turned to military purpose. He had seen American armies advance methodically across the Pacific, island by island, until Japan was encircled and then conquered. He had seen for himself the incomprehensible power of the atom bomb when he witnessed the test explosions at Bikini Atoll. While not shy in describing MacArthur's megalomania, he still admired what the general had achieved in Japan's reconstruction. What he saw when he covered the Korean War reinforced his belief that America was unlike other nations, a force for good and uniquely powerful. In a way, he thought America was like him, flawed but essentially true, strong enough to overcome all obstacles. Believing these things, having seen and written of them, he reflected what most Americans believed and had seen.

Beech was celebrated for his reporting from the Pacific and Korea. He and America were as one. But America's sense of itself was shattered by Vietnam. The worldview that had united most Americans, a view that included an instinctive antipathy to Communism, pride in America's industrial and military prowess, and certainty that America stood for freedom and justice, held fast through the earlier conflicts. It crumbled under assault first by intellectuals, and then by the anti-war movement in the 1960s.

Some historians, looking back, have been puzzled that so many Americans continued to support the war in Vietnam long after opposition to it had become a movement. It wasn't until Nixon took over that support for the war fell precipitously. But most Americans felt alienated by the social upheavals that changed their country. They weren't intellectuals. They did not read *The New York Times* or the *Washington Post*. Halberstam, Sheehan, Browne, Arnett, and the others were unknown to them. The anti-war movement left them untouched. If anything, they saw it as a threat to the established order. What they did read were the newspapers in which Beech's name was featured. Keyes Beech—the rugged kid from rural Tennessee who lived most of his life abroad—was in their eyes the more authentic American.

THE BEAUTIFUL SIMPLICITY OF WAR

CHAPTER I

Before the War

PULASKI

Keyes was not his first name. He dropped "William" early in his career to avoid being confused with other male members of the family, too many of whom were called either William or Walter, or both in combination. The name "Keyes" (rhymes with "eyes") came from his grandmother, Ursula Augusta Keyes, a formidable woman who bore her husband, Reverend William Branch Beech, seven children—three girls and four boys—that survived infancy. The girls married and settled close to home. The same was true of two of the boys, but a third, Cornelius, moved to Florida with his wife, Tommie Ann, son Walter Herschel, and daughter Mary. Walter Herschel would go on to have a rollicking career as a barnstorming pilot before applying what he had learned in the air to airplane construction on the ground. With partners he started the Beech Aircraft company, which, as Beechcraft, later merged with Cessna.

William Walter Beech, the fourth boy and the youngest of William and Ursula's brood, was born in 1870 or '71. He took up farming as a sharecropper on property some seven miles outside Pulaski, Tennessee, the Giles County seat, and married a local girl,

Leona Carden, in 1897. She gave birth to a daughter, Mabel, in 1905; a son, William Walter Jr., in 1909; and a second son, William Keyes, on August 13, 1913. Keyes's mother died in 1919 when she was just thirty-nine.

Keyes's father, now a widower, developed health problems soon after Leona's passing. He gave up farming in or around 1922 and moved with the three children to Florida. They stayed for a year with Cornelius's family in Tampa before moving across the bay to St. Petersburg. Mabel found clerical work in the classified advertising department of the *Evening Independent.* Keyes's father and brother went to work at the George G. Gill dairy. Keyes went to school.

Beginning in 1925 the family would move almost every year for a decade, a fact that reflected their difficult financial circumstances. Mabel remained employed at the *Evening Independent.* William Jr. went through a number of jobs, including clerk, counterman, and meat cutter, while supporting his wife, Dorothy, and, soon, two daughters. William Sr., meanwhile, responded to the question of his occupation in the 1930 census with the word "none." For the rest of his life he would be active in the local branch of the Church of Christ, in which his father had been a minister, but would never again be gainfully employed. In 1931 the family made another move, Mabel to her own apartment, the others to a place on Twelfth Street South. Two years later they were together again—Mabel included—at an address on Ninth Street. So many moves, and the strain of so many people living more or less on top of one another, must have been hard on them all.

Despite the domestic turbulence, Keyes did well in school and was active outside of it. The extended family was a factor in helping him to maintain a balance. A supportive community did the rest. From the inside pages of the *St. Petersburg Times* we learn, for example, that Keyes, as a grade five student at Glenoak School, recounted a story from Lincoln's life on Presidents' Day and that he was elected secretary of the Foursquare Club in November. A couple of years later, now promoted to eighth grade at South Side Secondary, he scored 100 percent in a spelling bee and was one of a troop of scouts detailed to welcome the ladies of the Parent and Teachers Council to their annual meeting. In the summers and at Christmas he returned to Tennessee to stay with family. It was on these holidays back home that he honed the skills he'd learned as a child: horseback riding, swimming in the local water hole, and sometimes shooting dinner with his .22 caliber rifle.

A fellow journalist and Tennessee native, Don Whitehead, recalled a time when "a stringbean of a youngster named Keyes Beech" joined playmates at a local landmark chanting together: "A head full of rocks or a head full of knowledge, I'd rather be at Goat Knob than any old college." Beech would remember with nostalgia listening to the June bugs on hot summer days, carving his initials into a beech tree by the hog pond, and dangling his feet in its cooling water. Between family stays and St. Petersburg's active community, life for the boy was okay.

The family, however, continued to experience financial stress. Keyes finally was obliged to drop out of school so he could contribute to the household finances. Mabel put in a good word for him at the *Independent*, and he started there as a copyboy in the fall of 1929. He was sixteen.

GREEN PARK BENCHES

Florida, south of the panhandle, was still a rough-and-tumble tropical frontier before World War I. An economy once based on grisly colonial-era agriculture—slaves, sugarcane, and cotton—struggled to establish a new identity by draining wetlands for cash crops and exploiting the peninsula's endless sunlit beaches as a destination for holidaymakers. A few visionary entrepreneurs had pushed a patchy network of railroads south to Jacksonville, Tampa, and even Miami as early as the 1890s, and a handful of fancy hotels had sprung up to serve an exclusive northern clientele. St. Petersburg, still a small town at the time, enjoyed something of an upswing before World War I, and the mood after the war was exuberant. But it was technological change, some of it the product of the war itself, that drove the economy. The coming of the automobile and the roads to accommodate them were transformative.

Beginning in 1922, Florida was seized by a boom that was reminiscent of the western gold rush. Above all, the excitement was focused on real estate. The attraction of accessible, cheap land, golden beaches, and reliably warm, dry winters would prove to be irresistible to hundreds of thousands of increasingly mobile Americans. St. Petersburg's population grew from around 14,000 in 1920 to more than three times as many a decade later. And when the real estate bubble burst, as it was bound to do, jokes about Florida property purchased hastily or sight unseen that turned out to be unreclaimed marsh or, worse, underwater, became an enduring strand of American folklore. A few got rich. And some got rich and then lost everything.

Noel A. Mitchell, like so many of the men and women who left their imprint on Florida between the wars, came from out of state. He was born in Rhode Island and spent his early years on the Eastern Seaboard. His instincts were those of a born showman. He worked in theater as an actor and impresario before moving on to running and then owning an amusement park in New Jersey. He was, by all accounts, a genial, ingenious, and eloquent huckster. He visited St. Petersburg in 1904, saw something that appealed to him, and moved there permanently in 1907. He fit right in.

He made shrewd investments. He built a hotel outside of town and a number of buildings inside of it. These included a two-story office block on Central Avenue at Fourth Street from which he conducted his real estate business. Because of his success in buying and selling beachfront property, he acquired a nickname, the

Sand Man, that stuck. He had an abiding, if subversive, interest in politics, running at different times for sheriff (on the slogan "hear no evil, speak no evil, see no evil"), mayor, and state governor. He actually served as mayor for a couple of years in the early twenties. His tenure was cut short by a scandal involving liquor—prohibition still being in force. But he was also known for his exploits in self-promotion and as a civic booster. He invested in the area's first golf course at Bayboro Harbor. He put money into the region's first regular airline service. He had vision and drive. He was regarded by some as a civic treasure and by all as an outstanding eccentric. He was known best of all for his green benches. Which weren't, in fact, green.

He noticed that people often stepped inside his office on Central Avenue just to sit for a while. Sometimes they asked for permission; often they didn't. But they gave him an idea. He bought fifty benches and placed them on the sidewalk outside his office. Lest they be overlooked, he had them painted bright orange. And to make sure their source was known, he had fixed to the back of each bench a sign that read: MITCHELL, THE SAND MAN. THE HONEST REAL ESTATE DEALER. THE MAN WITH A CONSCIENCE. HE NEVER SLEEPS. Soon other merchants were setting out their own benches with their own advertisements. They came in a variety of designs and a range of colors, and the overall effect was unsightly. In 1916 the mayor introduced a bylaw regulating their size and color. Which is how St. Petersburg came to be known for its ubiquitous green benches.

This was the city in which Keyes Beech was introduced to the newspaper business. Its permanent population was growing rapidly. So was the impermanent population, and the city strove mightily to find new diversions to keep the fluctuating numbers of visitors entertained. The Festival of States, which involved a parade and allied celebrations, was inaugurated in 1917. Major league baseball teams were invited by a committee struck for the purpose to hold their spring training in the city. Another initiative, the Million Dollar Pier, featured a ballroom where three thousand couples danced to the music of a big band on opening night in November 1926. The city's luxury hotels appealed to big spenders, but not all who yearned for a sojourn in the sun had that kind of money. An influx of "tin can tourists," so called because they camped in the open and made their meals from tinned goods, reached a peak in 1920. They took over a field at Eighteenth Street and Second Avenue South. The Chamber of Commerce objected to their presence, but Noel Mitchell—the incident fell into his brief tenure as mayor—welcomed them by designating the field a free municipal campground. His gesture was undone a year later by a less broad-minded mayor.

St. Petersburg, then as now, was a sports paradise. While Beech's daily routine as a copyboy centered on gofer tasks, including sharpening pencils and running reporters' copy to the editors' desks and, from there, to the compositors, he had the opportunity on his own time to cover school and college games and relay the scores to the sports editor. He also got to play. In the spring of 1930, the *Evening Independent* fielded a baseball team against the Lumbermen at Crescent Lake in which Beech, pitching for the winning side, held the opposition to six hits. In March 1936 he participated with a newspaper colleague in the second annual Press-Radio sailing races at the Big Bayou Yacht Club (they placed third in their class). His lean build and competitive character made him a natural athlete. And while, by his own account, he followed the classic apprentice journalist's path from copyboy to progressively more senior assignments—from the church dinner and lunch-club circuit, to the police blotter, and on to city hall, labor, and politics—it is not surprising that his first byline in the paper appeared on the sports page. He became for a couple of years a professional boxing aficionado.

Boxing was popular in St. Petersburg. Weekly fights held at the Disabled Veterans arena throughout the year often attracted a raucous crowd. This was the case on a Tuesday evening in September 1933, when a local welterweight, Lee Davis, fought Bob Wilson, a fighter from across the bay. Davis, a local favorite, had a reputation for employing techniques not sanctioned by the Marquess of Queensberry. He was expected to win, and Beech was at ringside to record the blows as they landed. He was writing for the first time under his own name, and he did his best to make it memorable:

> Lee Davis, a two-gated gambolier of the prize ring, has met his master. A slender blond lad, as game a fighter as ever trod the resin, rose up from certain defeat last night at the airport arena, wiped a crimson slash from his bleeding face and ended Davis' welterweight reign along the west coast with a blazing knockout in the sixth round. The bloody ring war made local ring history. A maddened crowd howled a dirge for Davis as blond Bob Wilson, a whipped fighter for four rounds, rose to fistic heights seldom seen and came back to drape the "bad boy" of the West Coast across the ropes in the sixth session, a thoroughly beaten fighter.

Davis did not take the decision well. Beech was on hand the following month when the local boxing commission voted to suspend him for taking a swing at the referee.

The sports pages gave some prominence to their writers—readers got to know them by name. They had license to give rein to a more florid writing style than was allowed in other departments. Consequently, when Beech graduated from sports to news, his name disappeared from the paper for a couple of years. It's not until 1935 that his byline turns up again, now attached to a variety of more or less oddball assignments. He interviewed Maurice Allard, for example, the captain of a "battered 65-foot auxiliary schooner," at dockside in Tampa. Allard was unhappy about the attention his planned expedition was attracting. He was especially grumpy at having been dubbed a nudist.

> "I can't see why all this fuss is being made," he declared indignantly. "We're not nudists, if that's what you think. D___ if it isn't hard to convince people of that. Since the Tampa papers have been printing all this stuff about us going to the Virgin Islands to set up a nudist colony people have been coming down here and looking at us like we were freaks. . . . We are sailing for South America and the islands to take up some land on which I have options. We don't know yet where we'll locate. We are farmers," Allard declared. "Yes, farmers, and all we want is to be let alone. We want to find some place where we can live our own lives. Nudism is only incidental. If some members of our colony want to go in swimming naked, it'll be all right. Tolerance is the thing—nudism, religion, tobacco, raw foodism and so forth."

Beech also interviewed a rising star in the opera world, soprano Rosa Tentoni, in St. Petersburg to take part in a music festival. He caught her off guard when he asked if she was planning to get married. "That can wait," she said definitely. Then, not so definitely: "Well, for the time being anyway. I can't be bothered with marriage—no, I don't mean that I can't be bothered. It's just that I think I have plenty of time to wait."

Tentoni did get married a few years later, to another singer, Joseph Royer. Beech, meanwhile, continued to get credit for occasional features—such as a front-page story about the fifty-second annual encampment of the Grand Army of the Republic, veterans of the Union Army in the Civil War, "their blue-clad ranks pitifully thinned by the grim reaper, Time"—while writing up routine news items anonymously, as was customary. Now and then, when there was a hole to fill, he authored a column called "Beech Combings." These columns consisted of political gossip, droll observations, and an occasional piece of unasked-for advice. In one, he claimed to have interviewed a "cadaverous and hopeless" drug addict, who told him that ruthless dealers will "slip a pill of strychnine in among the dope" if they suspect one of their clients is a snitch. In another, he reported on the ubiquity of gigolos who hung around in the town's high-end hotel lobbies in the hope of ensnaring the affection of a wealthy widow. "Sometimes," he wrote, "the middle-aged urge for youthful company assumes tragi-comic proportions. One wealthy widow has offered a young wife $15,000 to divorce her husband so she can have him. I understand the wife is holding out for $25,000, the romance-killer!"

Nineteen thirty-six was an eventful and in some ways pivotal year for Beech. His father, William Walter Sr., passed away at Mound Park Hospital on February 26. This can't have been a surprise, as he had been in ill health for years. The sudden passing of Beech's cousin, Mary Burns (the daughter of Cornelius and Tommie Ann), would have been more upsetting. She was just thirty-five. And then, even closer to home, the death of Beech's brother, William Walter Jr., was a shock. He died of blood poisoning that might have been treatable had the family been able to afford a physician's services. He was survived by his wife and two little girls. Like Mary Burns, Beech's brother was in his mid-thirties when he died.

The family had been living in yet another apartment, this one on Third Avenue, for a couple of years. Following William's death, Dorothy and the girls moved to their own apartment. Beech and his sister stayed put for the time being, but in 1937 he moved to his own place at 626 25th Avenue South. Mabel stayed behind, alone and then jointly with her husband after she married, for nearly a decade. It seems likely that less straitened economic times, as the state and the nation pulled out of the Depression, made these changes possible. It must have helped that the two surviving siblings were no longer supporting their father. It was also the case that Beech was rising through the ranks at the *Independent*. In June he was filing stories from the state capital, Tallahassee. The easing of the financial strain plus his elevated status gave Beech the confidence to get married. The wedding was held in August 1937.

Figure 1. Mildred Palmer Beech. Courtesy of Walter Beech.

His bride was an attractive young woman from a well-off family who could claim accomplishments of her own. Mildred Palmer was born in New York City, educated at Smith College (then and now a private institution exclusively for women) and then at the Sorbonne in Paris, France. The rising young reporter was a charmer. "Millie" Palmer was a catch.

Beech was getting more interesting and newsworthy assignments. In September he was in Alabama, following up on the murder of a St. Petersburg resident whose body had been found beside his car on a country road. There was a bullet hole in the car's windshield and a bullet hole in the victim, in whose hand there was a pistol whose butt was wrapped in a handkerchief. There was some evidence that the body had been moved from the site where the murder had taken place, and a man with a rap sheet involving rum-running had been taken into custody. According to Beech's sources, however, it was doubtful that the issue would be taken to court. The case would go unsolved.

A month later, Beech was across the bay in Tampa to attend a rally for the Communist candidate for president of the United States, Earl Browder. Things got ugly:

> Browder, short, middle-aged, mild-mannered, had just declared that "the chief issue of the 1936 campaign is defense of democracy" when the platform from which he was speaking began to heave from the combined assault of 10 to 15 attackers. As the platform tottered and the crowd of 400 or 500 roared with mingled indignation and approval, Browder and his aides neatly slid from the platform and disappeared. But the fighting in the rear of the platform continued. This reporter . . . rushed to the rear of the makeshift rostrum to watch the struggle. As he did so, he saw half a dozen men emerge from beneath the platform carrying the loudspeaker system; he saw a man identified as Constable Fred Newberger whip a gun from inside his shirt and bring it down on the head of a yellow-haired youth who was John Hovan, 20, Jacksonville, a Communist sympathizer. The youth fell flat on his face into the dirt, blood spurting from his head. Careful to keep his mouth shut and his hands still for fear he also would be clubbed over the head, this reporter saw the band of attackers wield blackjacks and pistol butts with deadly efficiency. The writer saw several persons clubbed, but in the

> melee could not establish identification of all those who were hurt or their attackers.

At least some of the attackers, it developed, were police officers in civilian clothes who, as "self-styled red-blooded Americans," had taken it upon themselves to run the Communist menace out of town. In this they were successful. Browder left by train for Detroit the same evening after telling Beech, "It is a disgrace to the city of Tampa . . . when it allows officers of the law to abet an illegal mob such as the one that assaulted us today." Charges were filed against three police officers, and Beech was among the witnesses expected to give evidence. It's not clear, however, that the incident ever went to trial.

There was an element of drollery (and poignancy) in Beech's report of the arrest for drunkenness of Noel A. Mitchell earlier in the year. The now-elderly showman, salesman, and perennial candidate for public office was discovered by a constable asleep on a park bench at the intersection that had been the locus of so much of his business career.

> Eccentric Noel A. Mitchell, former mayor and the man who originated St. Petersburg's famous green benches, was arrested early this morning for sleeping on one of them. Picked up at 12:40 a.m. while slumbering on a bench in front of the Hall building at Fourth and Central, Mitchell, whose most recent exploit was to announce for governor, was docketed at police headquarters for intoxication.

Mitchell fought the charge, claiming police persecution, and insisted that his falling asleep was a consequence of a rare condition. "I suffer with auto-intoxication," he told the court, "and after I eat a big meal I usually relapse into slumber. That is what happened to me the night I was arrested. I campaigned all day"—he was running again for governor—"and ate a heavy meal just before I fell asleep. I most certainly was not drunk." The judge was skeptical but indulgent. "I'll give you the benefit of the doubt," he said, and declared Mitchell not guilty. Mitchell died, aged seventy-seven, a few months later, his final bid for the governorship having failed.

If Mitchell's passing marked the end of an era, for Beech it was time for a new beginning. In December 1936 he and Mildred joined members of the Phi Delta Theta fraternity in celebrating the holiday season at the Sunset Country Club on Snell Isle. Millie's father was both a member and the author of a history of the fraternity. The kid who had dangled his feet in the hog pond back in Giles County was mixing with some of West Florida's most influential citizens. He had his own apartment and an attractive wife to share it with. Meanwhile, his career as a reporter was reaching a plateau. In the spring he would go again to Tallahassee to report on the goings-on in the state legislature. He would be filing stories about minor scandals—the accusation that former governor David Scholtz had accepted a bribe, an acrimonious debate about the appointment of senators' assistants—and the complexities of state legislation. The legislature sat for just a couple of months, and it may have struck Beech that the stage on which he was playing was too small. He had done well in St. Pete, but it was time to move on.

How Beech came to apply for a job on the staff of the *Akron Beacon Journal* is unclear, but he announced his intention to move to Ohio in May 1937 while the Florida legislature was still in session. A farewell party was held in his honor on a Wednesday night in mid-June. By the end of the month, he and Millie had put St. Petersburg behind them. He was a big-city reporter now.

HELL WAGONS

Akron in the mid-1930s was more than five times the size of St. Petersburg. Its major paper, the *Beacon Journal*, was the product of the merger, back in the 1890s, of the *Evening Journal* and the

Summit Beacon. It had thrived through most of the intervening years but foundered in the depths of the Depression when advertising dollars became scarce. For a time reporters accepted IOUs in place of wages. John S. Knight, known familiarly as Jack, inherited the paper from his father in 1933, precisely when conditions were at their worst. A lesser man might have thrown in the towel, but Knight was remarkable: an inspired editor and a visionary owner. By the time Beech was hired, in the summer of 1937, things were looking up and the paper's proprietor had plans to expand, not just the paper but his portfolio of papers. Beech timed his move well.

Beech had done serious reporting at the *Evening Independent*. It's where he learned the basics of his trade and found his voice. But his years in St. Petersburg had something of the character of a carnival: it was a resort town in the making, a place where people shed their worries and inhibitions, whether by dancing on the Million Dollar Pier or setting up tents in a tin-can encampment. Akron in the late 1930s was bigger and older: a solid, blue-collar town. It had its beginnings as a transportation hub built on a waterway, the Ohio and Erie Canal. Now it connected coast and heartland by rail and, increasingly, by road. It was an established industrial city dominated by rubber companies, where labor was organized and a force to be reckoned with. It was a city in which politics were complicated: both Communists and fascists could draw a crowd, and the Ku Klux Klan hovered in the background. It was a city, and a time, where an ambitious reporter could make his name.

Jack Knight recognized early Beech's ability to use a personal narrative to tease out the larger implications of a story, and Knight and his managing editor, Ben Maidenburg, threw Beech's way a rich variety of incidents to explore. Beech responded with solidly researched, cleverly structured articles from which his wry, what-a-world-we-live-in attitude was rarely absent. He accompanied a murderer to prison and exposed a marriage racket in a neighboring town. By the early 1940s, he was putting together short essays on subjects such as trucking and, with war impending, America's burgeoning fighting machine.

What desperation might have driven twenty-one-year-old George Wells to participate with three others in a holdup isn't clear. It wasn't the gang's first robbery, but it was the first in which a man was killed. The victim was a shop and restaurant owner, William Pantazis. All four of his assailants were armed with pistols, but according to the prosecution it was Wells who fired the fatal shot. Consequently, Wells's three companions were tried on a lesser charge and sentenced to life in prison, while Wells, the youngest member of the gang, was found guilty of murder in the first degree and condemned to die in the electric chair.

Wells maintained a tough-guy attitude throughout the trial. The jury was thought to have seen him as a defiant, glowering thug. His mien may have decided his fate. At any rate, it was the murderer's hard-boiled façade and his intermittent failure to maintain it that caught Beech's eye when he accompanied Wells from jail to the penitentiary:

> During the three-hour drive to Columbus from Akron yesterday Wells laughed and joked. He was a "hard guy," as the anecdotes of his criminal career clearly indicated. But his sudden explosive laughter was tinged with a sort of hysterical bitterness as he "kidded" "ol Rog"—18-year-old Roger Kegg—who sat in the front seat of the sheriff's car.

Beech was with the murderer when he said a tearful goodbye to his mother in Akron. And he was with him still when the prison doors clanged shut behind him in the prison complex in Columbus. Wells's accomplice, Kegg, was whisked away to the prison hospital to be examined, while Wells was taken directly to his cell in the "death house." As Beech observed: "There isn't much use taking a condemned man to a hospital."

Of all the stories Beech covered on the crime beat, the one that strikes a contemporary reader as most surprising was his inside account of the marriage racket that operated across the state line in Wellsburg, West Virginia. The business was well known, but, according to the *Beacon Journal*'s editors, it was "often denounced" but "never exposed." Wellsburg was the destination of choice for young couples who sought for whatever reason to get married fast, without the bother of a marriage license or the three-day wait that was generally required before a wedding could take place. It functioned with the collusion of local authorities, who accepted bribes to ignore what they may have regarded as minor illegalities. "It's simple," one of the gangsters explained. "All you have to do is hand out five bucks here and there. They've all got their hands out."

Beech broke the story by getting the minister who performed the ceremonies to open up to him. Reverend H. W. Best explained in a series of "as told to" articles that ill health had forced him to give up his church duties and find an alternative source of income. Fortuitously, he was approached by Martin Joyent, one of the principals of the local taxi firm. Joyent's offer was attractive: an income of $35 to $50 a week to perform marriage ceremonies on demand. His assurance that the business was on the up-and-up should have been treated skeptically, but Best was in a jam. He was sick, out of work, and had a wife and child to look after. So he agreed to Joyent's terms and moved from Wheeling, where he had been living, to Wellsburg, where Joyent and his associates insisted he purchase one thousand dollars' worth of furniture for his new apartment, "in order to put up a good front for the couples," or so they said. The debt tightened the gangsters' grip on the hapless minister. His need for cash to repay the loan and their knowledge of what he was doing gave him little room to maneuver. He was trapped.

The business thrived. Over a couple of years, Best claimed, he married an astonishing 3,911 couples. As he became familiar with his clients and their circumstances, he came to realize what he must have suspected from the start: that the activity in which he was engaged was one no minister of God should have had a hand in. "I was in pretty deep," he told Beech, "deep enough to know about illegal marriage licenses; a forged marriage certificate; threats in the middle of the night; hundreds of secret marriages that never should have occurred. And there are indications that in some of these marriages 'white slavery' was the primary purpose."

When, at last, burdened by debt he couldn't afford and a conscience that oppressed him, Best confronted his captors in the taxi company office, his complaints were met with threats that soon escalated to violence. Three thugs came at him with flailing fists and a blackjack pulled out of a desk drawer. Best attempted to escape through a window, which he half opened, but was roughly hauled back by his attackers, whom he then fended off with a chair. But it was his shouts for help on the chance they would be heard by a neighbor, a plumber, that finally caused his attackers to back off. He escaped, badly shaken. He was ready to tell what he knew.

Beech, having listened to the minister's tale, approached the gangsters himself. They proved amenable to being interviewed, apparently comfortable in the knowledge that local authorities would protect them. They were not so amenable to being photographed. Martin Joyent explained disarmingly that his wife would "razz him" if his picture appeared in print. Beech and the newspaper's photographer really wanted a picture, however, and arranged a setup. The photographer, Jerry Heiman, parked his car in front of the taxi company office and sat there, waiting. Beech approached Joyent, and the two men settled on the front step of the taxi company office to chat. When Joyent saw Heiman, still in the vehicle, lift up his camera, he leapt to his feet and tried to grab it. Beech grabbed his arm and pulled him off. Joyent turned and scrambled into the office. Beech got into the car. Joyent, enraged, emerged from the office with a blackjack in his hand. He stepped onto the running board as the car pulled away from the curb. . . .

Figure 2. "the exact moment when a bad guy sensed that a swell deal was about to go sour." © Jerry Heiman – USA TODAY NETWORK via Imagn Images.

> He brought the blackjack down on the windshield with terrific force, showering Heiman and me with broken glass. Through the hole in the windshield he made several attempts to strike me with the blackjack and then dropped from the running board. From a window in the sheriff's office across the street in the courthouse, a deputy watched the entire proceedings without any attempt to interfere.

Heiman's photograph, which was printed on the front page of the *Beacon Journal*, shows the two men seated on the sidewalk. Beech appears to be speaking. Joyent is drawing on a cigarette while glancing warily at the reporter. It was worth the risk to get the picture: it captured the exact moment when a bad guy sensed that a swell deal was about to go sour.

Beech ground out crime stories regularly through the years, almost always with a twist. He interviewed a juvenile gang leader just after his arrest who worried that his brush with the law would put the kibosh on his plan to join the navy. He wrote a detailed review of a selection of booklets that promised their purchasers a program for winning at the illegal but flourishing numbers racket. After confessing that a pamphlet called "Lucky Stars" described a system he found incomprehensible, he proceeded to examine the competition:

> "Harlem Hal" is the ace expert of "The Advance," but if you don't like "Hal" you can have your choice of selections by "Mutuel Murray," "Stocky Yardin" or "Cycle Charlie." If you prefer a system, "The Advance" offers the following: "Londi's 7-up," "Mme. Futura" and "Beaver Brown." Personally [Beech concluded], we like "Harlem Hal."

In August 1938 Jack Knight purchased another Akron paper, the *Times-Press*, and at the same time launched a Sunday edition of the *Beacon Journal* to fill the hole the *Times-Press* had occupied. The new Sunday paper initially had a two-person staff, with Ben Maidenburg as editor and Beech doing the rest. Beech took the occasion to launch a column for which, over the next few years, he won a substantial local following. In his weekly Biography in Brief, he sketched the lives and achievements of a wide swath of Akron society. Occasionally these columns gave him another vantage point from which to examine the interplay of crime and the social fabric by serving up portraits of some more or less shady characters as well as the individuals whose job it was to preserve order. He wrote, for example, about Curt Raleigh, whose father, Pat, was a policeman:

> Old Sgt. Pat Raleigh, for 25 years a member of the Akron police department, never wanted his boy to be a cop. There was, he said, no future in it. So it was with deep regret that old Pat saw his boy ignore his advice and join the force. In fact, the story goes, old Pat felt so strongly about the matter that two years later when his boy came up for a physical examination he went to the right places to have him disqualified.

However disappointed he was by this rather underhanded turn of events, Curt bounced back, first entering into partnership with another entrepreneurial-minded soul to preside over a combined restaurant (on the ground floor) and gambling den (in the basement), which flourished until closed by "the heat." Undaunted, he next became part owner of another outfit, the Walbridge Club. Raleigh, Beech wrote, had "formed a simple business philosophy: Regardless of the laws, people are going to gamble. This being so, Raleigh might as well provide the facilities as anyone else." Raleigh, according to Beech, wasn't averse to placing an occasional bet himself. He was also something of a legend when it came to partying. He and friends reportedly set out by train from Akron to attend baseball's 1936 World Series in New York:

> Raleigh and party started a poker game as soon as the train left Akron. As the train neared New York the game was still going. It appeared that the first series game scheduled for the following day would be rained out. A Pullman porter who was rapidly getting rich on tips backed up the weatherman for fear the players would decide they needed sleep. As the train rolled into Pennsylvania station, Raleigh and his companions refused to disembark, retiring to their berths instead. They woke up that afternoon in the Long Island railroad yards with the opening series game half played.

The Walbridge Club operated two gambling joints, one in East Akron, which was closed by the law, the other in nearby Boston Heights, where its illicit activities were ignored because, as civic officials pointed out, "the club is furnishing employment for local residents." Raleigh, Beech continued, "makes no pretense about his business, but would prefer not to discuss it. In his 20 years as a gambler he has never been subjected to the indignities of a 'pinch.'" He was married, Beech concluded, and the owner of a toy bulldog named Jiggs.

On the side of rectitude and propriety, Beech profiled Ervin Delano Fritch, a judge who rather than campaign for office relied on his reputation as a scrupulous arbiter of the law. The diminutive judge cut an eccentric figure. He wore an "ancient brown eyeshade held together with paper clips" to shield his eyes from overhead light.

> His only concession to judicial dignity is to put on his coat when he takes the bench. If the courtroom is not crowded, Fritch will prop his feet on his desk. Attorneys are sometimes startled in their arguments to look up and find themselves talking to a foot and a disreputable looking eyeshade with two stray wisps of hair hanging over it.

Fritch was an avid fisherman who, with friends, made an annual trip to the French River in Canada, where he usually chose to fish alone. Once, one of his friends returned to camp unexpectedly and was startled by what he saw:

> The dean of Summit county common pleas court emerged from his cottage with a woman's bathing suit, left at the camp the summer before, nattily knotted about his middle. In his hand he held a saucer, and on that saucer there was a bar of soap. Going to the riverbank, the judge took an anchor rope and lashed it around his waist. This safety measure completed, he then ventured a few feet

> offshore and he began to scrub himself with great vigor, jumping up and down in the water to wash off the soap. Then he jumped a few times just for fun.

When Beech invited the judge to comment on the story, Fritch responded "with some asperity" that the rope was merely to help him maintain stability while standing on slippery rocks. He had known how to swim, he said, since he was a child.

Over the course of these years, the availability of increasingly affordable and reliable vehicles was gradually changing the way Americans lived. These changes also posed a threat to public safety. The *Beacon Journal* had fun at Beech's expense when it sent him to New York to attend a seminar devoted to accident prevention. En route to the event, their reporter was tagged for speeding: "Safety Envoy's Face a Bit Pink," said the headline in the next day's paper. Beech confessed to exceeding the twenty-mile-per-hour limit but complained of police perfidiousness, labelling the spot where he was stopped in Lebanon, New Jersey, a "speed trap."

There weren't just more cars on the road, there were more trucks. In October 1938 Beech wrote a five-part series of articles describing his journey to New York and back with a "line hauler," a salaried long-distance truck driver. His companion was Wally Meusel, and the vehicle was a tractor-trailer carrying a mixed load consisting of "everything from whisky to razor blades to books." Meusel had an enviable record: only one accident in a seven-year career. It came about, through no fault of his, when a speeding car ran into him as he was pulling out of the terminal. The incident constituted a rude intrusion into a world that, as Beech came to see it, was self-contained and, if not idyllic, nevertheless complete. If a "truck-man" ever had a bad dream, Beech speculated, it was

> a nightmare of sour faced weight inspectors, relentless highway patrolmen lurking behind every curve, drunken drivers, big city

> traffic, and the ominous sway of a huge trailer that is beyond control and pulling him off the road to oblivion. But if he dreams of paradise, it is of an endless expanse of level concrete, peopled only by himself and a few friendly souls of the same trade. There are, at proper intervals, places where he may buy gas, coffee and lemon meringue pie.

For insurance reasons, drivers were forbidden from picking up hitchhikers, a prohibition that they viewed with regret. Things had been different during the worst years of the Depression, a time when "it was not uncommon to see stranded chorus girls 'thumbing' their way from Chicago to New York." Meusel and his fellow truckers harbored wistful memories of the era. "Some of'em," Meusel confided to Beech, "were mighty pretty." The comment elicited an unasked-for response from another driver who was listening to their conversation at a truck stop: "'So help me,' he breathed with a sigh that wrenched my heartstrings, 'I'll never forget that little blonde I picked up outside Buffalo. She was so damn cute,' his voice trailed off ecstatically. He was lost in the past and we were respectfully silent."

Beech would rediscover the romance of the road four years later in very different conditions: "The roaring sound from inside the Blue Mountain tunnel on the finest highway in the world grows steadily louder. Soon the headlights from the giant tractor-trailer begin to pierce the night. Now the roaring reaches a crescendo. There is a sudden whoosh as the big truck emerges from the tunnel onto the open road."

America was at war, and Beech was reporting on the transformation of a stretch of pavement from civilian to military use. The Pennsylvania Turnpike, a new four-lane highway through the Allegheny Mountains from the Ohio boundary to New Jersey, had become an essential component in the national project:

> All day long, all night long the 160-mile Pennsylvania turnpike echoes to the passage of trucks laden with the materials of war.

> They pass through the turnstiles at the rate of 1,000 every 24 hours; one every 86 seconds. One out of every 10 is from Akron. Trucks carry daily over this super-highway 21,000,000 pounds of freight valued at more than a million dollars. From Akron there are bomber parts, gun mounts, gas masks, rifle barrels and scores of other articles.

This was romance with a difference. The power of the big trucks was no longer harnessed to commerce but had a higher purpose. Beech's prose betrays his excitement. It had been building for years.

Political ferment in Akron in the late 1930s was, in some degree, a reflection of the ratcheting tension across the oceans, where the rise of fascism in Europe and Communism in the Far East challenged the democracies with which America identified and to which it was sentimentally and financially connected. Occasionally, someone passed through town who made the overseas contention tangible. In September 1937 Beech interviewed an assistant manager of the Goodyear Tire and Rubber Company who had just returned from China, which was in an undeclared war with Japan. He bore scars from an attack by a Chinese plane on the liner that was scheduled to bring him home. The liner, the *President Hoover*, was tied up in the Yangtze River not far from a pair of Japanese warships. The *Hoover* was clearly identified—an American flag had been spread across the upper deck—so it was unlikely that the assault was unintended. The motive of the attackers was unknown.

Such incidents got Americans thinking. The problem of preserving the peace or, if such efforts failed, of staying out of the ensuing war was an ongoing preoccupation. "As martial music echoed through downtown Akron," Beech wrote in November 1937, "as the city celebrated the signing of the World war armistice, steps to prevent future wars were being aired last night with sharply divergent views in a war crisis forum in the Y.W.C.A." The speakers included a professor who condemned all foreign involvement and an army reservist who, on the contrary, argued that America's alliances were its best defense. A pastor of the Universalist Church denounced violence as a means of settling disputes, and a student, who identified himself as a radical socialist, called for an uprising by the people if they were called upon to fight. Members of the Council for Peace Action, which had convened the meeting, resolved that America's participation in any future conflict should be decided by a popular vote.

Events in China were unsettling. Of more immediate concern to Akronites were developments in Europe. Hitler's escalating aggression over the years had led successively to Germany's occupation of the Ruhr, the Austrian Anschluss, the takeover of the Sudetenland, and then, in summer 1939, the threat to Poland's territorial integrity. In late August Hitler announced his intention to seize the port of Danzig and then launched an invasion on September 1. Britain replied with an ultimatum requiring Germany to withdraw by 11:00 a.m. on September 3. Where the sympathies of the *Beacon Journal*'s staff lay while all this was happening was plain. Beech stayed up through the night of September 3—the time difference between England and Akron meant that in Akron the ultimatum would expire at 5:00 a.m.—watching the reports roll in from the wire services. He wasn't alone. There was a crowd around the printers. Someone broke the silence: "Whyinhell don't they get this damn war started?" Another said: "It'd be just like Hitler to send a note at one minute to five saying, 'Hold on, boys, I didn't mean it.'" The minutes ticked by:

> At 5:15 a.m. an A.P. bulletin from Berlin says German Foreign Minister Von Ribbentrop received British Ambassador Sir Neville [*sic*] Henderson to give him Germany's answer to Chamberlain's last warning. 5:17 a.m.—the A.P. says from London that the deadline passed without any reply from Germany. Doesn't that mean the war is on? 5:22 a.m.—Chamberlain says Britain is at

> war with Germany. That is what we are waiting for. Outside it is getting brighter. The sun is coming up, and it is red.

Beech's instinctive opposition to Germany's aggression reflected his patriotism, his personal inclination, and the editorial stance of his paper. His position with respect to Communism was more circumspect. When the notorious American labor organizer and Stalin apologist Ella Reeve "Mother" Bloor came to Akron in March 1938 after a three-month sojourn in Russia, she got a satirical reception from Beech. The seventy-five-year-old Communist had assured a crowd of some four hundred sympathizers that the show trials in Russia were fair, that Stalin was no dictator, and that the Soviet press was not a "controlled press" but rather the "people's press." Beech noted that the audience was supportive but there was a dissident among them:

> Some unruly fellow in the third row back—Fascist, Trotskyite or perhaps even a capitalist—threatened for a time to create a disturbance with unintelligible bursts of heckling. Trouble was averted when an irate lady in the seat behind him gave him a sound whack over the head with her pocketbook. He shut up and said no more.

He struck a similarly indulgent note three years later after the Japanese attack on Pearl Harbor when he ran into some faces that were familiar to him:

> Useless but well-meaning citizen that I am, I went down to city hall the other day to volunteer for civil defense, and who should I spy but my old friend and comrade, Amos Murphy. Amos is the secretary of the Summit county Communist party, and seeing him reminded me that where there's a Murphy there's likely to be a Wenger. Sure enough, discreet inquiry revealed that Sigmund

> Wenger, who goes by the title of education director for the party in these parts, had also registered.

In what he wrote for the paper, Beech was apt to describe Communists as wrongheaded dupes and harmless cranks rather than an imminent danger to the republic. This had been true in his days with the St. Petersburg *Evening Independent*, when he interviewed Earl Browder. It would be true for as long as the Soviet Union was supported by America's allies in World War II. This is not to say that Beech ever viewed Communism sympathetically, only that his opinion, skeptical from the start, hardened over time.

His experience as a union rep marked an early step in the hardening process. In June 1941 he attended the American Newspaper Guild convention in Detroit as president of the Akron branch of the guild. It was a highly contentious gathering. For one thing, Australian-born Harry Bridges, founder and president of the International Longshore and Warehouse Union, was a featured speaker. Bridges was fighting off attempts by the FBI to have him deported as a Communist. The central controversy roiling the meeting, however, wasn't Bridges's battle with the authorities; it was the political orientation of the guild's national executive. Beech traveled to Detroit on his local's behalf with the express intention of voting for an explicitly anti-Communist leadership slate. Much later, he cited the convention as the place where his education in Communism began.

He was in his attic apartment at 118 Mayfield Avenue in Akron when "Elmer Davis' Indiana twang" broke into the New York Philharmonic Sunday broadcast to report that Japanese planes had struck Pearl Harbor. One positive outcome of the attack, he later claimed, was that he never finished writing the detective novel he was working on. But Beech did not immediately volunteer to fight. He remained at his desk at the *Beacon Journal* for another year, turning out stories about the local implications of the overseas struggle and ominous signs of what lay ahead.

The topics to which Beech turned his attention ranged from the functioning of the local draft board to the volunteer work of lawyers giving legal advice to conscripts. But nowhere is the newspaper's—and Beech's—clear understanding that Germany was an enemy that had to be defeated more clearly enunciated than in a series he wrote based on his tour of a handful of army bases. His admiration for the men he encountered there was obvious. And his fascination with powerful engines, already reflected in his trucking pieces, took a military turn when he camped out with an armored brigade at Fort Knox. Maybe it was an inspired editor who wrote the headline. The two-word term for a tank doesn't come up in Beech's text. But the piece was sufficiently stirring that the paper advertised his adventure ahead of time, asking readers, "Did You Ever Ride in a HELL WAGON?"

Beech, full of martial spirit, explained what it was like:

> You don't give a damn about anything. You are a living part of the armored monster in which you are riding. You just hope that something gets in your way so you can crush it. . . . We glided down an embankment, nosed upward, crushed a few inoffensive saplings and came to rest beneath a tree. The sense of power that comes from riding in a tank is almost overwhelming. There is nothing that so aroused the destructive instinct. I can see how even the most peaceful citizen could be transformed into a killer once he gets inside one of these mechanical monsters. I had an intense desire to pull the trigger of the machine gun in front of me. Nothing would have happened, because the gun wasn't loaded, but I didn't know that then. . . . I wondered what it would be like to be inside a tank when it was fired upon. Sergeant Funk told me. "It makes the hair rise on your neck," he said. "Sometimes in maneuvers we shoot at each other—machine gun bullets, of course. The bullets sound like rain on a roof."

Beech did not sign up until the end of 1942. It seems likely that he enjoyed his job as a reporter too much to give it up, even in a patriotic cause. No doubt the fact that he was married was a factor. He changed his mind when he discovered that the job of reporter and rifleman could be combined. The Marines initially called the writers they sent into battle "press sergeants." But it would be as a "combat correspondent" that he would serve until the war's end.

CHAPTER 2

War in the Pacific

THE BIRDS ON BETIO

They would miss Beech at the *Beacon Journal*. And Beech would miss Mildred. She had a job (as training director at a department store, the M. O'Neil Co.) and was active in society. There were dinners to host and attend. There were community events. Beech in his capacity as president of the Akron Newspaper Guild was involved in organizing the annual Gridiron Dinner. Mildred organized events for the Smith College alumnae club. Together they shared a house in a pleasant, leafy neighborhood with a Scottish Terrier named Tammy. (The little dog was something of a local hero, having once alerted neighbors with its barking when Mildred caught her hand in the wringer of their washing machine and fainted.) For Beech to be away from home for an extended period would be—as it was for all who went to war—a strain.

The role of combat correspondent was new, the brainchild of the Marine general in charge of public relations. Brig. Gen. Robert L. Denig's plan was to place two combat correspondents in every regiment. As the anonymous author of the introduction to a Marine publication put it later:

Figure 3. Beech in Washington, DC, following basic training, March 1943. Courtesy of National Photo Archives, no. 127-N-302827.

> It was their job to report the activities of the men in their outfit; to be in on the fighting; to go places where the regular war correspondents were not allowed, or did not choose, to go; to have access to restricted and confidential information which helped them to understand the problems of an operation; to be a Marine first and a writer second. Their material was made available to the press, radio and magazines of the United States and was widely used throughout the war.

The same writer made clear his view that these reporters were unlike other Marines:

> The Combat Correspondents were about twice as old and half as rugged as their fellow Marines. Most of them had been

> working newspapermen when the war broke out. They traded a green eye-shade for a helmet and wheedled their way into the Corps in spite of ulcers and varicose veins. They had the rank of non-commissioned officers and the gall of a rear-echelon second lieutenant, and they kept their typewriters in better condition than their rifles. Most of them are back, now, at their desks in the city room, interviewing public relations officers looking for jobs.

Whether or not the reporters were less rugged than their fellow leathernecks, they still had to undergo the exacting, not to say brutal, nine-week training regime required of all Marine recruits. Beech reported to the recruiting office in Cleveland on December 12, 1942. He trained at Parris Island through December and the first two months of 1943. In mid-March he was in Washington, DC, where his indoctrination as a combat correspondent was interrupted by a bout of measles, and by the end of the month he was back in Akron on furlough. From there, he took the train to the West Coast, where he was given orders to join the Marine 2nd Division, elements of which had taken part in the invasion of Guadalcanal. In May he was at sea, bound for New Zealand.

What the Marine Corps hoped for, and the correspondents delivered outside of combat, were stories that cast a positive light on the leathernecks' lives: their ingenuity, their skills, and their high morale. The pace of life, whether it was aboard ship in transit or in base camp awaiting assignment to a combat zone, was excruciatingly slow. Beech hinted good-naturedly at his frustration in a message to a colleague back in Akron:

> I suppose men have been saying it in every war since Caesar's time, but I can't help thinking that the worst part is the waiting. If only you could go ahead and fight and take your chances on getting out alive and get it over with. If you didn't survive, that

> would be too bad. If you did, swell. But the way it is, war is like a football game played with a month between quarters.

Over the course of the months-long posting in New Zealand, he filed gently admiring stories about the men he was encamped with. He wrote, for example, about an ornery chief cook who normally barred anyone from his galley but made an exception for the bugler who had to be up each morning as early as he did. He wrote about a corporal, a specialist in code and radio communications, who had just learned "through underground channels" that he was about to be promoted to sergeant, and was pleased by the prospect. He wrote about a Marine with a "booming baritone" voice who, within earshot of the enemy on Guadalcanal, had entertained his comrades with rousing renditions of favorites such as "Old Man River" and "The Road to Mandalay." No ordinary crooner, this artilleryman had studied music in New York and sung in music festivals across the United States.

Beech had been assigned to an artillery regiment. One day that September he watched from an observation post "atop a hill in the middle of a marsh" as the gun crews fired practice rounds that passed over his head:

> When the batteries in our rear opened up you could hear the shells coming over. They made a swishing sound, like a flock of swallows in flight. You could hear them and felt that you could see them, which of course you could not. But through binoculars you could watch where they landed and see the earth and water spout into the air.

Toward four o'clock, Beech noted, there was a phone call. Mr. Murphy, a local farmer whose routine had been disrupted by the Marines' presence, requested permission to drive his cows through the target area. "Mr. Murphy could," Beech reported, "but it was inadvisable. Mr. Murphy decided to wait."

Thus, over the course of the summer and fall the 2nd Division was kept occupied. The veterans of Guadalcanal, their ranks decimated, trained with the green recruits like Beech who had been shipped in from the States to bring the division up to strength. It was time well spent among people who were glad to see them. The New Zealanders appreciated what some of the Marines had been through and knew why they were there: their fates were intertwined.

In late October the idyll came to an end. The 2nd Marine Division was loaded aboard transports at Wellington's port city, Port Nicholson. They weighed anchor on Halloween. A week later the ships hove to off the island of Efate in the New Hebrides, where they were joined by the naval vessels that would give them cover in the coming operation. Beech and his fellow Marines didn't know yet their ultimate destination—the betting below decks was on Wake Island. Only when the armada left Efate was the secret shared. They were to seize from the Japanese a tiny atoll in the Gilbert Islands—Tarawa.

The fight for Tarawa was a bloody, close-quarters affair that came close to ending catastrophically. That it nearly failed can be traced to a number of mistakes and miscalculations, including an inadequate preliminary bombardment; a series of communications breakdowns; and the failure to account for a neap tide that left landing craft stranded on an outlying reef. It succeeded because some things went exactly right. These included the performance of the relatively new amphibious LVTs (Landing Vehicle Tracked, known colloquially as amtracs) and the timely support provided by two destroyers that sailed perilously close to shore in order to unleash their fire on Japanese positions. Some individuals—riflemen and tank crews—also made a difference by their acts of heroism. The toll the battle exacted, however, was sobering. The Marine Corps 2nd Division suffered a thousand casualties a day at Tarawa, the highest casualty rate sustained by any division in the war.

Beech was as ready as anyone could be. Like any other untested recruit, he had been anticipating the day when he would first come under fire, wondering what it would be like and how he would respond. He knew that there was to be a naval barrage before they landed. They had been told it would be devastating. Nevertheless, the thunderous roar of the battleships' 16-inch guns, backed up by those of the accompanying fleet, shook them. Beech and two companions were standing in the forward gun turret of their troopship in the early dawn of D-Day. "We chortled with unholy glee," he reported, "while our warships covered the Japanese shore positions with a blanket of fire." No enemy planes were in the sky. Perhaps everything was going to plan. Then, suddenly, there was the swishing sound of a shell overhead and a burst of spray fifty yards off the ship's bow. The men hit the deck, and one of Beech's companions turned to him and exclaimed, amazed: "Would you believe it! They're shooting at US!"

This first piece from Tarawa continues in a similar vein, reflecting something of the giddiness of men awaiting a momentous test. Beech picked up their wry barbs and throwaway comments as they watched and waited. A Marine gunner, who had been extolling the beauty of life in the Ozarks, paused to assess his chances of being killed by estimating the number of men going into battle. He reckoned the odds were "some thousands to one," and then added, "Of course, if they start whittling us down, the odds will get less and less." A sergeant grumpily reminded the gunner that, on learning how many Japanese were supposed to be on the island, he had worried there wouldn't be enough to go around. A sailor then complained that all the planes in the air appeared to be American. He wanted to try out the ship's anti-aircraft armament. "Personally," said another seaman, "it won't make me mad if we don't have to fire at all."

Beech was meant to land that day with a section of the 10th Artillery, the regiment he had trained with in New Zealand, but problems were soon apparent. There were not enough amtracs available to meet transport needs, so the deficit was filled by older Higgins boats whose deeper draft made them more likely to crash on the reef. An unexpectedly low tide made this even more likely, and enemy fire from shore reduced the number of both kinds of landing craft further. Two sections of artillery (each section consisting of two 75-mm pack howitzers and their crews) were successfully loaded onto amtracs and made it to the beach by late afternoon. Another three, loaded onto Higgins boats, made it as far as the reef. From there the cannoneers were obliged to break the guns down and carry them on their shoulders and backs, sometimes through shoulder-high water, and reassemble them in darkness. This was no small achievement. The howitzers, originally conceived of as a weapon to be carried by mule, weighed more than a thousand pounds. Their heaviest component weighed more than two hundred. Thanks to the men's efforts, by the next morning the officer commanding the onshore operation, Col. David M. Shoup, and Col. Presley M. Rixey, the artillery officer who landed with him, had guns at their disposal, tucked behind a berm cut into the coral sand by a bulldozer that somehow survived the landing. These guns would provide valuable support.

Beech wasn't there to see them. The demands being made on the landing craft were heavy and their losses considerable. What with the Higgins boats that never made it past the reef, the amtracs that broke down, and the landing craft of all description sunk by enemy fire, there was no capacity to spare. One combat correspondent stranded on a troopship rated low as a military priority. He could only plead, fret, and wait.

"I didn't get ashore until the third day," he later told friends back in Akron, "although journalistic pride impels me to state that I tried to get there sooner." He most likely landed with the 4th Battalion, 10th Marines, which took up position early on November 22 on the neighboring island of Bairiki. The 4/10, under Lt. Col. George

Shell, had been assigned to support a blocking maneuver led by Lt. Col. Raymond Murray's reserve battalion, the 2/6. The artillery on Bairiki would get a somewhat unusual assignment, to fire over the head of its forward observer on the eastern tip of Betio, in order to strike at the Japanese behind him. The observer, as Rixey later noted, "was looking into their muzzles." It was an eventuality that Beech had seen them rehearse months before.

The battle was largely over when Beech landed. At least it was clear that the Marines would soon control the island. Still, not all of the enemy had been routed. Hundreds of rikusentai—the Japanese equivalent of Marines—remained in blockhouses and bunkers from which it would have taken days to extract them. The Japanese made the task easier the night Beech landed by launching a series of coordinated counterattacks against their adversaries. The Marine guns played a grim part in annihilating them. A later policing of the ground turned up a grisly profusion of body parts. In a letter Beech hinted at but did not dwell on what he saw:

> That night the Japs launched their counter-attack. Our artillery blasted the hell out of'em. I was with an artillery unit in case you didn't know. I spent the night in a ditch, which the Japs had dug as a tank trap, about 50 yards behind the front line. The sky was criss-crossed with artillery, naval and machine gun fire. It was like Fourth of July at Portage Country club, only bigger and better.

He made light of what he had been through:

> The next morning I took a walk. I found a marine lying in a foxhole and asked him if this was the front line. He was dead. I found another marine, a live one this time, and asked the same question. He said he guessed it was and if I had a match he had a cigarette. We lay in his hole and smoked and wished we had some beer. There was sniper and machine gun fire all around, although

> it wasn't coming very close to us, and unless it does come close you don't pay much attention to it.

The marines were still mopping up the resistance when Beech filed another, more thoughtful piece:

> A bird flew in from the sea, making bewildered circles and uttering shrill cries, finally poising delicately to drink from the dark pool at the bottom of a bomb crater. Betio wasn't the peaceful tropical island that the bird had known. It was the third day after the Marines had landed and nowhere was there anything but the feel and smell of death.
>
> Except for a few pillboxes and an occasional sniper, the center of the rough triangle that is Betio had been cleared of enemy resistance. There was still heavy firing from the apex of the triangle but where we were nobody paid attention to it. Of the countless coconut palms only a few remained standing, and these were ripped and torn by shellfire. The ground was a welter of burned out oil drums, of blasted pillboxes, corrugated tin roofing, shell casings, coconut logs, twisted weapons and blasted machinery. . . . The Jap dead lay in heaps in and just outside the pillboxes and bunkers. Not all of them had died at our hands. Rather than surrender, many had placed the muzzles of their rifles against their heads and pulled the triggers with their toes. Most of the Marines who died lay on the beaches, their bodies washed by the waves.

Before he left Tarawa, Beech filed another story about a bird, an oddball story that developed something of a life of its own. A lieutenant from his regiment approached him as the battle was winding down and invited him to write about a duck that had fought heroically on the day they landed. Beech replied rather testily that he was tired, not feeling well, and there were bodies all around and to hell with the duck, or words to that effect. But the lieutenant persisted. The duck had been acquired by the unit in New Zealand, stolen or traded and originally intended for dinner, but it had become instead their mascot. All right, said Beech finally, I'll interview your duck. And the lieutenant replied that, no, that wasn't possible just then, because the duck was drunk. Beech, now sold on the pitch, set off in search of a photographer, who was as reluctant as he had been but came around, and together they found the duck. It was indeed drunk, "just sitting there making odd clucking sounds. He couldn't even produce an intelligible quack." And the story Beech wrote described how the duck, known as Siwash, had landed with the Marines and, according to its owners, attacked and defeated a Japanese pig, suffering minor wounds in the encounter. The lieutenant proposed to apply on the duck's behalf for a Purple Heart. The story was widely reprinted. The portrait of Siwash even appeared as Picture of the Week in *Life* magazine the following January. Beech came to wish that this wasn't the story from Tarawa he was best known for, but he still managed to turn its telling into a party piece.

The story of the two birds, the one that circled its devastated habitat in seeming confusion, the other that triumphed in its battle with a pig, sums up Beech's response to Tarawa as well as anything. He comfortably inhabited the role of a Marine, tough though not insensitive, and that of a reporter, with an especially keen sense of the absurd. There's no doubt, however, that the experience affected him. There would be time at sea, and then more time in a new camp, to process what he and his fellow Marines had been through and to share it as much as they cared to. Their destination, when they left Tarawa, was not New Zealand but Hawaii. They arrived there to find a camp already constructed by Seabees on the Parker Ranch in the northwest corner of the Big Island. "It was like any new camp anywhere, raw and ugly," wrote Beech, "and it was to be our new home for nobody knew how long. Somebody yelled disconsolately, 'Take me back to Tarawa.'" Later, another Marine, having checked the place out more thoroughly, said thoughtfully: "With a little more planning they could have picked a worse spot."

Tarawa Boom De-Ay

PUBLISHED BY AND FOR THE MEN OF THE SECOND MARINE DIVISION

January 6, 1944 — No. 1, Vol. I

Division Gains Fame At Tarawa

OKAY, MR. TOJO, YOU ASKED FOR IT!

TWO MARINES pose for a picture, but only one of them knew it. Standing over the dead Japanese Imperial Marine is a U. S. Marine, Private John H. Jennings of Columbia, Miss. It all happened when the Second stormed Tarawa Atoll and showed Tojo's Marines a few new tactics in modern warfare. (Photo by Sgt. Larry Burns, Division Photographer.)

Week's News In Review

(Continued on Page 2)

'Rec' Program Offers Varied Activities

Swimming, Fishing And Boating Plus Sports Planned For Men

By S/Sgt. Richard J. Murphy

(Continued on page 4)

Atlas, Alas, Is Little Too Late

General Smith Expresses Pride In His Outfit

Nation's Press Acclaims Feat Of Marines Who Took Jap Stronghold

By T/SGT. GENE WARD

(Continued on page 3)

Services And Turkeys Make Camp Christmas

Stateside Beer Takes Sting From Wind; Men Open Old, New Mail

(Continued on Page 4)

WARNING!

A WORD FROM THE GENERAL

To the Officers and Men of the Second Marine Division:

The beginning of the New Year, when our Division is again assembled in one camp, is an auspicious time to inaugurate the publication of a Division periodical.

In spite of the dispersion of the units of this command in the past, a remarkable spirit of unity has obtained, which I believe will be furthered by the systematic dissemination of news from the various organizations of the Division.

The Second Marine Division, under the guidance of Divine Providence, has made an enviable record during the less than three years of its existence. It has participated in two major engagements that have given the nation the names Guadalcanal and Tarawa to stand beside the Halls of Montezuma and the Shores of Tripoli.

It has been attached to two Amphibious Corps and has added lustre to the fame of each. It has been stationed on the territory of an allied nation and by its conduct has built up a spirit of cooperation and friendship that will be lasting and mutually beneficial to our respective nations. All in all, the Second Marine Division has lived up to and added to the traditions of the Marine Corps in peace and in war.

For the New Year, the record of our past performances must serve to inspire us to even greater achievements. We must continue on the road to decisive victory in order that our country may again enjoy the benefits of peace and security.

JULIAN C. SMITH
Major General, U. S. M. C.

Figure 4. First issue of *Tarawa Boom De-Ay*, January 6, 1944. Author's collection.

Such dour comments were to be expected: the men groused to entertain one another as much as they did to convey dissatisfaction. Their time in the camp, to which they gave the name Tarawa, was to be a period of recovery for the division. New recruits were taken in and new officers appointed. For Beech and the other Marine correspondents, it was a time to write feel-good pieces, to reassure the folks back home about the life their husbands, sons, fathers, and brothers were leading, and to issue what amounted to press releases about the awards being handed out to those who had distinguished themselves under fire. For the benefit of their peers, they turned out a camp newspaper, dubbed *Tarawa Boom De-Ay*. Beech was a Marine. His duty for the duration lay in writing articles that reflected well on the service. This he did.

THE FLAG

Life in Camp Tarawa may have lacked some of the amenities—especially, perhaps, access to a mixed-gender civilian population—that the division had enjoyed in New Zealand. But the Marines' 2nd Division was situated at a comfortable remove from hostilities in what amounted to a small town built entirely to military specifications. Twenty-five thousand soldiers were plunked down in the middle of nowhere or, more accurately, in a valley about twenty-six hundred feet above sea level between a pair of quiescent volcanoes. Here they reveled in the relative luxury of tents with plank floors, cots to sleep on, and hot meals from a fully equipped kitchen. They had electricity, refrigeration, paved roads, and water storage, and were able to share their luxuries, such as ice cream and chocolate, with the children living in the nearby village, Kamuela, for whom the treats were a novelty.

The villagers, numbering roughly 450, must have had mixed feelings about their new neighbors. The Marines brought noise, traffic, and occasional brawls but also company—lonely young men far from home who yearned for the small comforts they had enjoyed on the mainland. One resident of the village later recalled Marines in his kitchen canning fruit on his stove. Another invited members of the Marine band into his home where one of them played the piano. The Marines built a bridge over a stream by the school, supplied power when an electrical generator died, and rescued cattle trapped in hollows too deep for the beasts to climb out of. In their off-duty hours they engaged in team sports, organized a rodeo, played cards at night under electric light, and purchased at the Post Exchange minor comforts to ease their idle hours. It was a setting that fostered healing, where healing was called for, and a feeling of comradeship and esprit de corps.

At the end of April, Beech got a thirty-day furlough during which he returned to Akron and a welcome reunion with Mildred. He also stopped by the newsroom of the *Beacon Journal*, where a colleague remarked on the change that had come over him. "There was a day when I wouldn't have hesitated arguing with him over Sunday space allotments, baseball opinions, or what not," wrote the reporter. "I wouldn't want to tangle with him now."

Beech didn't go back to Camp Tarawa just then. After he left, the 2nd Division shipped out to take part in the invasion of Saipan and Tinian in the Marianas group of islands. Beech instead had a new assignment. In June he joined the recently formed 5th Division at Camp Pendleton in Oceanside, California. He spent his time there getting to know his new comrades, participating in their exercises, and writing more stories about Marine Corps life. And then Beech did go back to Camp Tarawa, this time with his new division. He was an old-timer now, in a position to show his new associates around the base and village. The mood was different. The battle-scarred 2nd Division had used its Hawaiian interlude to recover and rebuild. The 5th—a large part of which were raw recruits, built around a core of veterans—was girding itself for what lay ahead.

The kinds of training to which the Marines at Camp Tarawa were subjected became gradually more focused. Besides practicing landings, they were required, for example, to scramble up the sides of a smallish nearby volcano, on which they bestowed the chummy name Buster Brown. Through December, they were given briefings in which they got to know the shape and topographical features of a "gourd-shaped" island. And then, at the end of January 1945, they were loaded yet again onto troopships. Beech, after a hiatus of more than a year, was going back to war.

Another voyage. This one was interrupted on February 8 with a stopover at Eniwetok in the Marshall Islands. Three days later the fleet dropped anchor off Tinian. The troops participated in a final rehearsal there, scrambling down rope netting into the landing craft and chugging toward the beach but not landing. The lead ships, the ones carrying the troops scheduled to take part in the first waves of the assault, set out on February 15. The men now knew the name of the gourd-shaped island for which they were bound. It was Iwo Jima.

There may have been no uglier piece of real estate in the Pacific Ocean. This was no tropical paradise. It was part of the Bonin Islands, closer to Japan than to the equator. In fact, it was part of the administrative district of Tokyo, a Japanese possession from long before the war. The Japanese called it Sulfur Island in recognition of its only useful resource. No more than a few hundred people had lived there, and it was easy to understand why. It was difficult to grow anything in the volcanic ash. Rain was the only source of potable water. And the sulfur deposits released fumes across the island redolent of rotten eggs. The terrain was exceptionally rugged. An extinct volcano on the southern tip, Mount Suribachi, rose 554 feet above sea level. From the mountain looking north, the island gradually widened and rose in a series of rocky terraces and plateaus to its fat northern end, about four and a half miles away. A beach landing was possible only on the eastern or western side of the island's narrow neck, in the shadow of the mountain. Any invader landing on the beach inevitably started at a disadvantage, overlooked by an enemy ensconced on higher ground.

The island's strategic value, from the Japanese point of view, was that aircraft based there could harass the Americans on the territories to the south that the Japanese had lost. The Americans, for their part, wanted a base situated close enough to Japan to park the fighters that could protect their B-29 Superfortresses on their bombing missions to the north. Afterward, some critics would argue that the seizure of Iwo—and the thousands of lives lost or ruined there—had been unnecessary. But at the time, the taking of the island was seen as an unavoidable step in the steady advance on the enemy's homeland. The airfields, once they were in American hands, were in active use to the end of the war.

If the Americans had doubts about Iwo Jima's usefulness, their Japanese counterparts did not. In June 1944, an experienced officer, Lt. Gen. Tadamichi Kuribayashi, assumed responsibility for the defense of Sulfur Island. With scores of engineers and hundreds of workers under his command, he began building what was arguably the most comprehensive fixed defensive system ever constructed. Kuribayashi's men opened and enlarged existing caves and blasted new ones in the mountain. These he used to conceal gun emplacements, observation posts, and fighting positions. He had his men mine and tunnel beneath the airfields—there were two completed and a third under construction at the time of the American landing—building underground galleries, at least one of which was five stories deep. Kuribayashi chose not to focus on stopping the attackers on the shoreline, the defenders' strategy on Tarawa. He assumed that a beachhead would be established. His strategy, instead, was to make the attackers' progress inland as murderously difficult as possible. To this end, he constructed three defensive lines, each one with interconnecting pillboxes, bunkers, tunnels, spider holes, anti-tank ditches, minefields, and mortar trenches, and each taking advantage of such topographical features—hills, hollows, and open fields—that gave the defenders an advantage. Every built structure was camouflaged and protected. Kuribayashi knew that there would be a preliminary attempt to soften the island from the sea and from the air. The pattern of attack was well established.

What the Marines had learned from experience was that no amount of preparatory shelling was enough. It hadn't been enough at Tarawa. And it wasn't enough at most of the islands that had fallen in the intervening year. Lt. Gen. Holland M. Smith, commander of the expeditionary force, came close to living up to his nickname, "Howling Mad," in discussions with the commander of the task force assigned to pummel the island from the sea. Smith wanted a sustained barrage over the course of a week or more. What he got was three days. Granted, this was preceded and accompanied by intermittent bombardment by planes as well as ships over a period of months. But even the air force conceded, after studying follow-up photographs, that the preliminary working-over "had no appreciable effect in the reduction of the enemy's well-prepared and heavily fortified defensive installations." There was some evidence that the early bombing merely spurred the Japanese to step up the effort to make their defenses more nearly impregnable.

Three Marine divisions—the 5th, 4th, and 3rd—would take part in the assault on Iwo Jima as part of Maj. Gen. Harry Schmidt's V Amphibious Corps. Schmidt's plan called for the 5th Division to land on the eastern beach, cut across the island to isolate and then seize Mount Suribachi, and then wheel to the north in support of the 4th Division, whose mission from the start was to overcome the defenses arrayed around the airfields and beyond. The 3rd Division was to be held in reserve. It was understood that the fight would be tough, likely to take a number of days. No one anticipated that it would take as long as it did.

The attack began, as it had against Tarawa, with the thunder of guns and the rumble of bombs in the early hours of the morning. Beech's first dispatch on February 19 contained echoes of the earlier battle, but he was an experienced observer now.

At 3:00 a.m. he and his companions were roused by a shrill whistle and the call over the loudspeaker, "Up all hands! Up all hands!" Beech, groggy from shortened slumber, went to the head and splashed water on his face before making his way to the mess. They had been promised steak and eggs, but there was only steak, he noted irritably, no eggs. When breakfast was done, he climbed to the boat deck where it was still dark and the air "moist but warmer than the day before and the wind [had] died down." He climbed the gangway to the bridge. He could make out other transports as black smudges against the gray shimmering sea. He saw bright flashes on the horizon. A voice in the darkness said, "They've been firing like that all night. I'd hate to be those Japs." After another series of flashes, a sailor commented, "There won't be a Jap left alive on that island." Beech had heard this before. He said, "That's what you think." He turned and went back below. It was six o'clock, three hours before H-hour. He was still sleepy, he said, and didn't give a damn.

He was no longer assigned to an artillery battalion. Artillery had played a significant role in the earlier operation and would have a role in the coming one. But, for better or worse, artillery units rarely got the coverage in news bulletins—or, even after the fact, in histories—that rifle companies on the front line received. Now, as a member of the 28th Rifle Battalion, Beech would be in the thick of the fighting. He would get a better chance to show off his reporting skills.

What he could do in the first instance was describe what was before his eyes. He landed with the first wave about forty minutes past H-Hour, 9:00 a.m., on Monday, the 19th. He found, as others did, that the resistance on the beach was less than expected. The ground was soft. Men's boots slid into it ankle-deep, making progress arduous. Later, wheeled vehicles would get stuck and tracked vehicles struggle to obtain purchase. As the men moved forward, making it as far as the first storm-formed black-sand terraces, mortar and machine-gun fire began to exact a toll. Beech took cover. His initial observations reflect the detached, sardonic attitude that had infused his work back in Akron and, even earlier, in St. Petersburg. The incidents and snippets of conversation that caught his attention could be unexpected, but they also were reassuring: they tended to show how men strove to behave normally in abnormal conditions. His first dispatch, written from a foxhole about thirty yards back of the regimental command post, was filed just a few hours after he landed:

> Everybody drops into this hole coming or going. The fire is so intense all journeys must be broken many times as the runners seek momentary and partial safety in a shell hole. A few minutes ago a little black and white dog dropped in on us. He wore a camouflaged jacket. He carried two packets of carbine ammunition. His name is George. Navy Lieutenant (jg) Lawrence R. Grannis, 23 . . . just jumped in with us. "My first landing," he said. "I could certainly use a cold beer." A shell exploded a few yards away and a small fragment of steel plunked softly into the sand three feet away. "That came from over there," said Platoon Sergeant Joseph E. McGarvey, 31 . . . pointing to Mount Suribachi. "That's the trouble with this location," said Private First Class Richard E. Mathewson, 19 . . . "Every Jap up there must be able to see us." "It's time we were moving on," McGarvey said to Mathewson. "Pass the word on." Down the beach a wrecked amtrac tilts crazily. We can read its name: "Lena Horne." The sniper opened up again, a tiny but deadly sound. To our right the guns on Suribachi are still firing. Behind us, the roar of our Navy guns makes a thunderous reply.

The next day, D+1, he filed a story from a forward aid station:

> The first of the walking wounded came into the regimental aid station by himself. He didn't need to tell anybody what was wrong

> with him, for anyone could see that the flesh of his jaw was hanging by a piece. Some men turned their faces and went on talking while Lieutenant Charles W. Hatch, 27 . . . pulled the sagging flesh into place and wrapped a bandage around the man's head. Above the bloody jaw a pair of clear blue eyes darted from face to face. Their expression was unreadable. He might have been trying to smile, or it might have been a snarl. Two hospital corpsmen stood up to take the wounded Marine some 200 yards down the beach to be evacuated. He waved their hands aside and tried to talk, but only a strange and inarticulate sound came from what was left of his mouth. He shrugged and knelt down, a big, powerful man with blond hair cut so close to his head that you could see his sunburned scalp. While the corpsmen crouched beside him the wounded man tried to write in the sand, the loose volcanic sand. But as fast as his finger wrote the sand filled in what he had written, until finally in disgust he gave the sand an indignant brush with his hand and stood up. He was ready to go now.

More poignantly, Beech wrote on the same day about the death of S.Sgt. William T. Vessey, a younger man—twenty-four years old—with whom he had gone through basic training. Vessey, like Beech, was a Marine correspondent:

> If you will excuse the first person singular, I would like to tell you about my friend. He died about 15 minutes ago, but he had been dying for two hours, ever since that Jap mortar shell landed in the middle of our command post at 1 p.m. today. He was less than 50 feet from me but I didn't know he was there. . . . I went to the spot where the shell had struck. Half a dozen wounded lay there, patiently awaiting evacuation. I spoke to one of them, inquired about some more and moved on. It was raining. It still is. Somebody had tossed a poncho over the legs and body. The face was black with dirt, but here and there little white spots of

> skin showed where the raindrops had fallen. There was something familiar about the close-cut, wavy brown hair, the slightly curved nose, the firmly pointed chin with the suggestion of a dimple. I wiped some of the dirt away to make sure. I pulled the poncho back and quickly let it fall.

Some years after the war a friend of Beech, a CIA man who had known him in Saigon, told Beech's son Barnaby a story about Vessey's death. He said that Vessey was hit by a mortar round that blew off his legs and that Beech saw it and then, in a state of shock, rose from the hole in which they were sheltering and wandered around the battlefield, heedlessly calling for a corpsman. It's impossible to know in retrospect how these stories fit together, but there's no doubt that Beech was affected by the incident. Much later, when it came time to compose a memoir of the war, Beech wrote this:

> At Iwo Jima, when my best friend was killed, I wept. But I wept no more as my other friends were killed, one by one, day by day. Instead I felt like the little boy in a French motion picture I once saw. Because he stole money from his father's pocket, he was put to bed without supper. The family of eleven dined off mushrooms, which proved to be poisonous. The entire family died. At the mass funeral the little boy wept no tears. One might grieve for one, two, or perhaps three loved ones, he reasoned, but to grieve for eleven was too much! And so it was with me at Iwo. My capacity for grief had been exhausted.

The vignettes Beech was able to scribble or type in the thick of battle did not begin to give an overall picture of how the attack was developing. That picture was only dimly perceived by the officers overseeing it. What they saw in the first few days was discouraging. All units were taking heavy casualties, and some, especially the 4th Division in its mission to seize the first airfield, were stalled. Beech snatched what he could from the noise and confusion. He would use these stories to give color and texture to the more rounded accounts he composed later:

> On Iwo, where men lived with death, Marines laughed at strange things and let their feelings out. They roared when a Jap darted from a pillbox with a Marine in pursuit jabbing a bayonet at his rear. They laughed still louder when a second Marine cut down the Jap with his BAR [Browning Automatic Rifle] before the man with the bayonet could get there.
>
> One platoon of Marines surrounded a pillbox. Every time they tried to approach it, they were greeted by a barrage of grenades. The stymied Marines made catcalls to the Japs inside. Suddenly a Jap appeared on top of the pillbox and angrily set up a machine gun.
>
> "That guy couldn't take a ribbing," said one Marine after they shot the Jap.
>
> You don't pay so much attention to rifle fire unless it's close. Once, when three men dived into their hole as bullets began to kick up dust around them, a Marine walked past in the direction from which the fire had come.
>
> "Hey," called a voice from a foxhole, "there's a sniper up there."
>
> "So what?" said the Marine without looking back. "If there's a sniper up there why don't you shoot the bastard?"
>
> "That guy's from Chicago," said the foxhole voice bitterly. "Typical South Chicago."

By D+3, February 22, Beech was able to reconstruct some of what had happened in the preceding days. Easy Company had been charged with crossing the narrow, seven-hundred-yard-wide neck of the island in order to cut the mountain and its defenders off from the rest. It succeeded, but at a cost:

> Out of countless tales of heroism there came today the story of a Marine lieutenant and two enlisted men who fought their way through a maze of pillboxes, bunkers, blockhouses and machine gun nests to cross to the western shore of this island only 90 minutes after they landed on the east. When he hit the beach at H-hour four days ago, Second Lieutenant Frank J. Wright, 25 . . . had a platoon of 60 men. By the time he had crossed the island an hour and a half later two of the 60 remained with him and instead of being a platoon leader Wright was a company commander. Four of his company's officers, including the company commander, were killed or wounded as they attempted to follow him across.

Beech wove Wright's own words into his account of the action:

> "We weren't trying to run a foot race," said Wright, "but our orders were to get across the island as fast as possible, and that's what we did. The going was almost too easy at the beach. It was still easy coming up those terraces. But when we hit the crest of the ridge everything changed. What happened was that the Japs had withdrawn from the beach and the terraces and taken their positions on the ridge. Some of them had gone all the way down to Suribachi. I would move along ahead while Bechelli and Zuck kept me covered with their BARs. . . . As soon as I could see where we were going next I'd motion to them to come up. That way we made pretty good time, but we never would have got across as soon as we did if it hadn't been for the help the tanks gave us. We blew up some pillboxes but it was the men behind us who had to do most of the fighting. We were leading the way." At one point the three men came to an enemy 20-millimeter gun emplacement. There didn't seem to be a way around it, so Zuck leaped to the top of the emplacement and sprayed its occupants with his BAR, killing or wounding all of them. Later in those 90 dramatic minutes Bechelli did virtually the same thing.

Wright's company led the way. Other units followed them. But the mountain remained a bleak fortress that preoccupied the 28th for three more days. It wasn't until D+4, February 23, that it was secured. On the 24th, Beech made a passing reference to the raising of a flag on the summit in a dispatch that dwelt, not on that incident, but on the struggle that came before. (The passage in italics was crossed out on his typescript.)

> In the four-day battle that ended officially yesterday when the American flag was planted on Mount Suribachi, these things happened: A lone Marine charged an enemy pillbox and was met by a saber-swinging Jap lieutenant. The Marine grabbed the saber with his bare hands, took it away from the Jap and cut off his head. Two companies of Marines engaged in a grenade-throwing contest with the Japs, not daring to use rifles for fear of hitting their own men. When daylight came they counted 77 dead Japs in the area. One Marine took ten Japs with him in death. Alone, he stormed a pillbox and killed ten Japs before he himself was killed. *A Jap dived into a foxhole where Corporal Maurice F. Goodpasture, 21 . . . was standing watch. When Goodpasture's carbine failed to fire he held the Jap in his arms while another Marine shot him. When that failed to silence the Jap, Goodpasture grabbed a rifle and finished the job himself.* Two squads of Marines were isolated by enemy fire at the base of Suribachi 200 yards ahead of their lines. Two of the Marines were killed, eight wounded. The rest fought their way back in the darkness, dragging the eight wounded with them. . . . Marine demolition crews planted a 180-pound charge in a cave at the foot of Suribachi. A Jap picked it up and sat it outside the cave, then turned around and started back in. The Marines shot him and put the charge back where it belonged. . . . Sergeant Edward D. Jones, 30 . . . spoke enough Japanese to urge a wounded Jap to come out of a pillbox. The Jap refused, until Jones threatened to turn a flame thrower on the pillbox. The Jap,

> second prisoner to be taken on this island, told Jones his father runs a grocery store in Hawaii.

Beech climbed the mountain later in the day with Capt. Arthur H. Naylor of Fox Company, "a chunky blond man with no hat or helmet and a tear in the seat of his pants," as the mopping-up operation was still going on. The volcano had loomed threateningly over the regiment for days. There's no doubt its conquest mattered to the men who took it. When the Stars and Stripes was hoisted for the first time, men noticed. Many stood and watched. Some wept. But it was a moment only: the battle for the island was far from over. Neither Beech nor any other man that day had any idea how the story of the flag-raising would develop, how it would take on an extraordinary life of its own. The next day, February 25, Beech would get an inkling of what was to come.

That morning he received a summons from the command vessel, *Eldorado*, to attend a meeting with a fellow sergeant from the Corps and nothing less than the operation's most senior officers. Vice Adm. Richmond Turner and Lt. Gen. Holland Smith were men whom mere NCOs normally saw, if at all, from a respectful distance. But the officers had expressed a desire to shake the other sergeant's hand, and they needed Beech to compose a suitably fulsome record of the event. The other sergeant was twenty-year-old Ernest I. Thomas, known to his buddies as "Tommy" or "Boots." The reason the officers wanted to shake his hand, it turned out, was that Thomas had been one of the half dozen men who raised the first flag on Suribachi. Unknown to the men at the time, the flag-raising had attracted the attention not just of admirals and generals, but of the secretary of the navy, James Forrestal. Indeed, it went higher than that. The president of the United States, Franklin D. Roosevelt, had been advised of the incident, and he and his administration thought it might be exploited. They, unlike Keyes Beech and Boots Thomas, had seen a photograph. *The* photograph. The photograph that a diminutive Associated Press photographer, Joe Rosenthal, had snapped of the second flag-raising—a flag-raising in which Thomas had played no part. This was confusing. The confusion would get worse.

Both the first and second flag-raising were undertaken by Marines from Easy Company, of the 2nd Battalion, 28th Regiment. The first flag-raising was initiated by the battalion's commanding officer, Lt. Col. Chandler W. Johnson, who had brought a flag with him specifically for the purpose of signaling the accomplishment of his unit's primary objective. He sent a party of forty men up the mountain on the morning of the 23rd, first of all to make sure the mountain was secure (it wasn't, quite), and secondly to plant the flag. The patrol had been led by Lt. Harold Schrier, but he handed the task of hoisting the banner to Thomas. There were photographs of this first event too. A Marine photographer, Tech. Sgt. Louis Lowery, had called out instructions to the men to assist him by assuming an appropriately dramatic pose. It made a decent shot. But this was not the shot that caught America's imagination.

A few hours later, apparently at the direction of Secretary Forrestal, who was watching from a ship offshore, another party ascended the mountain with a larger flag. Joe Rosenthal joined them. He actually passed Lowery on his way up as the Marine photographer was coming down. Rosenthal knew that he had missed the raising of the first flag, which was the one with meaning to the men on the ground, but he figured he should have a picture anyway. So he slogged his way up the mountain and watched as another crew from Easy Company searched for and found a length of pipe, attached the new, outsized flag, and maneuvered it into position. He did not, as Lowery had done, call out instructions to the men who switched the flags. He stepped back some thirty feet, piled up some rocks to stand on, and snapped the picture as the flagstaff swung into place. There was more luck than art involved in the composition, although Rosenthal's experience should count for something. What he got, though he didn't know it at the time, was just about perfect.

He packed the film up and took it to the command ship that evening. From there, the film went to Guam for processing and review both by a picture editor and a military censor. Cleared by both, it was transmitted by radio back to the States. It first turned up on the front pages of American newspapers on the morning of the 25th. The same morning that Beech and Thomas were summoned to meet the brass.

Lieutenant General Smith greeted Thomas on the deck of the *Eldorado*. He posed with him for pictures. He intimated that Thomas was a hero. Thomas—unshaven and battle-begrimed as he was—then submitted to an interview with Don Pryor of CBS that was broadcast live to the United States. And then it was Beech's turn to ask the Marine some questions.

Neither Beech nor Thomas really understood what was going on. There was a photograph and Thomas was in it. (Only he wasn't in the photograph that people were making a fuss about. He was in the earlier one.) The flag-raising wasn't insignificant. Everyone's morale got a boost when the flag first fluttered in the wind. But it didn't make sense that his role in the incident made Thomas a hero, and yet that was the word that was being used. Beech took from this that his task was to establish Thomas's heroic credentials. He gave it his best shot. It's notable, however, that in the profile of Thomas he wrote that day, he alluded in the first line to his subject being "bewildered." Without doubt, the word described his own state as well:

> Marine Platoon Sergeant Ernest I. Thomas, 20 . . . is still bewildered by the things that have happened to him in the past few days. Thomas is the soft-spoken Marine who led his men up the bitter slopes of Mount Suribachi and planted the American colors at the summit. Shortly after his heroic deed, Thomas was taken out to the invasion flagship. There, the stubble and dirt of battle

Figure 5. Tech. Sgt. Keyes Beech, Lt. Gen. Holland M. Smith, and Sgt. Ernest I. "Boots" Thomas on board the *Eldorado*, February 25, 1945. Courtesy of National Photo Archives, no. 127-N-110299.

still on him, he met Vice Admiral Richmond K. Turner, head of the Iwo amphibious forces, and Lieutenant General Holland M. Smith, commander of the Fleet Marine Force, Pacific. The praises of high-ranking officers still ringing in his ears, Thomas was interviewed in a broadcast radioed to America. It was during this interview that Thomas insisted that others should be sharing the credit. "I didn't do it all by myself," he protested. "Those fellows who were with me ought to be out here, too." But it was Thomas who, when his platoon leader was hit, took over and led the Marines to the peak where the colors were raised. The story he told about the valiant fight was all about others, rarely himself.

Beech got almost nothing from Thomas about what happened on the summit, so he turned to asking about the fight that came before the ascent. Thomas, after all, had been in the company that trailed behind Second Lieutenant Wright, the platoon leader who found himself elevated to company commander in his march across the neck of the island. That hotly contested advance was an essential prelude to the seizure of the mountain, and the actions it entailed certainly involved acts of heroism. Thomas proved again to be a balky witness. Beech was able to extract only a few fragments of scenes that Thomas offered up as possibly newsworthy highlights. Beech was left to provide context as best he could:

> "On D-day plus three we attacked the hill," said Thomas. "First we had to pull out some barbed wire entanglements to get through. What we didn't know, because we couldn't see them, was that there were three or four pillboxes within twenty-five or thirty yards of the wire. I guess you could say we caught hell. We lost seventeen men out of forty-six in about forty-five minutes. That was when our platoon leader was wounded and I had to take over. After that, I don't remember much. I think I led some tanks up there to fire into pillboxes and caves. We were about one hundred and fifty yards from the foot of the mountain. I remember a Jap coming out of a pillbox and setting up a Nambu (a light machine gun) on top of it. I think about fifty of us shot him all at once. The Japs have got plenty of guts but they're stupid. They got a lot of us, but they could have got more if they'd been smarter. That guy coming out and setting up that Nambu wasn't smart. He was just crazy. Another thing I remember. That was a Marine climbing up on a pillbox with a demolition charge. A Jap came out of the pillbox—he didn't know the Marine was up there—and started to run away. This Marine leaped on his back and killed him with a knife."

Beech ended the profile with a thumbnail sketch of Thomas's background, where he was born, his education, his family. The article was no masterpiece. But then, the problems he faced in putting it together may have been insuperable. Both he and Thomas must have been relieved to return to their battalion that evening. There was a war going on.

The 5th Division got a few days' respite after Suribachi fell. The division wasn't entirely removed from the fray—the men still found themselves involved in skirmishes, and the heavy action was never more than a few hundred yards away—but their commanders had the opportunity to reorganize. The loss of so many officers led to promotions and changed assignments, and some cooks and clerks became riflemen to make up for the casualties. While the 5th regrouped, the 4th Division, reinforced by the 3rd (no longer in reserve), continued to plow its way slowly and painfully through the thickets of bunkers, pillboxes, tunnels, and gun emplacements on the central plateau. The obstacles they had to overcome acquired names that became part of Marine Corps lore: the Quarry, the Amphitheater, Hill 382, the Meat Grinder. On March 1 the 5th was ordered back into action. Their assignment was to move up on the left flank of the other divisions and drive the enemy into the sea. They too encountered obstacles that acquired names: Hill 362, Death Valley. Their lot was no less lethal than that of their comrades, as this dispatch from Beech indicates:

> Fox company's command post is in a shell crater on the left shoulder of a cliff on the forward slope of Hill 362. On the other side of that shoulder our men don't live long and the stretcher bearers, feeling terribly naked in their exposure to enemy fire, are working overtime. The faces of the men in the command post are familiar. They are men of the Second Battalion, 28th Marines, the regiment that took Mount Suribachi and raised the Stars and Stripes over the volcanic crater. But that was a long time ago, and this is another war on another end of the island. Twenty-five yards up the slope in full view of the C.P. [command post] there is a

> cave full of Japs. Fox company has been there since 8 a.m. today and the Japs keep throwing grenades into the C.P. The Marines have worked that cave over with flame throwers, demolitions, mortars and pack howitzers, but the Japs are very hard to kill and they continue to chuck grenades, like small boys with a pile of rocks. . . . It is difficult to talk in the C.P. The Jap mortars are coming closer, demolitions are exploding, our machine guns are rat-tatting and the Nambus are answering in kind. "Will the folks back home know what it's like out here?" It was Private First Class S. E. Olkoski, 30. . . . "Are you correspondents telling them what it's like?" I said we were trying, and crouched lower as shell fragments and pieces of rock began to rain around us.

The stories Beech filed from Iwo over the next two weeks continued to tread the narrow path he had scouted from the start. There are references to the horror the men witnessed and to which they contributed. Offsetting this are his observations of men's behavior under stress, the conversational asides, the quirks of character, and acts of selflessness and heroism. On March 12, for example, he described the situation at Captain Naylor's command post. "Except for a couple of days' rest," he wrote, Naylor

> had been on the lines since D-day, February 19. He is the only one of the original company officers left. His outfit has suffered more than 60 per cent casualties, but it is in no worse shape than many of the others. The Japs hadn't been able to slow him down, but dysentery had. He moved reluctantly, without his customary drive. He muttered something about one sniper holding up an entire platoon, then said: "I know what's the matter. Those guys are getting nervous. They can almost see the end of the island and they don't want to get knocked off now. Well, somebody's got to get knocked off."

In Beech's recounting, Naylor tapped a "thin, sharp-featured private first class" to call up the 3rd Platoon to get things moving:

> "I'm trying, captain, I'm trying, but that damned 'Able' Company keeps cutting in on our frequency," said the thin youth. Once a rabbit ran across his path and he became excited and exclaimed, "Oh! Wook at the wabbit!" Ever since then he has been called "Wabbit." "Wabbit" tried again but "Able" Company was so close it was like having two stations on your radio. "Wabbit" threw himself in the ground with a string of curses and beat his fist against the earth with rage and frustration. "Able," he screamed into the talkie, "will you get the hell off my line!" He listened for a moment and turned to the captain with an appalled expression. "You know what they said, Captain? They told me to go to hell."

A day later Beech noted a fleeting incident that doubtless reflected the image the Marines were happy to promote:

> There was a humming sound, like the buzzing of a bee, and a chunk of steel the size of a man's hand landed in the middle of the company command post. First Sergeant William J. "Gus" Geisendaffer, 34 . . . looked at the hot shell fragment, cooled it off with a squirt of tobacco juice, and remarked: "That one was getting personal."

Black humor continued to be a feature of the men's conversation. Beech noted Easy Company commander David Severance's amusement at the fatal expense of an enemy soldier:

> "You know these Jap grenades have to be 'agitated' before they are thrown," he said. "Well, we watched this Nip tap a grenade against his helmet in the usual fashion. Then he held it up to his ear. Nothing happened. He tapped it again and held it to his ear.

> Nothing happened. He tapped it a third time. This time it blew his head off."

By the end of the month, when it came time to sum up the operation in which he had taken part, Beech was perhaps less able to find levity in the experience. On March 24 he filed a story that focused on loss:

> The bodies of Marine dead are piled high in Death Valley. For four days men of the 28th Regiment, Fifth Marine Division, tried to take it by direct assault. They tried everything they knew and they failed. They failed because every man who set foot in that valley was as good as dead. . . . Death Valley isn't really a valley, although the Marines call it one. It is a long, winding gorge which extends from the northwest coast inland for about 700 yards. It is 200 yards wide. Its labyrinthine caves and tunnels are believed to house the Japanese command staff for the island.
>
> "I sent my men down there seven times," said Captain Robert B. Carney, 25. . . . "It was the hardest thing I ever had to do in my life. I told them each time that this time we would surely make it," Carney continued, "but I don't think they believed me. I couldn't blame them. I didn't believe it myself."

Beech's articles and others written by Marine correspondents did not hide the casualty rate—there was no concealing the butcher's bill when losses occurred on such a scale. Reporters working for independent news outlets were, in some cases, more explicit. Their reports caused consternation on the home front. So great was the uproar that Admiral Chester Nimitz issued a press release on March 16 stating that "the battle of Iwo Island has been won." The announcement, which was premature by about ten days, reflected the political pressure wrought by the losses. These were, in fact, virtually unprecedented: rarely had so many died in so short a time for so little real estate. Nearly 6,000 Marines were killed on Iwo; more than 17,000 were wounded; some 2,600 were judged to be suffering from battle fatigue. The Navy recorded 890 killed in action and close to 2,000 wounded. It has been estimated that the Japanese lost between 17,000 and 19,000 men.

Among those killed in action were a number of the men from Easy Company who had raised the two flags on Mount Suribachi. Colonel Johnson, the man who supplied the flag that signaled the summit's seizure, was killed by artillery fire on March 2. Louis Charlo, a Native American who helped plant the first flag, was killed in the course of the battle that followed. So were others among the flag-raisers who had served, to this point, valiantly but anonymously: Michael Strank, Franklin Sousley, and Harlon Block. So was Boots Thomas. Beech quoted another of the flag-raisers, navy corpsman John Bradley, when he wrote Thomas's obituary:

> "We were up on a sort of ridge," the corpsman said, "and we had to cross an open area. Before we jumped off 'Tommy' sized up the situation and said, 'It's going to be rough going over there.' But it wasn't so rough at first. I think we got across that open space without a casualty. 'Tommy' was up front, where he always was, when we came to a rocky area. Then we began to get rifle fire from all directions. There were caves all around us and we couldn't tell where the fire was coming from. 'Tommy' stopped beside a rock. He was holding his rifle straight up with the butt on the ground and was reaching for a phone when a bullet knocked the rifle out of his hand. You see, we had a wire-laying man with us to keep up communications. 'Tommy' didn't do anything but glance at the rifle. He just went on talking over the phone to the first sergeant. He was telling him he didn't think we ought to advance any farther without some protection from the platoon on our right. Then he got hit and pitched over. The telephone fell out of his hand. He never knew what hit him."

The men who were fighting were not much interested in the identity of the men who had raised the flag. But the question was being asked. Rosenthal's picture had aroused enormous interest, and messages were being passed down the line that required attention. It fell to Beech, among others, to see what he could do. By now he had Rosenthal's photograph as a reference. He knew that two groups of men were involved. But identification was problematic. Some were dead. And some didn't want to be identified. One of the group involved in the second effort, Ira Hayes, passed word to his fellows to keep him out of it. He was out of luck. Another of the group, Rene Gagnon, gave him up under pressure from officers whose seniority made them formidable interrogators. But even with a willing witness, putting names to men whose backs were turned to the camera or whose bodies were mostly obscured was a challenge. In the end, six names were made public: Franklin Sousley, Henry Hansen, Michael Strank, Ira Hayes, Rene Gagnon, and John Bradley. Of these, the first three had perished, and, as soon became apparent, one was misidentified. Hansen, who was in the first flag-raising group, was not in the second. His position was occupied by another Marine, also since deceased, Harlon Block.

The confusion didn't end with Block's belated recognition as one of the flag-raising party. A brilliant bit of photo analysis in 2014 led to further revision. It showed that navy corpsman John Bradley's place in the tableau was, in fact, occupied by another publicity-shy Marine, Cpl. Harold Schultz. And then, in 2019, the Marine Corps acknowledged yet another error: the figure so long identified as Rene Gagnon was Cpl. Harold Keller. Both Schultz and Keller survived the war. Like Ira Hayes, they didn't want any part of the publicity. Given what followed, their reticence was prescient.

THE SKY ROOM

The 5th Division was taken off Iwo beginning March 26. They would return to Hawaii and from there, after a respite, board transports bound for Okinawa in the expectation that the invasion of Japan itself was imminent. The detonation of two atomic bombs in August, the first on Hiroshima, the second on Nagasaki, rendered the invasion superfluous, and the invasion force became instead an army of occupation. In any event, Beech, for once, avoided a sea voyage. He and the three surviving men who had been identified as flag-raisers—Bradley, Hayes, and Gagnon—were about to be sucked into a maelstrom of publicity for which none of them was prepared. The US Treasury had been depleted by the war. A massive publicity campaign was envisioned to rebuild the country's finances. It needed only a galvanizing theme, and Rosenthal's picture was it. The Seventh United States War Loan tour was singularly successful in achieving its goal: Americans pledged $26.3 billion, almost twice what the Treasury had hoped for. But it was hard on the men who were called on to be the tour's chief shills. Beech, assigned to serve as their chaperone, was dismayed by the humbug that the tour entailed. Ira Hayes never recovered from it.

The photograph had been reproduced in virtually every newspaper and most magazines in the country. It conveyed at a glance the idea of a victory hard-won by men willing to sacrifice their lives. Everyone had seen it. Everyone admired it. For the tour, it was replicated in posters, on medallions, in pamphlets and ephemera. Plans were laid to make it the model for an enormous statue, later to be erected at Arlington cemetery, as a reminder of Marine Corps valor, of what they had won, and at what cost. On the tour itself, there would be reenactments in which the three Marines filled the starring roles. They were asked to do, again and again, what they were supposed to have done on Mount Suribachi, but this time in public squares and in stadiums, before thousands of civilians whose patriotism was aroused by the spectacle. Probably it was necessary. It undoubtedly served its purpose. It was also, in many ways, demeaning to everyone involved.

On May 24 Beech was flown from Iwo to Guam. From there, after a one-day delay because an officious naval ensign couldn't believe a dirty, unshaven leatherneck had legitimate claim to priority air transport, he caught a civilian flight to Washington, DC. The mode of travel was itself a novelty: this almost certainly was his first experience of commercial flight. More shocking still was to leave behind the carnage on Iwo, where corpses still littered the ground, and in an instant enter the clean, cocoon-like comfort of a modern airliner. While in transit he wrote an article that reads as the reflections of a man struggling to come to grips with disorienting change:

> Did they tell you it was a small world? Five days ago I was only 660 miles from Japan and at this minute (8:20 p.m., Tuesday, March 27, 1945) I am somewhere over Arizona, or perhaps it is New Mexico. Tomorrow I will be in Washington. That's how small the world is. This is one of the great airliners with soft maroon upholstery and seats that recline when you press a button. Not at all like the bucket seat job I rode from Iwo to Guam.

As he thought about what he had experienced, he was struck by an image: the sand on Iwo Jima's beaches:

> It is very easy to forget Iwo Jima here in this cozy little world five thousand feet above the earth, but the little things keep reminding me. Back there at the last stop when I pulled out my pocket comb the particles of black sand clung to the teeth. Not like the fine white sand of the beaches of Tarawa. No, there is something sinister and ugly about this black sand. Some of the correspondents called it volcanic ash. If it was ash, it was like no ash I ever saw. . . . Ash or sand, it certainly made tough going up those terraces. You sank into it up to your ankles. When I asked Lieutenant Colonel Jackson B. Butterfield where the going had been hardest for him, he replied, "Getting up those damned

> terraces." The colonel is short and chubby and isn't built for that kind of travel.

If the colonel was ill-equipped for the hike through shifting sand, such footslogging had been for some time Beech's accustomed lot. Now he found himself airborne, and he was no more suited to the air than the colonel was suited to the sand.

The piece, to this point, is disjointed. Beech was struggling to bring together vignettes from the battle and his rekindled sense of the America to which, with disconcerting abruptness, he was being returned. He landed on two stories: one about a Marine randomly robbed of his life, and one about a tough old sergeant who succumbed to a private's cheerful banter:

> The plane has landed and is taxiing up toward the brightly lighted terminal. A discreet blue neon sign advertises the existence of the "Sky Room." That sign takes me back to long ago—almost two weeks ago. "I" company was moving up behind "B" company to "mop up." "Mopping up" means that the battle is over—for everybody except those doing the "mopping up." Kugalowski, the demolitions man, was shot right through the head the day before I left Iwo. He was "mopping up," but Kugalowski is just as dead as if he were killed on D-Day. He lay there in a ravine in plain sight and we believed he was still alive because one of the boys said he saw him twitch. But nobody was about to go down there to get him so long as that sniper was registered on him. That was what the sniper was waiting for. Get the sniper first and then get Kugalowski.
>
> What was it the sign made me remember? Oh, yes. The "I" company men flopped down in a gully while two scouts went ahead to look over the ground. A tall young PFC busied himself making a gallon of synthetic lemonade. When he had finished he invited everybody over. The old gunnery sergeant didn't move.

> "Mooney," said the PFC.
>
> Mooney didn't look up.
>
> "Aw, Mooney," said the PFC, brushing the big, fat, blue flies away from the lemonade. "Come on over and be friendly. This is the Sky Room."
>
> Mooney grinned and got up and drank some lemonade.
>
> The scouts came back and conferred with the dimpled young second lieutenant, who had joined the outfit only three days before as a replacement. The lieutenant asked one of the scouts, a corporal, if he had drawn any sniper fire. The corporal said he hadn't, but that didn't mean anything. The enemy is patient and likes to take as many of us with him as possible. "I" company began to move out.
>
> I didn't have to go, so I stayed where I was, drinking the lemonade the PFC had given me and watching them file by, one by one, stooping low and moving fast as they went up over the embankment. They had been out of sight only a little while when I heard the fast rattle of a Nambu. Then somebody was yelling, "Corpsman! Corpsman!" in a hoarse voice. I told you I didn't HAVE to be up there.

The article would have benefited from editing. But it reflects the state of mind of a man emerging in a matter of hours from one of the bloodiest battles of the war into the soft embrace of American civilization without first having the chance to decompress. The transition was too quick. The chaos of battle and the comforts of the Sky Room were not easily reconciled.

Reconciling conflicting realities would be a challenge for all four of the men who were wrenched from combat and plunked down in Washington at the start of the tour. It may have been easier for Beech than for the others: he at least had no part in the pantomime reconstruction of the summiting of Suribachi. Of the putative actors, the navy corpsman, John Bradley, may have been the best equipped to deal with what lay ahead. He had spent the previous month binding the wounds of badly banged-up Marines, a task he had performed with courage and at enormous personal risk, a fact attested to by the leg injuries he had sustained that kept him on crutches throughout the tour. Rene Gagnon was another matter. He relished the spotlight, posing cheerfully for the cameras and embracing the hosannas rained down on them. He saw in the whole charade an opportunity for his own advancement. The third member of the party was the least well equipped. Ira Hayes was a dedicated Marine. His fellow Marines liked and admired him: he had shown himself to be a brave and efficient comrade. But he was made deeply uncomfortable by the attention. The people they met on the tour, including members of the press, could be thoughtless and crass. They drew attention to Hayes's status as a Native American, asking him questions that were insulting when they weren't racist, such as "How did you get a name like Ira Hayes, Chief?," and demanding "How many Japs you killed, Chief?" Hayes responded for the most part by clamming up.

He took refuge in alcohol. The writer James Bradley, quoting a wire-service correspondent, George McArthur, who in later years was close friends with Beech, suggested that Beech enabled Hayes's drinking habit: "Keyes was a big drinker. He was a drop-dead alcoholic until he joined Alcoholics Anonymous in the 1960s. He used to tell me that he and Ira drank every night on the Bond Tour and that his main job was to get Ira to the scheduled events."

McArthur's recollection, of course, is accurate: Beech was an alcoholic. But Beech had the ability to keep his drinking and his day job separate. He pursued his career as a reporter with single-minded determination, always intent on getting the story at whatever cost. The price of his drinking was paid, not by his employers, but by his wives and children. Hayes had no such ability.

In recalling this time years later, Beech remembered telling Hayes that "the War Bond drive was show business":

> Show business is make-believe. You make up stories, and it's all right because it's for a good cause. And in this show business you're representing the Marine Corps. So it's all right to drink, but during the day, when you have to meet the public, you got to straighten up and smile and do like the home folks expect you to do.

As for the reporters, Beech told Hayes, you can leave them to me.

All four Marines were plied with alcohol, along with rich food and exalted company, from the start of the tour in Washington, DC, where a luncheon was held in their honor at the Capitol, to the end (inevitably) on the Fourth of July. The fundraising got off to an official start on May 11 in New York, where the trio was called on to raise the flag in Times Square with Mayor Fiorello LaGuardia and Marine Corps Commdt. Gen. Alexander Vandegrift looking on. From there, they traveled to a succession of cities and towns in almost every region of the country: Philadelphia, Akron, Chicago, Detroit, Indianapolis, St. Louis, Tulsa, San Antonio, Austin, Portland, Seattle, Appleton, El Paso, Houston, Dallas, Phoenix, Tucson, Denver, Milwaukee, Atlanta, Greensboro, Tampa, Charleston, Richmond, and Norfolk, before finally returning to Washington. They didn't get far, however, before they lost Ira Hayes.

Beech was responsible for getting his weary band from one stop to another. He was their intermediary with the press: he had to make sure they presented the appropriate martial image while also protecting them from the public's more intrusive demands. Depending on the occasion, he sometimes introduced them himself and in the process encouraged the audience to purchase bonds in support of the war. Our fighting men "get sore as hell" at the notion that the war will soon be over, he told a crowd at the Loew's Theater in Akron on May 17. "Such news would be a great surprise to the guys getting shot on Okinawa tonight and tomorrow night. . . . Nobody out there is going to stop fighting just because people at home don't buy war bonds," he went on. "But they are going to know whether or not the Seventh War Loan is successful and will know whether or not the people at home are in back of them." And then, with the unsubtle suggestion that a failure to purchase a war bond (or several) implied an abandonment of men who were giving up their lives, he turned over proceedings to the three heroic survivors. Beech, again, was doing his bit.

He had another practical responsibility: to take care of the flag itself—the flag from Iwo had become a sort of sacred talisman. He assigned the task to Ira Hayes. "I [knew] if anyone tried to take it away from him," Beech explained, "he would've broken their arm."

Perhaps Beech hoped the task would infuse Hayes with a sense of purpose. If so, the tactic failed. Matters came to a head at Chicago's Soldier Field on Sunday, May 20. On what was billed as "I am an American Day" to welcome new citizens to the city, movie star Pat O'Brien was scheduled to act as master of ceremonies in the presence of a roster of Hollywood luminaries, including Humphrey Bogart, Lauren Bacall, Sonny Tufts, and Sophie Tucker. An hour of music was to be provided by military bands. General Vandegrift would be awarding a Silver Star to the mother of a Marine who died heroically on Guam. And, inevitably, the trio from Iwo would be asked again to climb a scaled-down replica of Mount Suribachi and plant the flag on its peak. Admission was free. There was every expectation that the stadium's seats would be filled. On Saturday night, Ira Hayes disappeared.

He was found by police on Sunday morning, wandering the Loop, and very drunk. Beech took him back to the hotel, poured quantities of ice water and coffee into him, and coaxed and cajoled him into a semblance of sobriety. There wasn't much time: the celebrations were scheduled to begin at 2:00 p.m. Somehow they made it to the stadium, and when they got their cue, Beech made sure that Hayes was securely wedged between Bradley and Gagnon in the back of the open-topped Cadillac in which they were ferried around the field. Hayes was clearly unsteady when they did their flag-raising routine and his condition was noted by observers, the Corps commandant among them.

> I was sweating blood when a voice behind me said: "I understand your Indian got drunk on you last night."
>
> I turned to make a nasty crack in defense of Hayes when I saw the four stars on General Vandegrift's shoulder. . . .
>
> "I know those Indians," continued the general. "We had lots of them on Guadalcanal and they were damned good men. But they aren't much for bond tours. How much longer do you go on with this?"
>
> "About a month, sir," I said.
>
> "My God!" the general shuddered.

The tour continued, but wheels were set in motion.

A couple of stops later they were back in Chicago. Beech and Hayes were summoned to the district Marine Corps recruiting office where Hayes was told he was being sent back to rejoin Easy Company. He asked if he could stop to see his family in Phoenix and was told no, he could not. Beech asked for and was given permission to call General Denig, in the hope that the general would intercede on Hayes's behalf. Denig responded, apologetically, that the order had come from the Marine Corps commandant. There was nothing he could do. "That evening," wrote one of Hayes's biographers, "Beech watched as Ira Hayes boarded the plane that would take him to the west coast. The bond tour had been 'an agonizing experience for him, he was extremely shy.' The hero worship, perpetuated by the media, would seal his doom. That was the last time Keyes Beech saw Ira Hayes. 'The only thing that ever mattered to him,' Beech would say later, 'was his mother and the Marine Corps.'"

Beech had few fond memories of the tour. "It was a circus," he told a reporter for *Us* magazine in 1985. "The three weren't really needed on the tour and I knew they felt awkward being trotted out like a Vaudeville routine." Bradley recovered from the shrapnel wounds that had made him lame. After the war he went home to Wisconsin, married, opened a funeral home, and fathered eight children. Rene Gagnon fared less well. He made the most of his celebrity, but between public appearances his work history was bumpy. When he died, in 1979, it was as the maintenance man in an apartment building in his hometown, Manchester, New Hampshire. Hayes survived the war but not the peace. He died of exposure and alcohol poisoning in December 1955, alone in an unheated cabin on the Gila River Indian Reservation in Arizona. His death can't be attributed directly to his experience on the bond tour, or to his discomfort with the fame that nagged at him in the years after the war. And yet, neither factor can be discounted. Nor can the experience of war itself: to some degree it wounded almost all who experienced it, mentally if not physically. Some coped more or less easily; others faltered in the attempt.

Beech, too, had difficulty adjusting to the peace. The "circus" of which he became a part in spring 1945 may, in its way, have scarred him just as the war did. Whatever role alcohol had in anaesthetizing him after all he and his fellow Marines had been through, he at least had recourse to another kind of therapy—he could write. And that fall, before he was demobilized, he wrote.

Beech had a significant part in the composition of two books that drew on his experience on Iwo. The first, *The U.S. Marines on Iwo Jima*, was published with impressive efficiency before the end of 1945. It was written by five combat correspondents, all of whom had taken part in the invasion, each attached to a different battalion. The five are credited with the text in its entirety, rather than authorship being assigned to specific chapters, but it is possible to trace at least some of Beech's contribution by referencing the pieces he had submitted previously as dispatches from the field. Chapter 5, "Suribachi," appears to be almost entirely his work.

The second book to which he contributed provided a potted history of the five Marine Corps divisions that served in the war. In *Uncommon Valor: Marine Divisions in Action*, Beech tells the story of the 5th Division from its formation in Camp Pendleton in January 1944 to its disbanding at the same camp two years later. *The U.S. Marines on Iwo Jima* has a raw, stitched-together feel to it, a strength as well as a weakness. Beech's profile of the 5th in *Uncommon Valor* combines material he gathered from others with his own observations. It's a balanced and tidy piece of work.

Beech, perhaps more than other Marine reporters, brought a bit of swagger to the items he wrote. The sergeant who cooled a fragment of shrapnel with tobacco juice was an archetype whose counterpart could be found later in comic books. Similarly, Beech's penchant for picking up facetious dialogue in dire situations, and his eye for the absurd and grotesque—his instances of "battle humor"—were habits not widely emulated by his peers. The dialogue and the incidents were real enough. When the private in Fox Company said, "Wook at the wabbit!" and so acquired a nickname, Beech was riffing on the cartoon culture familiar to his readers. When Captain Severance laughed at the Japanese soldier who blew his own head off through the careless manipulation of a hand grenade, he was not so much recounting a droll incident as inviting his listener to share his amazement at something that scarcely seemed real.

Beech, in civilian life, had mastered an approach to profiling personalities by picking up on quirky details. He applied the same technique to war. The technique served the same purpose for Beech the writer as it served for the men in the field. It created a space between the awfulness of what was happening and the people who somehow had to navigate a way through the experience. It represented an attempt to keep from being overwhelmed. In Beech's case, it might not have been entirely successful. From the shock of Tarawa to the unrelenting urgency of the almost interminable battle for Iwo Jima to, finally, the surreal circus of the Seventh United States War Loan drive, he had a hell of a war.

CHAPTER 3

Between Wars I

THE BOMB

The immediate postwar period brought a renewal of Beech's marriage, a new job, and—in short order—not one or two but three changes of scene. The obvious, tangible adjustment to civilian life in unfamiliar locations would be drastic. Adjusting to domesticity was no less a challenge. Going home after years of all-male company in military encampments could be felt as a welcome relief or as cloyingly oppressive. Perhaps both. The evidence suggests that Beech and Mildred were more than happy to be reunited at war's end. But then, as they worked out the actual conditions in which they would adapt to peace, the relationship changed. It takes no great psychological insight to conclude that Beech, for a time, succumbed to depression. Perhaps Mildred did too.

When Beech flew back to Washington at the end of March, he understood that two assignments awaited him: to chaperone the flag-raisers and to write Marine histories. Of the two assignments there's no doubt which one had greater appeal. Beech told the *Beacon Journal*'s city editor, Charles Miller, over a restaurant meal

Figure 6. Beech, 1948. Courtesy of Walter Beech.

two days after his arrival in Washington, that he had been brought back to write a book. He didn't mention the bond tour. It's entirely possible that he still hadn't come to terms with his return to civilization and that he hadn't fully grasped what a big deal the tour would turn out to be. Miller, in his profile, wrote that Beech was "still a little dizzy about it all." He noticed that Beech kept fingering the linen tablecloth as the two men faced each other, seemingly taking greater pleasure in the tactile sensation than in the food. In any event, the authorial task was what Beech looked forward to. It had the consequential side effect that he would not be returning to his battalion but staying in Washington. The move was welcome for another reason: Mildred was with him. She tapped him on the shoulder to speed the end of the interview with Miller. They had been separated for too long.

They had seen each other just once since Beech joined the Marines. After Tarawa, he had been furloughed for a month and spent most of April 1944 in Akron. Mildred still had her job at the M. O'Neil Co., but she dropped everything to join him in Washington. The war wasn't over yet. The chance to be together was too precious to be missed.

The book projects kept him occupied through the summer, past VE Day and the Japanese surrender, into the fall. He used the time when he wasn't writing or correcting galleys to renew his contacts with the civilian press. He chose not to return to the *Beacon Journal*. Instead, he accepted the post of Washington correspondent with the *Honolulu Star-Bulletin*. The segue could not have been neater. Within days of his discharge on October 17, 1945, he was turning out articles on the Washington political scene. Most of these were routine. All had a bearing on the military, and most on operations in the Pacific. The proceedings of a congressional committee investigating corruption, for example, produced particularly juicy items of interest to Hawaiians. Testimony before the Mead Committee revealed that a naval officer had diverted some one hundred thousand dollars' worth of meat from a supply depot in Pearl Harbor to restaurants in Honolulu and pocketed the proceeds. The naval legal team that might have been looking into this activity attended a party thrown by the officer at which a pig was roasted. Unwittingly or otherwise, the lawyers and other guests tucked into evidence of the crime.

A story like this was diverting, but the means by which it was gathered, which mainly entailed hanging around government buildings and picking up press releases, was tedious. Beech soon concluded that he wasn't cut out to be a Washington-based political reporter. Jack Knight and the *Star-Bulletin* came together to offer him a way out: the *Star-Bulletin* agreed to "loan" Beech to the foreign news service that Knight had set up based on the editorial staff at his Chicago paper, the *Daily News*. Beech would be their military affairs correspondent writing from Honolulu. The Chicago paper was a good fit. Beech was Tennessee-born and Florida-raised; he had matured as a reporter in Ohio, but the character of the *Daily News* suited him. It was the city's largest-circulation newspaper. It was smart, scrappy, inclined to be irreverent, and, at heart, as tough as nails. Its foreign staff, whose reports eventually were syndicated to some seventy papers across America, was top-notch.

Mildred, eight months pregnant, flew from Washington at the end of December to set up house on Green Street a few blocks from the waterfront in Honolulu. Beech, not wanting to give up their car, drove it to San Francisco and watched it being loaded on the Matson Line freighter *Mokihana*. The ship was delayed by a storm in which crew members were injured. It finally reached its destination on January 2. Some three weeks later, on January 26, Beech became a father for the first time when Mildred gave birth to an eight-pound, four-ounce baby boy, Walter Keyes Beech, to whom they gave the nickname "Thumper."

Over the next four years Beech's focus would shift, like that of his readers, from a preoccupation with the winding down and refocusing of the nation's military machine to the emerging threat of Communism and Communist-inspired nationalism abroad. For more than a year he was assigned solely to military matters and remained based in Honolulu. In mid-1946 his "on loan" status with the Honolulu paper came to an end. While the *Star-Bulletin* then and for years after was one of his most faithful subscribers, Beech would serve solely as a correspondent with the *Daily News*'s foreign staff. In the spring of 1947, he moved to Tokyo as regional bureau chief with responsibility for goings-on in Japan and Korea. A year after that, he was reporting from China, as Chiang Kai-shek's Nationalist forces ceded territory to the Communists, and by 1949 his remit embraced the Philippines too. As the years passed and his responsibilities were expanded, his writing assumed an air of worldly authority. By 1950 he was an acknowledged Asia hand.

The pieces he wrote at the beginning of this period must have felt like a continuation of his war service. He wrote movingly of a return to Camp Tarawa, then in the process of being dismantled. He made a tour of Pacific battle sites, including Saipan and the Marshall Islands. He noted, in passing, that the Marshallese demonstrated shocking skill at baseball, which Americans fondly regarded as their national game. "Native teams have defeated navy players so consistently," he wrote, "that the latter don't like to discuss the matter."

Beech didn't see the dropping of the atomic bombs on Japan or their immediate aftermath. He was, however, one of the cadre of reporters who watched the tests conducted in 1946 in the vicinity of Bikini Atoll. The US military was itself still striving to assess the uses and capabilities of their new weapon. Scores of ships from the once-mighty Japanese navy were brought to the test site to be used as targets. Journalists there to observe the bomb's destructive power were bunked on board the *Appalachian*, an amphibious force command ship similar to the *Eldorado* on which Beech had interviewed Boots Thomas the year before. There were a number of preliminary tests in June, which failed to greatly impress the press corps. The explosion on July 25 was something else:

> The most spectacular sight man's eyes have ever seen came today when the world's fifth atomic bomb was exploded in the center of a 75 ship target fleet in Bikini lagoon. A titanic force with an estimated strength of 400,000 one hundred pound depth charges rent the waters of the lagoon and sent a plume of water shooting into the sky for more than 8,000 feet. Forty thousand ton battleships were tossed about and even lifted clear of the water by a giant water hammer traveling at 7,000 feet per second.

He had known, like everyone else, what had happened at Hiroshima and Nagasaki, but this was something he witnessed himself. It made a lasting impression.

Beech was visited that summer at his home in Honolulu by a fellow Marine, a sergeant major who had seen fighting in some of the toughest battles—Guadalcanal, Tarawa, Iwo Jima—"always with an assault outfit." A rumor had gone around Iwo that he'd been killed or wounded. In the circumstances the notion was plausible but, as it turned out, unjustified. "I'm too old and ornery [to be killed]," said the sergeant major, a claim that Beech saw fit to confirm. Now the sergeant major was having a hard time adjusting to peace. He complained that he'd been made to eat with the WAVES back on the mainland. This offended his sense of the proper order of things. "Everything's all fouled up back there," he said. "The sergeant major is in his middle 40s," Beech wrote. "His face is long and thin and no amount of exposure to the elements will take away that pallor." The sergeant major, like everyone, had heard about the atomic bomb. He knew that Beech had witnessed what it could do. He wanted to know what Beech made of it.

> I looked at him and thought about the bomb. They seemed a million years apart; they belonged to different ages. "It's here to stay," I said finally. The sergeant major is on his way to China. There's shooting out there and he wants to be in it. It doesn't matter who's fighting who or why. Besides, the sergeant major thinks it will take a long time for the atomic bomb to get out to China. Out there it's still the kind of war he understands.

Beech continued through the spring to track the changes wrought by peace on America's armed forces. He wrote a series of articles from military installations in Hawaii—some of the sites repurposed, others to be taken down. He dug deeply into newly released documents to write a five-part feature on the "inside story" of the attack on Pearl Harbor. He returned to Kwajalein in the Marshall

Islands to report ruefully that a thatched hut that once housed the press club had been turned over to a women's sewing circle. And he noted that middle-ranking naval officers based in Pearl Harbor were distressed to have their access to military transport curtailed. As a cost-cutting measure, most officers no longer could call for a jeep and driver to chauffeur them to a golf game or party. Peace hurt.

Beech made the move to Tokyo in May 1947. Mildred and Walter stayed behind. Perhaps for Mildred, having moved from Akron to set up house in Washington and then in Honolulu, it was one move too many. Or the prospect of having to adjust to life in a foreign land was too much. Or it may be that their relationship was fraying. Beech had been away for long stretches: it may well have seemed that his pursuit of a peacetime career had taken precedence over establishing a domestic routine. The life of a foreign correspondent, constantly on the move, can put a strain on any marriage, and Beech had a roving eye. In any event, when he landed in Japan, Mildred and the boy weren't with him. He was on his own.

MACARTHUR'S JAPAN

He landed in a nation under military occupation, governed to all intents and purposes by one man. Gen. Douglas MacArthur had assumed what amounted to vice-regal powers. SCAP—Supreme Commander Allied Powers, of which MacArthur was chief—was established to manage Japan's transition from its recent imperial past to its hoped-for democratic future. Beech's beat was still in large part with men in uniform, but because he was now a civilian, special measures were put in place so that he was assured of access and a respectful reception in offices from which civilians normally were barred. With other senior correspondents he was informally accorded the rank of brigadier general. This was a dizzying status, Beech confessed, for a former sergeant of Marines. It wasn't to last. Over the course of the next couple of years, as Beech repeatedly challenged the secrecy and arrogance of MacArthur's regime, the rank, so arbitrarily bestowed, was just as capriciously taken away. No longer a nominal brigadier general, he was busted to nominal colonel. Beech bore the indignity with aplomb.

As Tokyo bureau chief for the *Chicago Daily News*, he had assigned to him a Japanese interpreter and one-half of an office on the fifth floor of the Mainichi newspaper building in central Tokyo, which he shared with the correspondent from the *New York Herald Tribune*. If the office was modest, his living quarters in Kugenuma were not. He and a fellow correspondent, John Rich of the International News Service (INS), took over a "twelve-room California-mission-style mansion that belonged to a purged minister of commerce and industry who was also business manager" of the newspaper the *Asahi*. The minister was exiled to a walled-off "Japanese" section of the house, while the two newspapermen enjoyed the attention of the five servants, a lush garden, and an array of modern amenities, all courtesy of SCAP. This would be Beech's home for the next five years.

Beech made it his first order of business to explore his new territory. He traveled the length and breadth of the islands, reporting on what he described as communal living, amounting to a form of rustic communism, on the edge of Honshu, and rampant corruption, comparable to Chicago in the era of Capone, on Kyushu. "Tokyo itself," he wrote, "was as visually depressing in 1947 as some of its social aspects. Large-scale reconstruction had not yet begun. Children played baseball and vegetables grew where great buildings had stood until the American bombers came." Conditions were improving but, as Beech came to understand, MacArthur was apt to exaggerate his regime's achievements. An ironic tone colored some of Beech's dispatches:

> It is inconceivable that a man of General MacArthur's greatness and proven integrity should deliberately present a falsely optimistic picture of the occupation of Japan. It is almost equally

> inconceivable that a man with every source of information at his disposal does not know the facts of life in Japan. And yet, unless MacArthur is the most magnificent optimist of all time, the latter seems to be the case. In the quiet atmosphere of his ivory tower on the sixth floor of the Dai Ichi [where SCAP was headquartered] . . . the supreme commander leads a sheltered life.

Beech soon made up his mind to distance himself from the palace guard of correspondents whose professional output was crafted to maintain friendly relations with MacArthur and the senior officers, mostly veterans of MacArthur's wartime campaigns, by whom he was surrounded. MacArthur cultivated a privileged few—Earnest Hoberecht of United Press, Russell Brines of Associated Press, and Howard Handleman of the International News Service, among them—by giving them tips and interviews in exchange for mainly favorable coverage. Beech's wary antipathy to MacArthur's reverential circle would become more pronounced in the months to come.

Beech spent most of December in China, bouncing from Shanghai to Nanking and on to Peking and the port of Tsingtao. The United States had a significant presence in the region where, for the duration of World War II, Japanese armies had held sway. The American interest lay partly in supporting the Nationalists against the Communists and partly in maintaining a strategic presence in the western Pacific. There was plenty for Beech to write about. The flood of refugees fleeing the Communists, the fraught relationship between Chiang Kai-shek and his American backers, and the corruption that the chaos gave rise to all provided the correspondent with colorful and sometimes offbeat material.

He stumbled on what may have been the most compelling sign of a precipitous decline in Nationalist fortunes when he hooked up with one of Chiang's generals on the way from Nanking to Peking. The general's name was Chen, and he was accompanied by his aide, a colonel, and a "leathery old ex-sergeant" there in an advisory capacity. They were waiting for a flight—a wait that lasted for days—and played cards to while away the time. "My mistake was to beat the general at gin rummy," wrote Beech:

> —seven games straight. The general got red in the face and tore the cards into tiny pieces. He later apologized for this display of petulance, but as we were getting off the plane at Tsingtao he kicked his aide on the shins. The colonel stood erect and took his kicking like a good soldier, probably because he was wearing knee length boots, which I suspect were equipped inside with shin guards. The old sergeant merely looked bored and said: "He's going to break his foot one of these days."
>
> Tsingtao, a port city built largely by the Germans before World War I, is currently notable for its thousands of refugees from the civil war and the dozens of clip joints whose sole purpose is to separate American sailors and marines from their dough. The general wanted to do the town. We walked into a place which truthfully advertised itself as "the most modern and up to date clip joint in Tsingtao."
>
> The establishment was populated mostly by Chinese army officers and their girl friends. Gen. Chen spotted another general who proved to be a classmate of his. On his arm the second general wore a White Russian blonde, who wore a mink coat that reached her ankles. It developed that the general was chief of staff of an army about 100 miles away. When I asked what he was doing in Tsingtao, he replied with engaging candor that he had set up temporary headquarters there. I nodded understandingly.
>
> When the plane did take off for Peiping Gen. Chen was ready for another bout of gin rummy. I declined out of consideration for the colonel's shins.

In professional terms, Beech put his first year in the Far East to good use: he was finding his feet. Personally, however, he reached a kind of nadir. Mildred and Walter had gone back to the mainland—to St. Petersburg, not Akron. In November Mildred filed for divorce. Beech drifted. There can be little doubt that he was drinking. He had a "stupid" affair in Tokyo and, on his sojourn in China, he took up with prostitutes. "I was no longer sure of what was right and what was wrong," he wrote later:

> I wanted absolutes to cling to, but reason rejected absolutes. Black and white blended into a confusing gray. Days were something to be endured; nights would bring forgetfulness of a sort. For the first time I knew that awful feeling that all men must experience at least once in a lifetime—to stand in a room full of people and feel utterly and absolutely alone. I was [he concluded, with a characteristic flash of self-awareness] dangerously close to feeling sorry for myself.

Beech surely knew the difference between right and wrong even as he made choices that offended that understanding. What's more likely than his having lost any moral sense is that he was hammered finally and forcefully by the effects of what he had gone through in the war. His delayed reaction might be thought of as a symptom of post-traumatic stress syndrome. It could also be thought of as depression. There can be no doubt that it was real and debilitating.

Sometime early in 1948—February or March—Beech pulled himself together sufficiently to follow his wife to the States and patch things up. Mildred and the boy flew from St. Petersburg to Tokyo on April 1. The divorce suit was dropped. The restoration of the relationship survived the summer, but September found Mildred with two-year-old Walter in Honolulu, "principally for the bathing." Beech passed through Honolulu, after a trip to the mainland, but there was no reconciliation. Mildred and Walter departed from Hawaii in October not for Japan but for the States. Through it all, Beech kept working.

He was among a small number of correspondents to take on in earnest MacArthur's coterie and its penchant for image control. For Beech, the breaking point came when he was repeatedly denied information to which he felt he and the American public were entitled. He asked how the US Army would make up the $80 million it lost earlier in the occupation in illegal yen-dollar transactions. He asked to see a report on the extravagant expenses incurred when Emperor Hirohito went on tour. He wanted to know what proportion of the war material taken from Japan at the beginning of the occupation had been returned. All items were relevant to a larger question journalists legitimately ask of government departments: how much was all this costing? In every instance Beech was told that the answers were classified. The army would tell him what it felt he needed to know, nothing more.

In June 1948 Beech wrote an article describing an unsatisfactory briefing given to reporters by Maj. Gen. Hugh Casey in which the officer, MacArthur's chief engineer, declined to respond to questions about the costs the army had incurred in its building operations. Casey told Beech that "the people of Chicago are not interested in details of such a story." Beech, irritated, replied that he would not presume to tell Casey how to build a bridge and expected Casey to let Beech decide what information was important to his readers. Beech, at the major general's request, followed up by putting his questions in writing. These went unanswered, leading Beech to publish his complaint.

Casey, seemingly determined to confirm the truth of Beech's charges, responded to a version of Beech's article that was published in the *San Francisco Chronicle* by writing an intemperate letter to the editor in which he accused Beech of "professional incompetence" and "sensation mongering." He went on: "It would appear that, in reality, he [Beech] hoped to uncover some sensational story by reviewing the exact costs in dollars and yen of multitudinous projects and subfeatures of the program including the exact amounts of US materials expended on each feature, specific items and value of Japanese war stocks returned to the Japanese and miscellaneous related detailed information." This was precisely what Beech wanted. His relationship with the Dai Ichi remained strained.

TWO HUNDRED COMMUNISTS

Russia was seen as a threat to the West in these early postwar years. China, so recently wracked by civil war, was discounted. And the threat Russia posed—through its influence on China and other countries—was a recurring theme in Beech's dispatches, whether he was writing from Japan, Korea, or—near the end of the summer—Honolulu. He observed the election campaign in Japan's provinces, where he found candidates adopting novel techniques to attract attention. "One candidate," he reported, "has established campaign headquarters aboard a life raft anchored near a canal bridge. From this point he harangues passersby while defending the raft from mischievous boys. Another candidate is stumping the countryside from the back of a cow—this being, by Japanese tradition, the 'year of the cow.'" The Japanese public, he noted, appeared to be largely indifferent. They believed that their elected representatives were thoroughly corrupt and understood that real power resided in MacArthur's eyrie atop the Dai Ichi building. They then showed their dissatisfaction by electing a surprising number of Communist candidates.

At the end of March 1949 Beech was in Seoul, where he interviewed a missionary whose wife had been murdered—supposedly, and perhaps inevitably—by Communists. The Republic of Korea capital held few attractions for the visitor. Beech described it as "a refugee-swollen city of more than 1,000,000 people, dirty and dusty, surrounded by treeless mountains." It was terribly poor. Americans especially had to watch out for thieves. He related a probably apocryphal story about one of his countrymen, wary of local lawlessness, who slept with a pistol under his pillow. He woke in the night to see a figure loaded down with his belongings about to disappear through an open window. He reached for his weapon only to find that it, too, was gone.

In July Beech traveled to St. Petersburg, where he saw his sister and her husband and dropped in on old friends at the *Evening Independent*. In a speech to the Rotary Club he described the situation in Japan as confused, the pull of Communism from the Chinese mainland having had a powerful effect—more powerful than the countervailing pull from America. "The Chinese peasants did not support the Nationalist government," he said, "because of a feeling that their lot could not be worse under the Communists and might even be better." As for MacArthur, Beech said, the general had achieved a great deal. The problem was not that MacArthur had achieved so little, but that he claimed to have changed so much. It wasn't realistic to think that so ancient a country could be so easily transformed.

Beech hadn't traveled all the way to Florida just to give speeches, however. He was combining work—showing the flag for the Chicago Daily News Foreign Service—with personal business. He wanted Mildred and Walter back. He made his pitch but left disappointed. Their marriage was over.

On his return journey to Japan he stopped in at the *Star-Bulletin* newsroom. A strike had paralyzed work on the docks, and the story was big enough to be of interest to both his present and previous employers. He joined the picket line, renewing his acquaintance with Harry Bridges, the Australian-born Communist and founder of the International Longshore and Warehouse Union, whom he had encountered at the Newspaper Guild convention before the war. Bridges was still fighting civil actions by the authorities aimed at either deporting or imprisoning him. (They succeeded in neither endeavor.) Beech heard him confidently assure a policeman that, if everything went well, the cops would get a raise too. The cop grinned.

Beech also talked to the territorial governor. It turned out that Ingram Stainback had a thing about Communists, having become aware of the threat they posed when Bridges's union, the ILWU, declined to support his candidate for Congress three years earlier. Stainback showed Beech a list he kept in his desk drawer of the two hundred "known Communists" in Hawaii. His list predated by six months the more infamous one to which Joe McCarthy referred in a Lincoln Day speech in Wheeling, West Virginia.

The advance of Mao Tse-tung's forces and the inauguration of the People's Republic of China had a lot of people worried. It was a fraught time. America had thrown in its lot with the Nationalists and wasn't about to reverse the decision. The freighted question of "who lost China?" would haunt American politics for a generation. The fact that such a question could be asked reflected a mostly tacit conviction that America had amassed sufficient power to "lose" a nation of several hundred million people an ocean away. The presumption, in retrospect, is remarkable. But Beech himself was witness to the change in America, from the largely self-involved, long-suffering Depression-era country he grew up in to the towering world power it had become by 1949.

America had not won the war single-handedly, but it would not have been won without her. Beech certainly understood this—he believed it in his bones—just as he appreciated the significance of the atom bomb. He had seen battleships tossed like bathtub toys at Bikini Atoll. He had seen the islands in the Pacific where Marines had fought and died transformed into sprawling military bases, a visible, palpable, and potent presence stretching from Manila to Okinawa and beyond. No less impressive, notwithstanding his semi-satirical criticism of its chief architect, was the American investment in Japan. If America could remake defeated, prostrate Japan into a thriving, democratic ally (and, granted, Beech had his reservations), then anything was possible. Why not China too?

Beech did have reservations. But what he saw and recorded in his hundreds of dispatches from 1945 to 1949 was the gradual winding down of a military machine aimed at Japan and the simultaneous emergence of the new confrontation, no less potentially dangerous, with the USSR. The same evolution was transforming relations in the West. The Cold War, first presciently signaled by Winston Churchill in his March 1946 "Iron Curtain" speech, achieved a chilling reality two years later when Russia imposed its blockade on the city of Berlin. America and its allies had put a war behind them. It wasn't yet clear if another one lay ahead.

In May 1950, from his perch in Tokyo, Beech wrote a remarkable article in which he set out a trenchant answer to the China question. In essence, he said, in having triumphed in the war, America had failed to offer a positive program to the nations they had liberated from the Japanese. America gave the Philippines its independence and persuaded the Dutch to do the same in Indonesia, but what, he asked, has independence brought but political chaos, widespread corruption, and economic collapse? In Indochina, he observed, America had chosen to recognize the appointment by the French of Bao Dai as emperor. "It doesn't really matter whether Bao is a French puppet, which he is or he wouldn't be there," Beech wrote. "The important thing is that the Indo-Chinese think he is a French puppet."

A kind of innocence partly explained American ineffectiveness:

> One reason we have failed in Asia is that we can't believe that people really starve to death. We are too well-fed to believe it. I found it hard to believe myself until I saw it happen in China. Millions will starve there this year under the Communists. And some Americans will say, "See what heartless brutes the Communists are. They're letting millions of people starve rather than take food from us." But I saw enough in China to convince me that if I were a Chinese peasant I would wish to be a Communist. Not that I would know anything about Communism. But because whatever the Communists offered couldn't be worse and might conceivably be better than what I had under the Nationalists.

It had been a mistake to back Chiang Kai-shek, a mistake compounded because America continued to back him even after his retreat to Formosa. The same mistake was being replicated in South Korea, where Syngman Rhee was holding elections only because of American pressure. Similarly, America had thrown in its lot with Filipino President Elpidio Quirino, whom Beech described as "a shifty politician whose office is stained with the blood of murdered voters," and with the playboy Bao Dai in Vietnam. There was surely a better way. "It could be that the answer is to help people rather than governments," Beech wrote: "To back a revolution instead of buck one. That could get us into an awful lot of trouble. But we are already in a lot of trouble out here. And we're getting the bejabbers beaten out of us every day. Do we go on taking a beating? Or do we try something else?"

This was a theme to which Beech would return from time to time in the years ahead. Sometimes it would seem that America never backed the right side. But then, as things turned out, it wasn't always easy to line up with the side that merited backing.

Beech was back in Japan at year's end, in the mansion he shared with John Rich, ready to indulge his now confirmed status as an unattached male. This, at least, is the implication of a society notice that appeared in the *Honolulu Star-Bulletin* that spring:

> From Tokyo we hear that Miss Linda Mangelsdorf is enjoying keenly life in Japan. The versatile daughter of Mr. and Mrs. A. J. Mangelsdorf left here last fall to take a position with the army. An accomplished linguist, Linda is finding her study of the Japanese language very handy. But it isn't all work and no play for the attractive Honolulu girl. She writes of many gay outings including parties given by Keyes Beech, *Chicago Daily News* correspondent, at his beach home.

There was every likelihood that 1950 would be an eventful, life-changing year.

CHAPTER 4

War in Korea

THE BEAUTIFUL SIMPLICITY OF WAR

The Korean War ended in stalemate, a condition that remains unresolved as these words are being written some seventy years later; so it's not surprising that it's the static condition that sticks in our collective memory. But in its first year, from late June 1950 through to late spring 1951, the war was not static at all. Movement was nearly constant. This was never a "police action," the term employed by President Truman to fudge his failure to obtain from Congress a declaration of war. The Korean conflict was a conflagration that leveled cities and towns, made refugees of hundreds of thousands of civilians, and ultimately took millions of lives. It was a war that United Nations forces came close to losing. What they won was no victory, but a standoff.

The North Koreans, given direction and arms by their Soviet ally—including, in particular, modern T-54 battle tanks—crossed the 38th parallel into South Korea on June 25, 1950. The American presence in the South had been stripped to an advisory rump of a couple of hundred officers and men, leaving the Republic of Korea (ROK) army to fend off the invasion. They were ill-equipped for the task. Among other handicaps were the anti-tank rockets, or bazookas, supplied to them by the Americans. These World War II-era rockets simply bounced off the T-54s' sides. The relative imperviousness of the tanks combined with the element of surprise, which was total, contributed to the rapid collapse of South Korean defenses. The rumble of guns could be heard inside Seoul within a couple of days of the war's start.

President Truman acted fast to declare US support for the South Koreans, but the rout was already underway. The Americans stationed in Seoul, members of the Korean Military Advisory Group (KMAG), joined the masses of fleeing South Korean soldiers and distraught civilians crossing the Han River on the road south. Over the following weeks, South Korean and American forces fell back to a series of defensive positions, first to the town of Suwon on July 1, and from there to Taejon, which fell on July 20, and thence to Taegu and finally, at the beginning of August, to Pusan on the southern tip of the peninsula. The Pusan perimeter, hastily contrived by 8th Army commander Gen. Walton Walker, using a patchwork of ROK divisions and American infantry units brought in from occupied Japan, barely held on as more reinforcements piled into the port. There was a real chance that the North Koreans would push the defenders into the sea. These first few months of the war, when armies panicked and ran, re-formed, advanced, stalled, and retreated again, were thrilling, confusing, chaotic, and perilous. Of the seventeen Western correspondents who were killed in Korea, all but three lost their lives in the first couple of months. It was a time when a reporter who survived could make his—or her—reputation. Beech was among the handful who made the most of the chance. He found the prospect exhilarating.

For better or worse, his experience in the Pacific had marked him. He tried domestic life after he was demobilized and shied away. He tried reporting from Washington, DC, was bored by it, and fled to Honolulu. He didn't stay. His subsequent appointment to Tokyo proved to be congenial. He found satisfaction in exploring Japan, and then China, Korea, and the Philippines, all places that yielded colorful stories. But war, when it erupted, offered something more that he yearned for: danger, of course, but also relief from the conventions of civilized society. He suspected that he saw a similar impulse in some of his fellow correspondents when they gathered on the tarmac at Haneda Airport, awaiting transport to Korea on June 25. "None of the men said so," he wrote later,

> but they were secretly glad. Without exception they were veterans of the last war, either as correspondents or soldiers, and they had stayed on in Japan because they did not want to return to the familiar humdrum of life in America.
>
> But with the passing of the years domesticity had caught up with them even in Japan. Wives and children had come from the States, or had been acquired on the scene. They had acquired houses, servants, insurance policies, refrigerators, responsibility, and respectability. Now they were being rescued from all this, at least for the time being, by the unknown dangers, the uncertainty, the beautiful simplicity of war.

Beech was still exhilarated during the initial retreat from Seoul. He was standing on the sandy shore of the Han River, wondering how he'd get across ahead of the enemy, when he turned to Burton Crane, the *New York Times* correspondent. "I hate to say this," he told Crane, "but this is the first time I've felt alive since Iwo." He would repeat this sentiment two months later, when he lay in a ditch under mortar fire on the road back to Seoul. Someone called out for assistance in rescuing a wounded soldier. He got up and helped and then afterward mused on the impulse that led him to respond:

> Now I didn't have to get up. I was a goddamned civilian in this war and I didn't have to get up. Nobody was going to order me

around now. I could go where I pleased and do what I pleased. Well, if that was the case, what was I doing here? Did it please me to be lying here in this ditch? It did not. Then what was I here for? For money? They don't pay that kind of money. Newspapers especially don't pay that kind of money.

I turned over on my back and lit a cigarette. Maybe I was here because I liked it.

Maybe he did. Beech was in the prime of life—he was thirty-six years old when the war began. He was lean and fit. He had a secure and respected position with an established news organization. He was technically still married but by now permanently separated from Mildred. His relationship with Linda Mangelsdorf had yet to be formalized, leaving him as attached or unattached as he chose to behave. He was comfortable in a military environment and friends with any number of Marines and soldiers. Officers he had known as young men now occupied more senior positions. He was experienced enough in battlefield conditions to understand what was happening and to assess the risks accurately. Granted, survival in war required luck as well as smarts, but Beech had been lucky. When his friend John Rich got the call from the office in Tokyo alerting them to the outbreak of hostilities, when both he and Beech were at Kugenuma, Beech grumbled at the interruption to his weekend but didn't hesitate. He was more than ready to go to war.

The Korean War, as Beech experienced it, had four elements. First, the frontline reporting: the dispatches that earned him accolades. He described battles in stripped-down, matter-of-fact prose that had vivid immediacy. With good reason, his articles often were featured on the front page of subscriber newspapers. Second, he was blunt in calling out the weaknesses and occasional failures of American forces. His criticisms caught the attention of readers and provoked the anger of officials. He had established himself as something of a gadfly in MacArthur's Japan. The scope of his skepticism widened with the disasters he witnessed in the first months of the war in Korea. Third, he remained his news service's senior Far East correspondent and returned at intervals to report from Tokyo. At such moments he would step back and editorialize on the war's status. A few of these pieces are notable, if only to remind us that the war's outcome was not known to its real-time witnesses. A present-day reader may be jaded, but for participants the ricocheting events in Korea had the capacity to shock, worry, and surprise.

A fourth aspect of Beech's Korean experience requires notice: his relationship with Marguerite Higgins. There's some reason to think that Higgins single-handedly improved the work of the correspondents—all men—with whom she competed. They, Beech not least among them, could not bear to be outdone by the singularly pugnacious, pioneering reporter, almost certainly the first woman to succeed in insisting on her right to cover American or Allied armies from the front lines. Beech sized her up early as a kind of human hurricane best endured in the eye. Both benefited from the other's proximity. She pushed him to up his game; he pushed her to assess risk cagily. They became an item. Both were among the six who shared a Pulitzer Prize.

HIGGINS

Marguerite Higgins was five years younger than Beech. Her background was exotic, at least for a girl who went to school in a suburb of Oakland, California, between the two world wars. Her mother was a French aristocrat effectively disowned by her family when, during World War I, she took up with an unpedigreed Irish American who volunteered for the air arm of the French army. They met in a shelter in Paris as bombs exploded above them: She was enthralled by his heroics; he was enchanted by her beauty. Their war was romantic, the peace that followed anticlimactic. They thought life in the Far East would offer compensatory excitement and moved to Hong Kong, but his job with a trading firm was disappointingly routine. This is where Marguerite was born, however, in relative comfort, with a Chinese amah to look after her. She picked up some Cantonese to go with the French she learned from her mother: languages would come easily to her in later years. When, as an infant, she came down with malaria, she and her mother sought respite in Indochina, in the cool and salubrious highland town of Dalat. This early interlude was the basis of her later claim to have acquired a childhood affinity for Vietnam.

Her parents, Laurence or "Larry" and (confusingly) Marguerite, moved back to the United States for Maggie's sake, to ensure that she got an American education. Larry struggled to find a fitting occupation, landing eventually on selling stocks, a career that crashed with the stock market in 1929. After a spell of unemployment he took a position with a bank. The family got by but didn't prosper. Marguerite made Maggie's dresses by hand, taught her and some neighborhood children to play piano, and ultimately cut a deal with the headmistress of the exclusive Anna Head School for Girls in Berkeley, California, to teach French in exchange for Maggie's tuition. Maggie's continuing status as a student depended on her achieving a consistent "A" average, a hard condition, but Maggie, the darling only child of a couple in straitened circumstances, managed it with ease.

She became accustomed to being indifferent to the things that made her different. She accepted her status as a poor student in a rich girls' school: the experience served mainly to make her intensely competitive. And she accepted the more or less quiet opprobrium caused by her father's drinking, which led often to loud arguments, and her mother's theatricality, which sometimes degenerated into hysterics. Her friends thought Maggie callous when her mother fainted and Maggie calmly stepped over her on the way to fetch an ammonia-soaked cloth, but for Maggie this too was routine. If her family taught her anything, it was that the consequence of outlandish behavior is disapproval by some, which she found bearable, and admiration by others, which she enjoyed.

From the Anna Head school, Maggie went on to the University of California at Berkeley. Always the competitor, she sought acceptance in the prestigious Alpha Phi sorority and was shattered when turned down. Her parents' notoriety may have been a factor in her being blackballed, but her own reputation—there had been a scandal involving a sleepover with a boy—was a factor too. For a time, she found consolation by assuming a leadership position in a rival sorority, Gamma Phi Beta, but her outlook on life, which came to embrace, among other things, Bertrand Russell's arguments in favor of free love, led her to lose interest in high society. Going low, she turned to journalism instead.

The *Daily Californian*, the university newspaper, was set up to serve as a tiered training ground for would-be reporters. First-year students were given entry-level assignments and overseen by more senior students who acted as mentors. As they progressed from one year to the next, they were rotated through beats and assumed greater responsibility. The student staff approached their assignments seriously and collegially, were supportive of one another's efforts, and took collective pride in the paper they turned out. This, at any rate, was the ethos of the organization. It wasn't Maggie's way. Collegiality and collective action in pursuit of a common goal were, to Maggie, incomprehensible concepts. She used every advantage, not excepting her pert good looks, to establish her primacy as a reporter, even if it meant stepping on others along the way.

In her senior year she fully expected to be named editor of the paper. She felt that she had earned the promotion and said as much to friends. She was crushed when, again, she was let down by her peers. She took on the less prestigious position of night editor with such grace as she could muster. When she graduated (cum laude) from Berkeley in spring 1940, her ambition was settled. Eschewing the local scene, she set out to make her mark on a bigger stage. She packed her bags and took the train to New York.

She may have been the only one surprised that neither *The New York Times* nor the *Herald Tribune* hired her instantly on her arrival on the East Coast. She also may have been the only one unsurprised when she secured a reporting job with the latter paper a couple of years later. The fact that there was a war on, and that many male reporters volunteered for service, leaving vacancies behind them, created opportunities. But Higgins would have found a way even without a war. She obtained by guile and pertinacity interviews that others failed to get. She put in long hours and seized opportunities as they arose. She formed alliances with men who, in their innocence, sought to give her guidance. The reporter Robert Shaplen, later well known as a Far East specialist, claimed he was the first *Herald Tribune* reporter to befriend her. He was just one in a long line. The patronage of the wife of the paper's owner also helped. All of these factors contributed to her progress, but Higgins's talent—for straight-ahead reporting if not for graceful prose—was what mattered most.

There was (and is) a hierarchy in the profession of journalism. Editors have power and columnists have influence, but the role of the foreign correspondent, especially in wartime, has a glamor that sets it apart. Higgins soon chafed at the job of city reporter. She yearned to be where battles were being fought. This was a tall order at a time when women were strictly barred from battle zones. Nevertheless, she got close, shipping out for Europe in September 1944. In December she celebrated the New Year with the throng in London's Trafalgar Square. In February she bantered with Ernest Hemingway in the Hotel Scribe, the correspondents' Paris headquarters. In March she wangled a place in a junket arranged by the 8th Army after it crossed the Rhine River. In April she joined forces with *Stars and Stripes* reporter Peter Furst, and with him witnessed the liberation of Buchenwald concentration camp. At the end of April she and Furst accompanied American troops as they entered Dachau. According to an article Furst wrote at the time,

Higgins, "blonde, 23-year-old war correspondent for the *New York Herald-Tribune*, was the first person actually to announce to the prisoners"—in French, English, and German—"that the Americans had arrived, and that they would soon be free." A Polish Catholic cardinal, prisoner in the camp, hugged and kissed her. Her story made the *Herald Tribune*'s front page.

After the war, Higgins remained in Europe, initially as assistant to the Berlin bureau chief, and then as his replacement. She covered the trials of the most prominent Nazi war criminals at Nuremberg and later traveled daringly behind the Iron Curtain, an experience that left her with an abiding abhorrence of Communist regimes. The Berlin post was a prestigious one. It also turned out to be the kind of break that journalists dream of, giving her the platform from which to report one of the major international stories of the postwar era: the Soviet blockade of Berlin and the American-led airlift that relieved it. Over the course of the nearly year-long crisis, she became accustomed to seeing her byline featured prominently above the fold on the *Trib*'s front page. This struck her as only right.

Her meteoric rise (she was just twenty-eight at the time of the airlift), and the means by which she was thought to have achieved it, made her enemies. One of her detractors was Toni Howard, a correspondent for *Newsweek* also based in Germany, who would soon marry a colleague at the magazine's Berlin bureau, Jim O'Donnell. O'Donnell, an experienced correspondent, generously shared his knowledge and some of his contacts with Higgins. Sometimes, as their respective publications adhered to a different schedule with a mainly distinct readership, they shared leads, always on the condition that they wouldn't scoop each other by premature publication. No doubt O'Donnell appreciated Higgins's charms (presumably to the annoyance of Toni Howard), but he wasn't blinded by them. On one occasion, when he uncovered a particularly piquant story, he was prepared to stand by his agreement with Higgins, but he also took care to protect himself.

The tale as recapitulated by Higgins's biographer, Antoinette May, went like this. O'Donnell had a line on a story that he shared with Higgins on condition, as usual, that she not publish it before him. The story was too good: she couldn't resist filing it ahead of time. He got wind of her duplicity and contrived to let her know that the story had fallen through, the source on whom it depended had recanted. She panicked and had the story pulled as it was going to press—a costly maneuver. He went ahead, and the story, a big one, duly appeared in *Newsweek*, leading Maggie's editors in New York to wonder what on earth had possessed her to have the story pulled. Was she drunk?

Toni Howard doubtless got the story from O'Donnell. It seems likely that it became something of a party piece retailed at gatherings of journalists in the postwar years. In any event, Howard incorporated a modified version in a novel she wrote, in which a woman closely resembling Higgins—the guileful and alluring Berlin bureau chief of a New York newspaper—reneges on an agreement with a fellow reporter, precisely as Higgins had cheated on O'Donnell, and is similarly humiliated. But Carla MacMurphy, the shameless "Mata Hari of the Headlines," carries on conniving, without morals and without shame. Howard's book, *Shriek with Pleasure*, is classic pulp fiction, a period pocket book with a lurid cover. It's a pitiless hatchet job that gives a devastating impression of the way Higgins was regarded by her peers. It was published in spring 1950 and so coincided exactly with her transfer from Berlin to Tokyo, where the *Herald Tribune* and the *Chicago Daily News* shared an office. She landed there in May of that year, annoyed because she thought the assignment would be a backwater after the excitement of Berlin. But Higgins had a knack for being in the right place at the right time. She had done it again.

ESCAPE FROM SEOUL

Beech, in his memoir, wrote that Higgins's arrival in Tokyo had an immediate impact on the community of resident correspondents.

Figure 7. "Carla MacMurphy would do anything to scoop a headline—lie, cheat or betray the men who confided in her." Author's collection.

Howard's book, he suggested, was greeted by journalists with ribald hilarity. And he complained that her propensity, as his newly arrived office mate, to pick his brain and bird-dog him on his daily rounds pushed his patience to the point where he was looking for a new, Higgins-free base of operations. There may be an element of embroidery in this account. There's not much doubt that her new colleagues had been tipped off as to her identity as the model for Howard's protagonist. The reception they gave her may well have been cool. But they didn't have much time to form an independent impression of her character. She didn't turn up in Tokyo until the second half of May, barely more than a month before the Korean War began. And as Beech in particular did a good deal of traveling in May and June, it's fair to wonder whether she had the opportunity to irritate him to the degree he implies. (Granted, it's possible he traveled precisely to escape her.) Whatever the reality, Higgins and Beech headed their respective newspapers' Tokyo bureaus when war broke out and their response was identical. They leapt at the chance to cover it.

Getting there turned out to be a challenge: military transport, to the extent that it was flying into the Korean capital at all, was directed chiefly at extracting stranded American personnel rather than inserting random correspondents. The first gaggle of reporters Beech joined at Haneda Airport boarded an aircraft that turned around mid-journey and headed back to Japan, the pilot citing news that Kimpo airfield outside Seoul was under attack. After further efforts to hitch a lift from Haneda proved fruitless—and after more than a day had passed—Beech made his way to an air force base on the southern tip of the island where transports were still shuttling in and out of Seoul. There he boarded a military C-54, whose pilot shrugged at the perversity of a civilian bound for a destination from which so many were desperate to escape.

Beech wasn't the only one so inclined. Three more correspondents piled in behind him: Burton Crane of *The New York Times*,

Frank Gibney of *Life* magazine, and Marguerite Higgins. This time they made it to Kimpo without incident. When the correspondents peered through the plane's plexiglass portholes and took in the scene below, they saw the smoldering wreckage of two airplanes, victims of earlier strafing, that had been pushed to the side, and a handful of figures near the terminal frantically waving bedsheets to signal that the airport was still in friendly hands. The pilot never cut the engines. As fast as Beech and the others disembarked, some thirty waiting Americans scrambled aboard. Minutes later the C-54, the last to leave Kimpo, was airborne once more.

It was 7:30 p.m. on June 27. The twenty-four hours that followed were wild.

A score of vehicles were parked outside the airport terminal, all abandoned by their owners, some with the keys still in the ignition. Gibney and Crane took jeeps, Higgins a Studebaker, and Beech a brand-new Dodge. Together they formed a ragtag caravan, forging a path through an endless stream of fleeing Korean soldiers and panicked civilians, some of whom cheered at their appearance. Higgins found the experience both moving and terrifying. Beech, similarly affected, honked his car horn and yelled incoherently. "The poor fools didn't know that we were merely four correspondents, and one of us a woman at that. I laughed like a loon and kept my hand on the horn. I was giddy with elation. Was I not a symbol of democracy?"

It was after 11:00 p.m. when they tracked down the officer in charge of the Korean Military Advisory Group. Col. W. Sterling Wright told them the North Koreans were some distance to the north of the city and that, while the situation was "fluid," they were likely safe enough to grab some sleep. The reporters correctly interpreted the word "fluid" to mean, as Crane put it, "nobody knows much about anything." Wright found accommodation for Higgins, while the three men bunked down in the officers' quarters. Their slumber was short-lived. At 2:15 on the morning of the 28th, they were woken by the ringing of the phone: the enemy reportedly was closing in from both east and west. The reports were partly true: Kimpo airfield west of the city had been overrun, and tanks had penetrated the eastern outskirts, but the North Koreans' main forces were not yet that close. Nevertheless, the reporters decided to move. The three men piled into one of the jeeps that Gibney and Crane had appropriated and joined the dense mass of Koreans bound for the bridge over the Han River. On the other side lay the way to Suwon and safety.

Their progress in pouring rain and pitch darkness on the crowded road was slow. Their jeep trailed a truck packed with Korean military police whose bulk was their salvation. They had just started to cross the river when the bridge exploded. Gibney's first thought was that enemy planes had bombed them. Beech guessed it was tanks. The truck in front of them was destroyed, the MPs inside it "blown to bits." Their jeep was thrown back fifteen feet, its windshield shattered, sending shards of glass flying. Both Gibney and Crane in front were badly cut. Beech, who was in the back, scrambled to assist them. He led Crane, blinded by blood, to the river's edge. There, on the shore, he washed Crane's wounds and improvised a field dressing from an undershirt. Gibney stanched the blood from his own cuts by drawing on the contents of his rucksack. This included, he later recalled, a pair of Higgins's slacks, "a rather jazzy blue and white" number, which she had asked him to pack when the air force made her divest herself of excess baggage. "She was very useful in that regard," he said.

The bridge that led south was no longer available. It had been destroyed, not by enemy planes or tanks but by panicky ROK soldiers who detonated the charges that had been planted in anticipation of the North Korean advance. The three men considered their options. They ruled out any attempt to swim across the river in the rain and darkness. They had passed houses earlier that had been occupied by KMAG staff. Bravely, they started cross-country,

Beech with his typewriter in one hand, the other on Crane, who was still wiping blood from his eyes. They had the benefit of guides: a pair of teenage Korean soldiers attached themselves unbidden to the party. One of them (they called him Joe) shared with them his faith that things would turn out for the best. "The American planes will come tomorrow," he said. "I could have cried," Beech remembered, "because I felt we owed those planes to Joe." They were soaked to the skin, and their path led them through rice paddies. Beech kept losing his shoes in the mud, and his belt buckle broke. He had to hold up his pants with the same hand that clutched his typewriter. Struck suddenly by the absurdity of the situation, he felt better. They trudged on.

They tried the doors of a couple of the American houses and found them locked. They might have turned away from another but saw a sliver of light under the door. They pounded on the door until it was opened. Inside they found two servants and a soldier waiting in vain for their employers' return. The Koreans, understandably frightened, let them in. They cooked them eggs and ham while Beech replaced the improvised dressings on the two bloodied correspondents with bandages. They half expected the enemy to turn up at the door and take them prisoner, but fortified by food and tumblersful of whisky found in a cupboard, they mooted another attempt to cross the river. The teenage Korean soldiers promised to show them a way.

Dawn was breaking when they liberated a pair of abandoned jeeps and drove by backroads, muddy tracks, and cross country to a point ten miles upriver from the blown Han bridge. They weren't alone. Thousands of Koreans, both soldiers and civilians, were struggling to make their escape. Gibney and one of the soldiers found a boat and rowed across the river. They came back with a Korean who was poling a raft that served, in Beech's words, as a "homemade LST." When the ramp was lowered, Beech drove his jeep onto it, and was astonished that the raft didn't sink. They pulled away from the shore, but not before a Korean farmer grabbed the side of the raft with one hand while holding the rope attached to his ox with the other. The captain of their improvised LST whacked the farmer's hand until enjoined by the Americans to let him be. Somehow both farmer and ox made it to the other side.

More paddies lay before them, but the jeep (they were down to one) was up to the challenge, and they made it onto a road that was packed with yet more refugees. Mercifully, the rain had let up. At around 10:30 that morning, they were greeted by a sight that must have gladdened Joe's heart. "Out of the cloudless sky came six United States B-26's in formation, flying north toward Seoul, only twelve miles away. The refugees, thousands upon thousands, stretching as far as the hills in either direction, clapped and cheered."

The correspondents met up with Colonel Wright and his party in Suwon. With them was Higgins. She wasn't pleased. The preceding hours had been an adventure for her too. She rode in a jeep behind Colonel Wright and the KMAG staff on a journey not unlike that of her colleagues, although they crossed the river at different points. Higgins ended up having to swim, and because they had abandoned their vehicles on the other side, they were obliged from then on to hoof it. She was eventually taken on board another jeep in which somehow she found a place among two American colonels, a Korean officer, and five Korean soldiers. It was an uncomfortable ride, but it gave her a chance to focus once more on her task as a journalist. Her reflections made her both anxious and angry. An American major had assured her back at KMAG headquarters that Beech, Crane, and Gibney had left the city ahead of her. No doubt they already were filing their stories with their respective papers. She had the same story they had: they were the only correspondents to witness the fall of Seoul. She couldn't bear to think that she had been scooped. When she saw Beech, she let him have it.

"Maggie was mad about losing the dress [a reference to lost luggage], mad because we'd left her, mad because we'd finally found a jeep and driven to Suwon while she walked most of the way," Beech later told Antoinette May. "She only calmed down when she discovered that we hadn't been able to file our stories either." The state of communications in Suwon matched conditions generally. Three ROK divisions on the north side of the river were fighting a rearguard action against forces that were overwhelming them. They were falling back fast. The result was barely contained panic. The correspondents got neither assistance nor sympathy from officials on the spot. The US ambassador to Korea, John Muccio, took a moment to summon them to his presence in order to tell them to go away. They were a nuisance, he said. They did go away. At least Beech, Crane, and Higgins did. They caught a military plane taking off from the Suwon airstrip and filed their stories from Japan.

Beech knew what his role would be in Korea. He would be covering the war from the front lines. Higgins had the same ambition, but there were obstacles in her path. While most of the troops she encountered, and a number of senior officers as well, admired her pluck, a handful of their seniors objected to her presence. And one correspondent in particular wanted her out. It was a fight that Higgins, of all people, was prepared to engage in. She would employ all the strategies she had honed over the years: she would summon allies, invoke public opinion, and, not least of all, act with courage to earn her right to do what the men did. As always, her fallback was her sex appeal.

She certainly knew she'd meet opposition. Even before their plane landed at Kimpo airfield, Frank Gibney had remarked to Beech that Korea was "no place for a woman." Beech had nodded his head sagely, but, having spent time in Higgins's company, added that however unsuitable it might be for a woman, "it was all right for her." Beech may have found her irritating in Tokyo, but at some point in their journey he formed for her an ungrudging respect. At no point in their escape from Seoul had she asked for any favor. The thunder of enemy guns hadn't fazed her. The flood of refugees had dismayed but not stopped her. The situation in Suwon would be no less perilous, and yet she remained stalwart. He was impressed.

The next two days in and out of Suwon—June 29 and 30—were as tumultuous as the days that went before. Both Beech and Higgins were back from Tokyo on the 29th, gathering what news they could of the enemy's progress. General MacArthur landed there too with the same intention and to meet with Maj. Gen. John H. Church, Ambassador Muccio, and President Syngman Rhee. Beech greeted him at the airstrip with the words, "General, I'm glad to see you here." He meant it: after the mad scramble of the previous two days, the general's presence was reassuring. Before he departed, MacArthur insisted on being driven to the Han River to make his own assessment of the situation. When he got back to the airstrip some hours later, Higgins caught his eye. They exchanged pleasantries and he offered her a ride in his plane back to Tokyo. She accepted the offer gratefully, both for the shot at an exclusive interview and to file the day's story at the other end. She was granted the interview on the flight—one that no other reporter was offered—and what she wrote was admiring. His visit, she assured the *Trib*'s readers, "dramatically buoyed the defenders' morale." Indeed, so great was his effect that "the panic that gripped the retreating South Koreans is now gone." MacArthur was not without charm.

If MacArthur's visit had indeed boosted the morale of the Americans in Suwon, it didn't last. By the time Higgins was back from Tokyo on the 30th, both the sky and the mood had darkened. MacArthur's departure left a void that Church and his staff failed to fill. In its place rumors circulated: of the ROK's utter collapse, of an enemy movement to surround the city, of a last-minute airlift to rescue them, of their imminent abandonment by the brass. At one point, the correspondents were told to grab weapons and be prepared to defend what they were told was their one possible avenue of escape, the airfield south of the town. They did as instructed, but Beech, even as he checked the clip on his carbine, muttered derisively: "Do they really think this handful of men can hold that airstrip? They're out of their minds." In fact, the enemy's advance was less rapid than rumored, the city wasn't yet cut off, no planes were coming to their rescue, and no firefight was fought on the airstrip's edge. The rumor that the brass were leaving, however, turned out to be true. When the news sank in that evening that Church and company had taken off down the road, leaving the correspondents to fend for themselves, they were furious. They weren't the only ones: scores of enlisted men and a handful of officers had been left behind too.

Beech still had the jeep he had ferried across the river. He would hang onto it over the coming months with murderous zeal: it gave him mobility in a war where mobility was everything and where the US military had no transport to spare. That night the jeep was their salvation. Beech drove with Higgins and two other correspondents in the back and a young sergeant riding shotgun down the long bumpy road to Taejon. It poured rain. None of them was wearing anything remotely waterproof, and they were soaked to the skin. In the small hours of the morning, the jeep lost traction in the mud and slid off the road. They needed the help of two farmers to push it back.

They found General Church early the next morning alone in his newly established headquarters. He had just received word from Tokyo that a task force was on its way. His remarks to the reporters reflected the then-still prevalent feeling that the Americans only had to show up to make the North Koreans turn and run. What if the Russians get involved directly? Beech asked. Then, said Church, "we'll fight the Russkies too." Both Higgins and Beech filed substantial stories in the next few hours. Hers sounded a hopeful note; Beech's was grim. The confused, ramshackle withdrawal from Suwon, in particular, was on his mind. The South Korean army, he wrote, had failed to hold back the enemy at the Han River. With its collapse, the retreat became general:

> The miscellaneous group of 232 American officers and enlisted men based at Suwon, 15 miles south of the Han fled. They made a panicky withdrawal to Suwon air strip a few miles to the south where they were told to defend the strip to the bitter end. Although this correspondent is no military expert this move caused him some astonishment. The strip offers no cover and could be easily surrounded by Communist units or strafed by the disagreeably active Yaks. As we departed from Suwon in unseemly haste, one lieutenant colonel was heard to say: "It looks as though we are completely isolated," and another stomped in shouting: "Let's get out of here." It is the considered opinion of this correspondent, now a veteran of two retreats in the Korean war, that this behavior was not only unnecessary but undignified. There followed a 70-mile all-night drive southward to Taejon, an event which I will always remember with distaste. We traveled in an open jeep in the driving rain leading the rear-guard convoy. It is most unusual for war correspondents to lead military convoys. But this is a most unusual war. Up to now it's been an American war with other people doing the fighting—and a very poor job of it, too. Now we are about to do our own fighting. It is to be hoped by all hands that we will do a better job of it.

THE DEFENSE OF TAEJON

The 8th Army, based in Japan, was preparing to move to Korea. Its vanguard was to be a battalion made up in part of two understrength rifle companies from the 21st Infantry, backed by a mortar platoon and one-half of a 75-mm recoilless rifle company. This was Task Force Smith, named for its commander, Lt. Col. Charles B. Smith, whose orders were to advance as far north of Taejon as possible, and hold the enemy there for as long as possible, while reinforcements were brought into play. Smith and his men were in Taejon early on July 2.

It wasn't only the US Army that was gearing up for the conflict. In New York, the *Herald Tribune* called up its most seasoned war correspondent. Homer Bigart had come up through the ranks of newsmen the hard way. His unprepossessing manner had, by all accounts, held him back. His thick spectacles gave him an owlish look, and his stutter misled some into thinking him slow-witted. He established a dubious record for the length of time he spent as a copyboy. Only reluctantly did his bosses send him into the street. When they did, he shone. He used his apparent diffidence to his advantage, asking the people he interviewed endless questions, often seeming to repeat himself but in the process digging deeper. His subjects felt sorry for him and went out of their way to be helpful, so that in the end he soaked up quantities of information far surpassing that gathered by his competitors. His work was increasingly appreciated beyond the *Herald Tribune*'s newsroom, and with America in the war he was sent overseas.

Bigart earned for himself an enviable reputation for fearlessness, fierce intelligence, and fine, often sardonic prose in the course of covering multiple campaigns in World War II. He was in Europe at the start, in Italy, and then the Pacific. He may have encountered Beech on Iwo Jima when he landed there in time to describe the battle's end. Awards were heaped on him, not least a Pulitzer Prize. He was famous, and the *Trib* was justly proud of him. The decision to send him to Korea was automatic. He was their prime war correspondent; of course he'd be there.

He was in Tokyo on July 2 when he ran into Carl Mydans, a *Life* photographer and writer. Higgins's name came up. Bigart said she wouldn't be needed in Korea now that he was on the scene. Mydans said he guessed Higgins was unlikely to welcome that news. Bigart doubled down with words to the effect that if she didn't return to her post in Tokyo, she would be fired. The *Trib*, as Bigart saw things, needed only one reporter in Korea. Him.

When a dubious Mydans relayed the threat to Higgins on his return to Taejon, the news dismayed her. Another threat, every bit as ominous, emerged at about the same time. Gen. Walton Walker, the 8th Army commander, considered women an impediment to the smooth conduct of operations. He let it be known that she was to be sent home. MacArthur deferred to his field commander and endorsed the order. These were powerful enemies indeed. Higgins set about marshaling her own forces. Mydans was firmly in her camp. A number of other correspondents, including Tom Lambert of AP and Roy McCartney of Reuters, accepted her presence equably. And Beech made it clear there was a place for her in his jeep. From that point on she could scarcely be dislodged from it. Certain officers supported her, chief among them Gen. William Dean, who arrived in Taejon on July 5 to take command of the city's defense. He told her he saw no reason to give her the "bum's rush."

Higgins worked doggedly over the next two weeks, turning out copy that was consistently colorful if overwrought. She filed an account at once sensitive and trite—"one young private said bitterly, 'What a place to die!'"—about a member of a bazooka team whom she claimed was the first American killed in Korea. (The US Army's official historian says not.) A sergeant told her how, in extricating his platoon, he had been forced to leave a wounded man behind. He gave him a hand grenade. "'O.K., Sarge,' the man told him. 'I don't expect to get out of here, but maybe I can take some of them with me.'"

She was in the field every day. Every night she returned to Taejon to file a story. The conditions were rugged. The correspondents camped out in the billet that had been assigned to them, sleeping on the floor and going short of provisions, while they waited for their turn to use the only phone. Beech later described what it was like to be a "special," that is, a correspondent like Higgins and him who were there not to report events as they happened (the principal job of the wire-service reporters), but rather to develop a narrative that conveyed a sense of the conditions and their significance. The agencies, he explained, with some hyperbole,

> have whole companies of men covering [the war] and they already have piled up copy six feet high. You sit down to write your story and the lights go out. You steal a flashlight and go on. You have to keep it short but being a special you have to get the color in. Your first take goes into the stack, then your second, third and fourth and you go off into the darkness to scrounge a cup of coffee and some rations. . . . You lie down on the floor wondering who stole your blanket which you stole from somebody else. You smell yourself and you stink. Just as sleep begins to creep up on you, your name comes up on the telephone list and you leap to phone your first take to Tokyo. There are no beats out here. Everyone can hear you phoning and if you have something they missed they not only can write it and get it through but sometimes are able to beat you to publication. So it goes through the night. The first take is cleared maybe at 8, the second at midnight, the next at perhaps 2 a.m. and the last at 5 or 6. Then it's time to go back to the front and do it all over again.

In the same dispatch, Beech took a moment to assure readers that he wasn't complaining. "In fact," he wrote, "I'm luckier than any other correspondent in Korea":

> I have a jeep. I am mobile. Remember the jeep I drove out of Seoul? The one that was nearly destroyed when they blew up the bridge under our noses? That's it. The noblest jeep of all. It can do things no other jeep can do. It can climb mountains, swim rivers and when I want to spend a night at the front, I turn it around toward division headquarters and tell it to go after water and oil and gas and be sure to be back in the morning. It always shows up. For some reason, as the other correspondents hitch-hike to the front, their most murderous instincts are aroused when they see me go by, master of my destiny, captain of my fate. Oh yes, they have tried to take it away from me. Once they stole it and

> abandoned it under shell fire. I drove it out again. The Army has tried to take it away from me but I remind them it would not be here if I hadn't brought it out of Seoul while others abandoned jeeps by the score and walked out. Right now, the jeep is in the custody of an air force colonel, a friend, at an unidentified strip in Korea, awaiting my return.

By staying at the front and away from Walker's headquarters in Taegu, Higgins avoided officious headquarters staff who might take it upon themselves to enforce the general's instructions and bundle her out of the country. At the same time, she established something of a beachhead in the front section—often the front page—of the *Herald Tribune*. Her stories had a different tone than the ones that Bigart began to file. Hers reflected her own excitement, which sometimes bubbled up in vignettes that smacked of melodrama. His had the quiet authority, precision, and elegance of a seasoned observer. In effect, Higgins and Bigart would come to complement each other. The paper would claim credit for featuring the exploits of the only woman reporter on the front lines in Korea and those of the most celebrated war correspondent of his time. The fact that they behaved as if they were rivals, far from undermining their work, enhanced it. Hanson Baldwin, the *New York Times* military correspondent, would later ask Beech plaintively, "Why are Homer and Maggie beating our asses off out there?" To which Beech replied, "That's easy—they hate each other. The competition is a lot fiercer between them than between me and you."

Whether or not the editors at the *Herald Tribune* guessed from the start the benefits of keeping both reporters in the field, they made no move to recall Higgins. On the contrary, when Higgins wrote to Helen Reid, spouse of the *Herald Tribune*'s publisher, to beg for her support in fighting General Walker's order, Reid came through in spades. The *Trib* issued a statement on July 18 extolling the outstanding work Higgins had been doing and arguing that it was high time that women be allowed to assume the same risks as men in reporting the war.

The statement came a bit late. Higgins finally went to Taegu on the 17th to plead her case with General Walker. She was intercepted by a member of his staff, who marched her to the airstrip and sent her to Japan. She landed there in time to learn that MacArthur, buckling to public pressure, was rescinding Walker's order. A couple of weeks later she was back in Korea and on the front lines.

Task Force Smith did not stop, but at least slowed down, the North Korean advance from Suwon south to the edge of Taejon. The defense of that city became the responsibility of General Dean, commander of the 24th Infantry Division and, since his arrival on July 5, commander of the expeditionary force, including Smith's team. His assignment was a thankless one. His division had languished in occupation duty in Japan since the Japanese surrender. Most of its veterans had retired from the military: only 15 percent of the men under his command had seen combat. They were short of mortars, munitions, vehicles, and, as it turned out, officers with leadership ability. They were outnumbered and outgunned. It was not surprising that they were forced back.

Reporters on the scene were conflicted. They were reflexively and unreservedly supportive of the American, and then the United Nations', intervention. They reported eagerly enough any sign that resistance to the North Koreans was stiffening. But many of them, like Beech, were veterans themselves. They knew what a well-led and effective outfit looked like, and they could see clearly the units that were failing. In any case, there was no way to disguise a retreat. A lot of reporting that made its way back to the States was, accordingly, critical. None more so than that filed by Beech.

It's possible to sense his initial reluctance to condemn even obvious deficiencies in the American intervention. When American troops were beginning to arrive on the Korean peninsula, he wrote that it was "inconceivable" that the North could stand against

American "ground, air and naval strength" unless the Russians chose to intercede. He found demonstrations of UN air power, when they occurred, encouraging. "American and Australian fighter planes came to the relief of our sorely harassed and depressed soldiers," he wrote in the lead-up to the battle for Taejon. "They shot up enemy tank concentrations 25 miles north of United States headquarters."

Nevertheless, a pattern of enemy advance and American retreat was becoming familiar. North Korean troops accompanied by tanks infiltrated and encircled American units that stood, faltered, and then pulled back, often abandoning supplies and equipment in the process. Green GIs and their ROK counterparts were unable to sustain an effective response. On July 9 Beech was sitting on a hill south of Chonan observing another retreat:

> As the Americans came down the road, off to the left 40 to 50 North Korean soldiers could be seen trudging along a path through rice paddies, bent on encirclement. Our people like to stick to roads. The Communists don't mind getting their feet in paddies, which, despite the fact that our forces currently are outnumbered, is the main reason we are constantly being outflanked.

No doubt Beech was channeling a sentiment shared by most of his countrymen when he wrote in early July that he hoped fervently the tide soon would turn, but there was "no denying that so far we have been getting our teeth kicked in." "Twice within three days," he added, "United States forces were forced to retreat, sometimes minus helmets, pants and shoes."

In mid-July, Beech, back in Tokyo, took time to review his notes and collect his thoughts. In promoting the piece on its front page, the *Chicago Daily News* reminded readers of Beech's May 8 article, the one in which he complained of his country's habit of bucking rather than backing revolutions. "Russian-managed Oriental peasants," Beech wrote, "have humbled the mightiest nation on earth."

Just think, he asked, if the Russians can achieve this with Koreans, then "the question naturally arises as to what they can do with millions of Chinese peasants." The Americans troops, he went on, were not prepared for what they were now finding themselves up against. Partly this was due to inexperience. He quoted a regimental commander saying, "No American division is worth a damn until it's been in battle. That was true in the last war and it's true now." The same commander "managed to hold a hotly contested hill only because he himself was up front leading his troops. 'They could not walk out on the high-priced help,' the officer said ruefully. 'Our casualties have not been so heavy. It is only that the men have a tendency to break and run when the enemy gets in their midst.'" Both the officer with whom he was speaking and Beech himself were restrained in the way they characterized this tendency, and Beech still argued that the situation would "be corrected as soon as the full weight of American might [could] be brought against the enemy." But, he added, only provided that "the American G.I.s are willing to face the sad but inescapable fact that in a war men must fight and die."

This grim observation was, in effect, endorsed by General Dean himself. The day before Taejon was invested, he told Beech that morale wasn't what it should be. "My men won't fight," he said. "I know the odds are against us and all that, but they still won't fight. I can't understand it." In the event, some did fight, and Dean did his best to show them how by his own example. But they had been through a lot. The three infantry regiments at Dean's disposal, the 34th, 19th, and 21st, each had been reduced in the preceding days to little more than a battalion. They were physically exhausted and mentally drained, a characterization that could be applied to Dean himself.

He had planned to set up an orderly withdrawal beginning on July 19. There was no thought that the city could be held for long against the two North Korean divisions (nominally three, but the third was itself badly weakened) that were bearing down on them. But General Walker landed at Taejon airstrip on the 18th to meet with Dean and demand a further delay. Walker was awaiting the arrival of reinforcements in the form of the 1st Cavalry Division, which he hoped would shore up the perimeter around the city. He needed more time. So Dean arrayed his depleted forces as best he could. Anticipating an assault following the now-familiar pattern, with heavy pressure on a central front accompanied by flanking movements and an attempt to block the rear, he sought to preserve an exit. Elements of the 34th were positioned to the north and northwest of the city; the 19th on a ridgeline facing the Kapchon River on its western flank; and the 21st to the east. It wasn't long before these preparations were tested.

The story of what happened on July 19 and early on the 20th is one of disintegrating defenses and a simultaneous breakdown in communication. The North Korean attack was a pincer movement: one prong drove down the Kongju Road toward the airstrip north of the city; the other challenged the 19th Infantry position along the Kapchon River. On both fronts the defenders were hard pressed from the start. The western line was breached early in the day, and later that afternoon Dean himself was at the front with two tanks, directing fire. He was back in Taejon later, where he joined the officer commanding the 34th Infantry, Col. Charles E. Beauchamp, who had moved his command post into the city from its initial blocking position farther north. Neither man was aware that the breach in the west was turning into a rout. Under increasing pressure, the 19th Infantry essentially scattered and took to the hills. Nor did Dean get word of activity south of the city on the road to Kumsan, where North Korean troops were setting up roadblocks. The envelopment of the city was well underway.

Dean was awakened at around 5:30 a.m. on July 20 by the sound of small-arms fire. Enemy tanks were in the city, and with them scores of infantrymen, who rode on their decks and then dismounted to set up strongpoints from which to snipe at American soldiers. Dean joined a team hunting tanks using the old 2.36-inch bazooka and then, later, another team armed with the new 3.5-inch version. Together they stalked a North Korean T-34 and, from a second-floor position, blew it up. "I got me a tank!" he was reported to have shouted. Just as he had the day before, the general commanding the 24th Infantry Division was going where, in most circumstances, he had no business being: in active combat on the front line.

Dean and Beauchamp took a break to eat warmed-up C-Rations in the afternoon, blissfully unaware of their rapidly deteriorating position. "It would be difficult to find a parallel to the bizarre situation," wrote the US Army's official historian, "the two commanders quietly eating their late lunch in the belief that their combat forces were still in battle position a mile or two west of the city, while actually the two battalions were scattered in the hills, completely ineffective for any defense of Taejon." They were equally unaware later that their escape routes south of the city were blocked and, in this state of ignorance, they set about organizing what they assumed would be a more or less organized withdrawal.

At around 5:00 p.m. a convoy of some fifty vehicles carrying mostly 34th Infantry personnel drove out of the center of the city headed for a road that they thought was still open. They were harassed by small-arms fire and then halted by a barrier of burning vehicles. Forced to flee on foot, a party of 125 started for the hills, becoming separated during the night and leaving scattered groups to make their way independently to what they hoped would be friendly lines. Some succeeded, either that morning or a day later. Some were taken prisoner. Others disappeared and were never heard from again.

Homer Bigart observed the battle from atop a hill overlooking the northern approach to the city. His account was typically dispassionate, considered, and in its implications scathing. He noted the ease, "overlooked" by the Americans, with which the sprawling city of 130,000 could be infiltrated. Once the North Korean troops were entrenched, they were able to cut access routes, destroy supply dumps, and direct their fire at isolated American units. He reported that no straggler line had been set up, with the result that "a number of soldiers who fled the city were permitted to wander aimlessly to the rear. Many of them still carried rifles and should have been promptly reorganized and sent back to assist in the defense, or at least, help secure and open the line for retreat."

Beech interviewed a "regimental commander," almost certainly Beauchamp, at midnight on July 20. Beauchamp described the battle his men had fought with enemy tanks before explaining how their escape went wrong: "The house fell in when I issued the order to withdraw," he said. "I wasn't worried so much about our retreat because I had sent back word I was coming out. . . . But there was some sort of mixup and we didn't get the support we had expected." Runners were dispatched who either disappeared or failed to find anyone to report to. Radio messages were lost.

There was no disguising the significance of Taejon's fall. Beech was explicit:

> The United States Army suffered its worst defeat of the Korean War yesterday. Taejon fell to victorious Reds from North Korea in a thunderous climax to a 15-day-old campaign. As trapped American forces attempted to fight their way out of the city explosive clashes could be seen. The Communists lost no time exploiting their victory. They moved south of Taejon to establish roadblocks of burning jeeps. They set up machine guns on high ground. One man who ran the gantlet of enemy fire and lived to tell about it was Pvt. Darcy Brady of Gassaway, W.Va. Brady brought back 11 wounded in one jeep. "They put up a roadblock of four jeeps and set them all afire," said Brady. "We were using our trucks to push the jeeps out of the way. Of course, they were

> shooting at us all the time." Brady talked like a man who had just driven through hell. "I wanted to bring back the wounded," he said, "but they have a lot more wounded up there."

Beech, like Bigart, noted with some disgust the number of troops running from the enemy:

> Standing alongside the road outside Taejon, I counted more than 75 stragglers. Most had thrown away their weapons and some were shoeless. Questioning disclosed that their unit had suffered two casualties, one killed and one wounded. Allied observers believe that there is nothing especially wrong with the American Army here that more fighting and less running wouldn't cure.

Beech also mentioned a fellow correspondent's dramatic encounter with an enemy sniper. An Australian reporter, Denis Warner, took the word of a party of South Korean military policemen that it was safe to enter the city. A gung-ho Texan he identified as Private Reuben Kimba volunteered to take him and a photographer in his jeep. What they saw as they entered the city, the extent of the devastation, made Warner wonder whether the word of the South Korean policemen—if they were indeed South Korean—was reliable. Nevertheless, they stopped and left the jeep to investigate and promptly came under small-arms fire. Warner, seeking cover, turned a corner leading into a narrow alley only to find himself staring down the barrel of a sniper's rifle. He threw himself to the ground as Private Kimba came tearing up behind him, a .45 pistol blazing in his hand. In Beech's telling, Kimba, "a fast man on the draw," took down the sniper. In Warner's later recollection, the sniper dropped his rifle with a clatter and ran "with the Texan's bullets flying around his ears." Bigart picked up the story too. His version reflects his accustomed unflappability. He also came up with a different spelling of Warner's savior's name: "Their guide," he wrote, "Pvt. Reuben

Kimball of Baytown, Texas, shot a Red infantryman just as he was about to draw a bead on a British correspondent." Bigart, of course, had the correct spelling of Kimball's name.

The fall of Taejon had a sad coda. General Dean departed the city on the evening of the 20th in a jeep that he turned over to a group of wounded men whose need for it, he reckoned, was greater than his. He boarded an artillery half-track, part of a convoy that, like so many others, was halted outside of town by a barrier made up of burning vehicles. He and the men with him were forced to find their way from there on foot. They took to the hills that cradled the city, hid in gardens and ditches from enemy soldiers, and crossed the Taejon River in the middle of the night. The going got harder as the hills gave way to mountains. The wounded among them struggled to keep up. Dean set off by himself to find water for the wounded men, slipped and fell down a steep embankment, banged his head, and lost consciousness. He woke badly bruised, with a broken shoulder, now cut off from the other men. He wandered on his own for thirty-six days before accepting an offer of help from Korean farmers, who betrayed him. For the next three years he was a prisoner of war.

"I SHOULD HAVE BEEN BLOWN UP"

In late July Beech filed a couple of articles detailing all that seemed to him to be wrong with the war effort. In one he described the helpless befuddlement of a particular battalion commander: "I saw one first lieutenant running a battalion when his commanding officer, a lieutenant colonel didn't know what to do." He enlarged on the story in his memoir. He, Higgins, and McCartney had watched as the drama played out:

> "I don't think the lieutenant colonel knows what to do," said Roy.
>
> We were all watching the lieutenant colonel and listening to what he said and trying not to be noticed. But the lieutenant

> colonel noticed us and he wished we would go away without saying so. For the truth was that the lieutenant colonel didn't know what to do. His men knew he didn't know what to do, but that was family. We were the intruders, spying on his weakness.

The lieutenant colonel was struggling to resolve a dilemma. Another company had requested help. To send help would mean weakening his own position. Their left flank would be exposed.

> The lieutenant colonel looked pleadingly at the lieutenant, but the lieutenant's eyes were politely questioning.
>
> There was a long silence; even the cicadas were suddenly quiet. The lieutenant colonel cast a sidelong look at the three correspondents.
>
> "Sir, may I make a suggestion?" said the lieutenant.

Beech had no sympathy for the senior officer.

> He was a lieutenant colonel in the United States Army and he had been given command of a battalion of several hundred men. If he didn't know his job he had no right to those silver leaves. Let him get the hell out of the Army and give those leaves to somebody who knew how to use them.

Frank Gibney, long after the war, described a similar but more dire incident. He was with Beech, Mydans, Lambert, and McCartney, all of whom were veterans of campaigns in earlier wars. They were following a column of infantrymen accompanied by officers in two jeeps when they paused on the crest of a hill overlooking a Korean village. "The officers," wrote Gibney, "fresh from service in Europe, thought it would not take very long to secure the village." The correspondents were not so sure. The village seemed oddly quiet to them. They suggested to the company commander that "he might want to send a small patrol ahead to explore the terrain. The North Koreans, it seemed to us, were given to ambushes and this was a very good place for one." The officers listened but were not bothered by the correspondents' concern. The commander said they were going ahead. The correspondents could come with them or not, as they chose. The correspondents talked it over. They got in their jeep and turned around. They checked on other units. They filed their stories in Taejon.

Later they learned that the company commander and his men had been ambushed. The two jeeps were destroyed by heavy-caliber machine-gun fire. There were casualties. Gibney did not report this story at the time it occurred. Nor did Beech elaborate beyond the single sentence about the lieutenant who effectively took command of a battalion in the same period. But the piece he filed on July 24 from Tokyo was forthright.

He told a story about a "mist-shrouded dawn" when he was driving his jeep on the road to Chonui. A sentry stopped him, said his orders were to stop everyone, but relented for some reason when Beech explained that he was a correspondent:

> We drove one mile to the deserted village of Chonui, where a blasted bridge stopped us. We got out and looked around. Half-a-dozen mines were planted like naked turnips on each side of the bridge. We got back into the jeep and backed gingerly out. Back at the battalion command post I casually mentioned to the battalion commander that we had driven to Chonui. "The hell you say!" he exclaimed. "That road is mined." The point is that I should not be here to write the story. I should have been blown up. More important, enemy tanks that came down that road a couple of hours later should have been blown up. This is just one illustration of how unprepared we were for the Korean war. American soldiers who bore the brunt of the North Korean attack, didn't

Figure 8. Beech, Marguerite Higgins, Reuters reporter Roy McCartney, and unidentified individual, Korea, 1950. Marguerite Higgins Papers, Special Collections Research Center, Syracuse University Libraries.

know how to lay mines. They don't know how to park their vehicles properly or how to space their vehicles in convoy. On more than one occasion I've driven at least three quarters of a mile

> past American trucks strung out bumper to bumper. One enemy plane could have blown the whole convoy to pieces. The American Army prides itself on communications yet our communications in Korea have been fantastically inadequate. . . . Speaking of Taejon, nobody has explained why, when it was obvious the city was about to fall, we failed to get out our heavy equipment, guns and ammunition. Back at Twenty-fourth Division headquarters I asked a colonel why. "I cannot answer that," he said. We left more than half a dozen 155-mm guns in Taejon, not to mention more than one 105 plus 10 carloads of ammunition.

Anticipating the likely response from the Dai Ichi, Beech admitted that his comments might be received coolly:

> It may be said with some truth that a dispatch like this gives aid and comfort to the enemy. Certainly it won't give aid and comfort to the folks back home. But this is not the time for Americans to be comfortable. Our one consolation should be that we discovered our inadequacies while we were up against a second-class enemy.

The reaction was not long in coming, and when it came it came not from the Dai Ichi but from the Pentagon. Perhaps surprisingly, the officer responding on behalf of Army Chief of Staff Gen. J. Lawton Collins admitted some weaknesses while denying knowledge of others. "We have no reports of such incidents of soldiers there in planting mines so they would not explode," he said. However:

> Communications have improved greatly in the last week. . . . Ignorance of arms is possible among green men. So is an inability to stand and fight. . . . And it is probable, because men had to be thrown in quickly, that they were not well trained.

In effect, Beech's angry analysis was confirmed.

Reinforcements were streaming into the country. By mid-August General Walker had put together a defensive line around the southern port city of Pusan. The loss of Pusan would most likely have marked the dissolution of the United Nations intervention. That didn't happen. But for a time it was possible to imagine a different outcome.

THE PUSAN PERIMETER

Beech and Higgins adopted a new routine over the next few weeks. Because the region around Taegu was a battleground for much of August, Pusan became their base of operations. From there they did their best to monitor the action wherever it was most intense.

At the beginning of the month Higgins spent a few days with Col. John "Iron Mike" Michaelis, the "handsome, hard-fighting commander" (in Beech's description) of the 27th Infantry, then engaged in a push against the Communists west of Pusan. Her story about a melee on the morning of August 3 would add to her growing fame, especially when it was amplified by Carl Mydans in the adoring profile he wrote for *Life* magazine. Mydans adored Higgins, and Higgins adored Michaelis, who appears to have reciprocated in kind. The US Army's official historian, Roy Appleman, less adoringly described the incident as unremarkable. The affair at Chingdongni, as Appleman termed it, was centered on Michaelis's regimental command post, a schoolhouse (which in Korea was often the sturdiest building available). This one was situated at the foot of a bluff, with a courtyard in front of it. On this August morning it was the site of a surprise attack.

Higgins was in the schoolhouse enjoying her second cup of coffee with the headquarters staff when the coffee pot on the table beside her exploded. Beech, who got the story from Higgins, added his own flourish when he wrote that "machine-gun bullets ripped through the building like jet-propelled hailstones." The room's occupants hit the floor. Keeping low, Michaelis and his officers worked their way from room to room before eventually reaching the door and the courtyard. Higgins and another reporter, Harold Martin, took a more direct route: they leapt through a window and found themselves under fire. The North Koreans had set up their machine guns on the bluff overlooking the building, and some GIs on the other side of the courtyard were firing back. Some of the GIs, apparently under the impression that the schoolhouse itself had been taken over by the enemy, directed their fire at the building. In the courtyard, a number of soldiers, startled from their slumber and finding themselves being shot at from all directions, took cover beneath jeeps and trucks. Michaelis, when he emerged from the schoolhouse, was able to bring order to the chaos, directing machine-gun units to attack the enemy, and in time the skirmish ended. In its aftermath, Higgins wrote modestly, "one correspondent learned how to administer blood plasma."

Appleman noted dryly in a footnote that Higgins's account (as well as that written by Martin for the *Saturday Evening Post*) was "somewhat colored." Michaelis was more appreciative. When, more than a month after the event, a copy of Higgins's dispatch fell into his hands, he was moved to write a letter to the *Herald Tribune* in which he described her "heroic" actions as having "saved the lives of many grievously wounded men." Higgins, however inadvertently, had committed the journalist's sin of making herself the story.

Beech, meanwhile, had taken the time to welcome the 5th Marine Battalion when it landed in Pusan and then follow it into battle. "The hill is nameless but not the Marines who died to take it," Beech wrote a week later. The Marines were following through on Walker's first counteroffensive, a thrust along the Chinju-Masan corridor on the southwest edge of the peninsula for which Walker had put together Task Force Kean, led by the officer commanding the 25th Division, Maj. Gen. William B. Kean. On the night of August 7–8, at Hill 255 east of Chingdongni, where Michaelis had so impressed Higgins, the Marines found themselves in a tough fight to keep open the road to Masan. "The Marines went up the hill, sheer and precipitous, Tuesday morning," Beech wrote:

> They met the Army coming down, happy and deserving of relief after four days of concentrated hell. "They opened up on us with grazing fire the minute we reached the top of the hill," said Pfc Howard M. Varner, 19, Danville, Illinois. "You cannot stand up under fire like that, grazing along at you about knee high."

Private John Hicks, nineteen, of Jacksonville, Florida, couldn't decide which was worse, the terrain or the enemy. Just as bad was the heat: as many men succumbed to heat prostration as to enemy fire. "Men were falling like flies," said Hicks. "I went down for water. The fellows up there are crazy for water. They keep dropping water to us from the air but the cans break open when they hit the ground and the water runs out. You can almost cry to see all that good water go to waste." The Marines took the hill, though the assault was costly.

While there was some positive movement in the southwest, UN forces suffered setbacks on the central front along the Naktong River. In attempting to break what had turned into something of a stalemate, Walker ordered the 5th Marine Regiment to be brought up from the southwestern front to augment his forces in the center. He planned an attack to open on the morning of August 17 with both the Marines, commanded by Lt. Col. Raymond Murray (whom Beech had known as an artillery battalion commander on Tarawa), and elements of the 9th Infantry under overall command of General Church. Beech would watch again as the Marines advanced against an entrenched enemy occupying a superior position, in this case a strip of high ground called the Obongni Ridge. The 9th Infantry were to assault the adjacent complex of hills called the Cloverleaf. The Marine attack started badly.

"The marines ran into their toughest fight of the Korean war

Thursday," Beech wrote, "and got a bloody nose." The 2nd Battalion, 5th Marines watched and waited as carrier-based Marine Corsairs set the bald summit aflame after artillery fire had softened up the area behind it. Then, at 8:00 a.m., four platoons numbering about 120 men stepped forward from the line of departure. Their task was to climb the steep slope and dislodge the enemy troops from the summit. Colonel Murray had argued against timing the Marine assault to coincide with that of the 9th Infantry. He saw the Obongni Ridge as a first step to taking the higher and, he assumed, more heavily defended hills that lay beyond it. That, he believed, was when the two forces could combine most effectively. This proved to be a miscalculation:

> I watched through binoculars [wrote Beech] as the antlike figures of half a dozen marines emerged from the red clay on the side of the hill and started upward. They couldn't see what I could see. There were 8 or 10 North Koreans waiting for them behind a clump of trees. I wanted to scream a warning.

The enemy were deeply dug into foxholes on the reverse slope of the ridge. The air attack had little effect on them. Only two-thirds of one Marine platoon, twenty of thirty men, reached the summit in a first attempt. They were pushed back. After another sortie by Corsairs, the Marines tried again, with a similar result, nine of fifteen making it to the summit before retreating. Colonel Murray reconsidered his earlier decision. Much of the fire that had impeded his men's progress had come from the Cloverleaf and a nearby village. A coordinated attack later in the day suppressed the flanking fire that had decimated the Marines, and the Obongni Ridge was taken.

Beech reported on the toll the assault had exacted. A corpsman told him that they had six ambulances shuttling to the rear all morning:

> An aging gunner sergeant, his hand a bloody mess, walked in and collapsed on a stretcher. "I got men lying all over that hill with their brains blown out and here I got hit in the hand," he croaked between swollen lips. "Somebody light me a cigaret, will you? I can't run bending over, that's my trouble. I guess I'm just too old for this war," he almost sobbed. A tall, black-bearded corporal with a bandaged face and shoulder walked into the aid station and a corpsman told him to sit down. "I can't," he said. "I got hit there too. But I might manage one cheek," he said, lowering himself gingerly.

Back in Tokyo on August 19, Beech may have been thinking of the scene at the aid station when he attempted to answer what he said was an often-asked question: How long would the war last? His answer, in essence, was that it depended on how seriously the United States chose to take it. With sufficient resources, he wrote, commanders in the field believed it could be ended in six months. But it seemed that the administration wasn't prepared to commit what was needed. People in Korea were frustrated "by Washington's apparent refusal to recognize the Korean war was a first class war. It may not be a first class war in any conventional sense. But Americans are going to be in for a rude shock when they see the casualty figures."

The Naktong front continued to preoccupy Walker, but battles were fought from one end of the perimeter to the other. Beech and Higgins worked hard to keep tabs on the wider campaign, sometimes paying particular attention to their favorite units. One day Beech found Michaelis at his command post in a concrete culvert under a highway south of Taejon. The colonel was always good for a quote. The "8th Army's handsome, fair-headed boy," wrote Beech, "interrupted a recent telephone conversation with headquarters to say, 'Just a minute, there's a tank running over me.'"

Occasionally, as a break from the rigors of battlefront reporting, the two correspondents were entertained by government officials. After one such occasion, as they were driving away from dinner at the American ambassador's residence in Pusan, Beech discovered the brakes on his jeep weren't functioning. Faced with the choice of driving over a fifty-foot embankment or into a concrete gatepost, he chose the gatepost. Higgins got the worst of it: a goose egg on her forehead and a probable concussion when she was thrown into the windshield. She was hospitalized, but only for the night. Incensed at the idea that Beech would head to the front without her, she insisted on going with him the next day.

By mid-August it seemed that UN forces were at last gaining the upper hand. At about the same time, Beech picked up rumors that MacArthur planned to exploit their advantage by launching an amphibious attack behind enemy lines. The site of the proposed maneuver was an open secret. "The enemy has only one regiment," Beech reported, "—and that of poor fighting quality—at Inchon, a port only a half hour's drive from Seoul. An amphibious landing in that vicinity would be profitable."

A couple of weeks later, correspondents were making arrangements to take part in the assault. Beech was assigned to a cabin on a transport, where he was joined by another correspondent, Joseph Alsop, who with his brother, Stuart, wrote an influential thrice-weekly column in the *Herald Tribune*. Their passage from Pusan took four days. On the night before D-Day, they settled down with a bottle of whisky between them and debated the issues of most immediate concern. Two came to the fore in Alsop's recollection: "which of the landing waves we should go in on (the dangerous first ones or the 'official' initial assault that followed); and whether Keyes should marry . . . Marguerite Higgins." Alsop argued for the first wave and for matrimony on the grounds that in each case it would be the "distinguished" thing to do."

How Beech responded is not recorded.

NIGHT AT THE CHOSUN HOTEL

When MacArthur celebrated his seventieth birthday back in January, Beech marked the occasion with a series of articles that managed to be both respectful and cheeky. He had long paid attention to the accoutrements that made MacArthur's presence distinctive: the battered cap he had worn in the Philippines, the creased leather flying jacket, the corncob pipe. He now remarked on MacArthur's bearing, how he acted the part of the great man. The general's routine, he wrote, never varied. He arrived at the Dai Ichi building each day in an immaculate black Cadillac. Looking neither right nor left, he stalked to the entrance, a tall, dignified, somber man, "wearing five stars and the brooding face of a man of destiny," before disappearing inside. Beech listed the titles to which MacArthur could lay claim: not just general of the army but also "illustrious American, Yankee Shogun, soldier-statesman," and added "actor-impresario."

Beech was acutely conscious of MacArthur's theatricality, his knack for prepping the stage on which he was set to perform. Beech acknowledged the strength of his character and the quality of his achievements, but he also noticed his overweening pride and the signs of age-related decline. MacArthur was flawed, but no journalist—and certainly not Beech—could ignore his news value. MacArthur was hugely popular in the United States and intended, even at this late point in his career, to exploit his fame to achieve higher office. He still believed he had a future in politics. Nothing less than the White House would do.

For this to happen and to reaffirm his military genius he desired another victory, but the Communists weren't yet vanquished. MacArthur tended to blame the 8th Army commander, Gen. Walton Walker, for the stalemate. He suspected Walker of being insufficiently bold. He intended the landing at Inchon and subsequent drive to Seoul to make up for Walker's perceived failings and to decisively change the course of the war. The seizure of the capital would be a psychological as well as military triumph that he planned to cap with a suitably impressive ceremony in which he would personally return the seat of government to the South Korean president, Syngman Rhee. After that he would focus on destroying the enemy once and for all.

For this purpose he put together X (or 10th) Corps. The new army corps consisted in part of the 1st Marine Division, which he needed for the amphibious operation, and the 7th Infantry Division, which would lead the swing south from Seoul to meet Walker's 8th Army and annihilate enemy forces caught in between. To command X Corps he selected his own chief of staff, Gen. Edward Almond, whom he knew to be loyal and obedient. To ensure that the landing and subsequent movements would have every chance of success, he diverted resources from the south. He was already making the 8th Army weaker by removing the 1st Marine Division from Walker's command. He made them weaker still by diverting supplies to X Corps: Walker's remaining forces would be short of ammunition and even food in the days to come.

The tension between personalities and their interests would become evident as the operation developed. MacArthur pushed Almond hard to achieve quick victories. Almond pushed the Marines. The Marines, in turn, soon had reason to question Almond's decisions. Nor was any love lost between Almond and Walker. It wasn't just that the 8th Army commander was annoyed at being deprived of men and supplies. He doubted that Almond had a solid understanding of combat fundamentals. He regarded him as impetuous and inclined to underestimate the enemy's ability while overestimating his own. Such cross-currents are not rare among commanders, but they hampered operations in the field. In some instances Almond's forces were pushed prematurely or without preparation into battles that were more costly than they should have been. The taking of Seoul's industrial suburb, Yongdungpo, was one such instance. Arguably, the battle for Seoul was another.

But to get to Seoul the Marines first had to take Inchon. While the 3rd Battalion of the 5th Marines landed early on September 15 on an outlying island, the main assault touched shore in the late afternoon. Beech and Alsop clambered down the rope netting into their assigned landing craft along with thirty Marines at around 3:30. It was so cramped that men's backpacks were pushed into one another's faces, their rifles shoved into their backs. Beech was seated, involuntarily, in another man's lap. Alsop, scrunched up beside him, complained that he was too old for this sort of thing. They landed with a platoon from the 1st Marine Regiment fifty-four minutes after the first wave. The waterfront was deserted. "It was the most uneventful beachhead I had ever made," Beech reported. What he saw when he looked around, however, was impressive. The city was in flames. Munitions were exploding:

> A blood-red sun dropped behind Korea's brooding black hills as Inchon burned in Uncle Sam's answer to the temerity of a half-pint Communist satellite. Silhouetted on the breakwater that protects Inchon harbor, Pfc John Meyers, 21, of Chicago summed it up: "It's so awful and—but it's beautiful." Across the harbor from where we stood this Friday night new explosions rocked Inchon and huge columns of flame boiled up against a sullen sky.

For Beech, who took such pride in America's achievements, and not least in its industrial and military might, the repeated retreats endured in July and the beginning of August had been humiliating. The prospect of going back to Seoul was something to be savored. He would refer to his earlier, hasty escape from the city repeatedly as the Marine 1st Division closed in on the capital. At Inchon on September 17, he remembered that on his last visit he had been unable to reclaim the laundry he had left at the Chosun Hotel before the war started. "Even as the Chosun moves," he wrote, "it should be ready by now." At Kimpo airfield a day later he noted that "it was good to be back for I was one of four correspondents who landed at Kimpo . . . two days after the war started." And as the Marines got closer to the capital: "It was a most enjoyable occasion for me, an ex-Marine, just as it obviously was for the active Marine participants. I had crossed the Han going the other way on a Korean raft the morning of June 28."

If Beech was pleased by the turn of events, MacArthur was jubilant. The supreme commander Asia Pacific had kept a low profile when the war was going badly. Not now. He stepped ashore on August 17 with an impressive entourage, including five generals and an admiral, even before the skirmishing around the airfield had been quashed. The illustrious party came across the corpse of a North Korean soldier. As Beech looked on, MacArthur poked the body with the toe of his boot. "That's the way I like to see them!" he said to the others. And then, turning to a doctor who was accompanying them, he added, "There's one patient you'll never have to work on, doc!" As soon as he was back on his flagship, USS *McKinley*, he issued a communiqué stating—about twenty-four hours prematurely—that Kimpo was securely in American hands.

Beech and Higgins were with the 5th Marines when they got lost between Inchon and Kimpo. The roads in Korea were often rudimentary, and the Marines, faced with a choice of dirt tracks, and with poor maps and no signs to guide them, were stymied. Beech found Kim, a young Korean woman, "well scrubbed and rosy-cheeked," who had put on her best dress and shoes to greet the Americans. She knew the way, she told him: she had attended GI dances at Kimpo before the war. The Marines took up her offer of guidance, and Kim climbed onto Beech's jeep at the head of the convoy. They moved at a good clip for several miles before suddenly coming under machine-gun fire. "We were out of our jeep and into the ditch before you could say Seoul City Sue," Beech wrote. "Then I heard a voice bawling 'get that jeep outta the way.'" His jeep was blocking the path of the tanks behind him. Only later did he learn why Kim was so keen to help them. The Communists had murdered her infant son—he had blue eyes. She had lost touch with her soldier "husband," but lived in hope.

Meanwhile, there had been no letup in the enmity between the two *Herald Tribune* colleagues. One day, as the Marines were advancing on Seoul, Beech found himself mediating between them. Bigart was sitting on one side of the road, watching the progress of the battle; Higgins was on the other side. Then she noticed that the *New York Times* correspondent was headed for the rear, presumably to file his story. "One of us should go back and file if the *Times* is going back," said Higgins:

> By "us" she meant either her or Homer. "Why don't you ask Homer what he's going to do?" I suggested. "No," said Higgins. "If I speak to him he'll just ignore me or bawl me out." "Well," I said, "I'll ask Homer if he'll talk to you." I walked across the road and said to Homer: "Homer, Maggie wants to talk to you. Will you talk to her?" Homer considered the matter with a gravity befitting the senior military correspondent of the *New York Herald Tribune*, then said graciously: "I don't see why not."

A few days later Beech was sitting in an onion patch on a hill overlooking the Han River, watching as the 3rd Battalion of the 5th Marines came across in amtracs, North Korean bullets bouncing off their sides. The tractor carrying the battalion commander, Lt. Col. Robert Taplett, got stuck in the mud, causing him considerable grief: "I died approximately one thousand times," he said later. He got across just the same, and casualties were relatively light. Twelve hours earlier, Beech wrote, Col. Ray Murray had briefed his officers. "We are directed to cross the Han River and move on Seoul, the exact time and place to be left pretty much to us. Now here's the plan. If it works I'll collapse from relief." As it turned out, his plan was good as far as the north side of the river. The North Koreans made their stand not on the riverbank but on the hills around the city. The 5th Marines would have to fight a series of battles to take the high ground before they saw the streets of Seoul. They would be delayed for another four blood-drenched days.

While Murray's 5th Battalion approached the capital from the west, Col. Lewis "Chesty" Puller's 1st Battalion had taken a more direct route to Seoul through its industrial suburb on the south side of the river. They had been pushed by Almond, who was under instructions from MacArthur to stick to a timetable that would have MacArthur handing over Seoul to Syngman Rhee before the month's end. There could be no question of a circumspect approach, one that might have slowed the advance but saved American lives. The battle fought in Yongdungpo's streets, where the defenders had the advantage, took a heavy toll on the Marines before the enemy finally pulled out. Puller's men crossed the river on September 24.

The North Koreans shelled the capital from the surrounding hills and sniped at its liberators from behind barricades in the streets. The Marines had been instructed to preserve what they could of the built environment, but this proved to be impossible. As the commander of a flame-throwing tank told Beech, "We came in here with a humanitarian viewpoint. . . . But we found that humanitarians go home in wooden boxes." Beech and Higgins followed C Company of the First Marines as they fought their way into the city on September 25. Beech had twisted a leg on his way to Puller's command post and was hobbling. Higgins, heedless of his discomfort, proposed to climb a hill surmounted by a ruined church that promised a panoramic view of the destruction below. Beech envisioned the story that Higgins would write: "Tonight in the gathering dusk eye stood on the crest of aye hill looking straight down into the smoking heart of Seoul as marines of Charlie Company. . . . In the little Catholic church nearby the bells pealed." To let her beat him up the hill was unthinkable, so he hobbled up behind her, his hurt knee "shrieking its protest with every step." His own lede was worth the climb:

> The tolling of church bells mingled Sunday night with the chatter of machinegun fire as night fell on the burning city of Seoul. Charlie Company, more concerned with securing its objective than with history, had set up its machine guns around a small shell-shattered Catholic church that topped the hill. "Please tell my folks I'm in church," said Sgt. William C. Shadley, 24, of Chicago.

The battle in the streets intensified on the morning of September 26. Beech, now with G Company, captured the intensity of the fighting:

> The marines fought their way into the heart of the capital to the accompaniment of steady machine-gun fire. Crashing of mortar shells and heavy artillery took their toll of civilians as well as enemy. Hundreds of hapless civilians have been killed and wounded. Navy hospital corpsmen are doing all they can for them after taking care of their own wounded. Marine tanks spearheading the infantry advance made hell-raising forays in the center of the city. Their 90mm guns blasted through sandbag roadblocks five feet thick. But exhausted tank crews had to withdraw to come up for air. Some passed out in their tanks overcome by the choking smoke of gunpowder.

MacArthur again anticipated the battle's outcome in a communiqué announcing that UN forces had "completed the envelopment and seizure" of the city. Even two days later, on the morning of the 28th, Marines were still mopping up. South Korean civilians and police simultaneously were involved in a different kind of operation, scouring the city for any of their countrymen who had colluded with the Communists. "Civilians emerged from alleys prodding in front of them an occasional frightened North Korean soldier," Beech noted. "I watched them beat one over the head. Beatings were the least of the collaborationists' worries. Hundreds were summarily executed and thousands more imprisoned. The brutality could be interpreted as an answer to the no less horrifying atrocities committed by the Communists. Nevertheless, many among the Americans looking on were appalled."

Colonel Taplett, whose amtrac had been stuck crossing the Han River, slept rough with the men of the 3rd Battalion in the capitol building on the night of September 27. He was acting on instructions from Almond to make the place secure for MacArthur's arrival. The scene was being set for the ceremony that the supreme commander had planned. That day, trim soldiers from the 7th Infantry began pouring into the city, their uniforms bright, their boots polished, ready to position themselves as his photogenic honor guard. They tried to bar Puller, who was unshaven and still wearing grimy battle gear, when he drove up to the Duk Soo Palace (dubbed "Duck Soup" by the Marines, naturally). Puller had to make explicit his willingness to run over the major who tried to stop him. But the signal had been sent: in MacArthur's view, the Marines' job was done.

That night, Beech set out to retrieve his laundry. He and Higgins were accompanied by a ragtag escort of civilians armed with one club and a Japanese rifle that wouldn't shoot as he steered the jeep through the ruined streets. The air was heavy with the stinging scent of gunpowder. In some stretches the heat from the fires was so intense that he worried his jerry cans of gasoline would explode. The distant clatter of machine guns echoed off the walls of gutted buildings. Flames glistened on what remained of their windows. Clouds of debris-laden smoke drifted overhead. In his retrospective account, Beech described how he "left Higgins sitting in the jeep saying that if I wanted to get myself killed it was none of her responsibility," and approached the entrance to the hotel warily, carbine in hand, not knowing what fate awaited him. He "could feel the heat from the fire that raged . . . on the opposite side of the narrow street. The steel shutters that covered the windows of this building . . . buckled outward and sent flakes of red-hot metal raining down." The great shadowed bulk of the Chosun had the aspect of a medieval fortress. There could be snipers training their sights on him even then. With sudden resolve he swung open the wooden gate and strode boldly inside. No enemy ambushed him. Instead, the entire hotel staff was arrayed on either side of the driveway. As if on cue they greeted his entrance with a full-throated cheer, their longed-for liberation realized at last.

The account he wrote at the time was less dramatic. In this presumably more authoritative version, he acknowledged that his liberation of the hotel was "no great trick"; the Marines had passed through the neighborhood minutes earlier. As he entered the hotel grounds, thirteen hotel employees rushed up to shake his hand—he was the first American they had seen since June. Higgins joined him almost immediately. Inside they learned from the manager how events had developed when the North Koreans took over. The Communist high command had made the hotel their headquarters, and Kim Il Sung himself had been a guest twice in the previous two months. With help from thirsty Chinese and Russian journalists, these dignitaries had exhausted the hotel's supply of gin. They did no structural damage, but when it came time to retreat they took everything of value with them, including the hotel register and the clock from behind the reception desk. Their depredations were thorough: Beech's laundry had gone with them too.

Beech and Higgins slept at the hotel that night, a flickering fiery glow in the sky outside their window, the sounds of war echoing in the streets. It was a celebratory moment. They guessed that their adventure together was just about done.

In the morning the generals arrived. Beech counted twenty-two stars on the crisp uniforms of the officers who landed in MacArthur's plane. It was a formidable array of brass that notably, as Beech observed, was missing the insignia of the Marine commanders who had actually fought for and seized the city. Just hours earlier, leathernecks had repelled an enemy attack four miles northeast of Seoul's boundaries with a loss of four killed and twenty wounded. The fighting wasn't over. But at least one Marine lieutenant colonel slipped into the capitol to take in the proceedings. Ray Murray, Beech reported, "whose nose still bears a mark where an enemy burst nicked it a week ago, watched the ceremonies with the wide-eyed interest of a kid seeing his first movie." It was indeed an impressive show. MacArthur's emotion-charged speech—tears were said to have rolled down his cheeks—ended with a recitation of the Lord's prayer. It was followed by a no-less-heartfelt response from President Rhee. And then the solemnity of the occasion was threatened:

> When glass from the shattered capitol windows came tinkling down, shoulders hunched and lesser mortals, including ambassador John Muccio, involuntarily put their arms over their heads. MacArthur, a dignified man, didn't even look up. From the gallery above faded wine-colored drapes whipped in the wind. . . . "It's safer up front," muttered an uninvited, bearded marine on the fringe of the crowd. "I'm getting outta here."

The question on everyone's mind as the month came to an end was how far north of the capital MacArthur's armies would advance. The wire services reported that MacArthur would demand the North's surrender and, failing that, was prepared to advance to the Yalu River and, if necessary, into Manchuria. Beech, from his office in Tokyo, claimed that sentiment among officials supported him. The Truman administration, made anxious by the possible intervention of China and uncomfortably aware of the limited United Nations' remit, had reservations about MacArthur's aggressive approach. But the issue was moot for the time being. Almond's X Corps, Walker's 8th Army, and South Korea's now-triumphant army corps proceeded to roll over the Communists on all fronts. Beech was content to leave them to it. The war had taken a toll on him. "When the war began," he wrote in his memoir,

> I weighed 150 pounds, about five pounds more than my normal weight. Three months later I weighed 122 pounds and I could literally count my ribs. . . . I lived like a coiled spring, without respite from the tension. I became taciturn and short-tempered. The story had become an obsession with me and anything that got in the way of that obsession drew my wrath.

It was time to take a break. While Higgins stayed on for another two weeks to observe the UN forces' advance, the Beech byline disappeared from subscribers' newspapers. As far as he—and almost everyone else—was concerned, the war had been won.

RAY MURRAY SHEDS A TEAR

She had it made. Higgins already was a celebrity in Korea. Soldiers, when they saw her on the road, whistled and cheered. Some of her colleagues were briefly nonplussed when they rode beside her, wondering why their appearance provoked such a riotous response. And then they understood. *New York Post* reporter Jimmy Cannon was said to have muttered ruefully, "Riding in a jeep with Maggie is like being a jockey on Lady Godiva's horse."

By the time of the Inchon landing, her fame as a frontline correspondent—and gossip about the froideur between her and Homer Bigart—had crossed the ocean. When she landed in Honolulu on the 19th of October, both news of her arrival and a photograph to prove it were featured on the *Star-Bulletin*'s front page. It was only a hint of the reception that awaited her on the mainland. Her friend and ally Carl Mydans had contributed a glowing profile of her that appeared in *Life* magazine earlier that month. Under the inevitable heading "Girl War Correspondent," Mydans wrote that she was a "small, slight blonde, sometimes described as winsome," and continued: "Miss Higgins already has become a legend, both in Korea and the US. In the war theater she has proved alarmingly brave, extraordinarily durable and pretty even in her fighting clothes." Mydans provided proof of the latter assertion with photographs of Higgins in army-issue dungarees and blouse, on the tarmac at Kimpo, sitting in a foxhole, leaning on a jeep, and smiling with the bruise on her forehead that was the product of the jeep's encounter with a gatepost in Pusan.

Beech later called Higgins the "best combat buddy" he ever had. He concluded a chapter devoted to their time together by describing her, soberly, as "better than 90 percent of her detractors" and a "good newspaperman." They had done good work together.

It's likely that Beech and Higgins crossed paths again in Seoul as she was leaving and he returning on October 16 or 17. Beech was annoyed when an officious American colonel tried to bar him from taking a room at the Chosun Hotel. Senior officers had moved in and made it their private club. Beech overcame the colonel's obstruction, but only after calling him a "desk clerk" and going over his head by summoning the support of the 8th Army's chief of staff. Beech's affection for the Chosun had taken a proprietorial turn.

North Korean troops were on the run. The Americans and their allies were, by all appearances, coasting to a hard-won victory. Back in Tokyo, Beech laid out what he saw as the lessons learned and the benefits earned. American prestige, as he saw it, was enhanced. The United States had shown its willingness to support a friend whose freedom was threatened. Its armed services, meanwhile, had discovered how unprepared they were. But the discovery, fortunately, was made when they were tested against an inferior foe. There was time to make amends. A day or two later Beech reported confidently that American troops would be home before Christmas, maybe even before Thanksgiving. MacArthur, Beech said, was personally committed to seeing Americans withdrawn as soon as possible and Korea returned to Koreans. For GIs, an early departure would be "the best Christmas present of all. Korea is pretty hard to take, particularly Korean winters."

Beech, along with MacArthur and the armies under his command, was caught short by developments that November. Beech, in particular, missed most of a battle that became a Marine Corps legend: the epic confrontation at the Chosin Reservoir.

Retired Gen. S. L. A. Marshall devoted a preliminary chapter in his book *The River and the Gauntlet* to the stunning intelligence failure that led MacArthur to miss entirely the surreptitious incursion of Chinese troops across the Yalu River. Beginning in mid-October, thousands, and then tens of thousands, and ultimately some three hundred thousand Chinese troops made their way south. Weeks passed before elements of these forces were detected. And even when encountered, Army intelligence guessed that the Chinese mission was either diversionary or defensive. Only when engaged at division level late in November was the situation properly understood.

General Almond had ordered a two-pronged attack to push the North Koreans to the Yalu River. His own X Corps, led in part by the Marine 1st Division, was to move up from the coastal city of Hungnam in the east, while the 8th Army approached in the west. The Marines engaged with Chinese forces almost immediately just north of Hungnam, fighting a furious five-day battle before the Communists broke contact on November 7. The Marines proceeded cautiously after that, meeting with occasional harassment as they approached the Chosin Reservoir. Initially directed to carry on up the east side of the reservoir, they were told on November 25 to turn to the west, with the aim of joining up with the 8th Army. This didn't happen.

On November 27, Chesty Puller's 7th Regiment seized the town of Yudam-ni, and Ray Murray's 5th Regiment followed through to spearhead the prescribed westward drive. What followed was some of the bitterest fighting of the Korean War. Some thirty thousand Chinese emerged from the surrounding hills and closed in on a Marine force barely a third the size in subzero conditions and on rugged terrain that favored the enemy. The Chinese had the advantage in numbers but were poorly equipped: they suffered from the cold no less than the Americans and lacked the Americans' air power and artillery. Marine Corsairs and howitzers played a crucial part in extricating the two regiments from their peril, but the driving snow and freezing temperatures threatened the two sides equally. "It was so cold," Beech wrote later, "that men's feet froze to the bottom of their boots and the skin peeled off when the socks were removed; so cold that men had the feeling their faces would pop; so cold that men who might have died from loss of blood didn't die because the blood congealed and the bleeding stopped." The number of casualties was horrific.

On November 29, forced onto the defensive and aware that they were in imminent danger of being encircled, the Marines were ordered to change direction. To their lasting credit, they succeeded in battling their way from Yudam-ni back to the fork in the road where they had first swung west, and then to Hagaru-ri, where they were able briefly to regroup. It was a triumph of sorts, given the trap they had walked into and the conditions that complicated their escape. They had had to climb mountains in the dark. They had had to endure temperatures that made the discomfort of a rest stop as taxing as continuous marching. Night fights stole what sleep they might otherwise have seized. To march in cadence into the town, as they did, after all they had been through was a tribute to the officers who led them and the men's discipline and fortitude. But the two regiments had suffered some fifteen hundred casualties.

Beech landed at Hagaru-ri on December 4, when the air force was involved in a challenging operation to evacuate as many of the wounded as possible, in the shortest possible time, using an airfield that was technically too short for the planes that employed it. Its success was a logistical triumph. The Marine commanders, meanwhile, were fierce in describing what they had been through. Puller, talking to Beech, uttered a sentiment echoed by his colleagues, though the wording varied with the telling: "Remember," he told Beech, "whatever you write, that this was no retreat. All that happened was we found more Chinese behind us than in front of us. So we about-faced and attacked."

At Hagaru-ri on the 4th, Beech was with other correspondents "in the darkened corner of a wind-whipped tent" as Colonel Murray briefed his men on what lay ahead in their march to Koto-ri. Beech and Murray were friends, but because his face was half-hidden by the hood of his parka Beech went unrecognized until the meeting was ending. "Keyes! What the hell are you doing here?" Murray asked when he saw him. "Damned if I know," said Beech. "I can think of lots of places I'd rather be." "You should have been with us at Yudam-ni," said Murray. "You'd have gotten a story there!" Beech replied, "I'm damned glad I wasn't."

When the tent had emptied and they were alone together, they spoke more frankly about what they had been through. Beech was forthright about decisions made by the higher-ups: "Almond had to know he was sending the Marines into a trap," he told Murray. "I've said it before and I'll say it again. Almond is the meanest son of a bitch, inside the military or outside of the military, I've ever had anything to do with. But he loves to give medals." They shared a drink and Murray told Beech more of his recent tribulations. The recollection got to him and he cried. "I hope he won't mind my reporting that he cried," Beech wrote, "because he's a very large Marine and a very tough guy. He cried because he had to have some sort of emotional release, because all his men were heroes and wonderful people, because the next day he was going to have to submit them to another phase in the trial of blood and ice. Besides, he wasn't the only one who cried."

In Hagaru-ri and then at Koto-ri to the south, Beech pieced together an account of the ten-day action that made much of the hardship and heroism the Marines had exhibited. They didn't break, he wrote. They kept their units' cohesion. They brought out their wounded and many of their dead, though it cost them dearly, and the means by which they achieved these feats were grim. Both dead and wounded often were tied down over the hoods of trucks and jeeps. The cold left them "frozen stiff as boards," according to a navy doctor. For many who survived, the damage wrought by frostbite would be a permanent scar or debility. A Marine sergeant musing on what they had done together summed up their achievement: "It was impossible for us to get out of here. We were surrounded, encircled, and cut off. But we never got the word. That's us, we never got the word."

Beech didn't stay at the front for long. From Seoul he sent a bitter dispatch questioning a MacArthur communiqué that claimed UN forces' morale remained high "despite their smashing defeat by Chinese troops." "Evidently the general and I haven't talked to the same people," Beech wrote. "The atmosphere around 8th Army headquarters is about as cheerful as a wake. So far as news is concerned, the lid is on. Nobody wants to talk." As a sign of what was coming, he reported that GIs had chucked correspondents out of their beds in the press building next to the capitol. The troops had been told to pack them up. It was just as well, said a British correspondent. After all, he wouldn't want the beds to fall into the enemies' hands to be used against them.

Beech joined other correspondents on January 3 to watch as Seoul fell into Communist hands for the second time. Higgins commandeered a jeep and a reluctant GI driver from an artillery outfit. Besides her and Beech, two other correspondents climbed aboard, Hal Boyle from AP and Dwight "Pepper" Martin from *Time*, and together they toured the city. It was an inferno once more, but this time the inhabitants had started the fires, a gesture that might have reflected spite or despair or a simple determination to deny the Communists a material victory. The Americans, for their part, had already decamped. They had fought pitched battles in the streets of Seoul just a few months before, and the toll had been considerable. Now, Beech surmised, they had decided it would be smarter to fight the Communists from the other side of the river.

The inhabitants themselves were nowhere to be seen, and while the boom of big guns, both Chinese and American, could be heard in the distance, the streets were eerily still. The correspondents pulled to a stop in front of City Hall and paused to watch a building being consumed by flames, when they heard a keening wail above the crackle of the fire and the crash of falling masonry. A small boy was crying in front of the building, "crying in a way that twisted a knife in your heart. He was the loneliest boy in the world." It was Pepper Martin who said what the others were thinking: "Well, we can't leave him here." And Martin, a big man, swept the boy up into his arms, wrapped him in blankets, and tucked him between the other passengers in the back seat.

They made other stops that afternoon: the capitol building, now deserted, and the drive that led to the president's residence, where the gates were locked. Martin got out when they came to an apartment block that had served as a press billet and recovered a box of chewing gum from the room he had slept in the night before. Then they drove north of the city and found "Iron Mike" Michaelis at his command post: his 27th Infantry was part of the rearguard covering the American withdrawal. "There are lots of Chinese up the road but so far there's no sweat," he told them. He seemed comfortable in the "living van" that his rank did not technically entitle him to, but which he had nevertheless acquired. Finally they drove back into the city and to the Chosun Hotel. It was supposed to be off-limits and the staff were all gone, leaving it empty but open, and Beech, who was sad and angry about the abandonment of the city and about the way the day had gone, was determined to stay one more night with Higgins in his old room, "with the red light of burning buildings flickering on the walls . . . and the tinkle of falling glass and the sound of the not-so-distant artillery in my ears." Perhaps the familiarity was soothing. He slept well.

CHAPTER 5

Between Wars II

THE PULITZER

Beech was on his way back to the States on April 11, 1951, when he heard the news that MacArthur, too, would be returning to the mainland. MacArthur had, at last, been dismissed by the president. Beech had also been summoned by his employer, but the circumstances were different. His career, unlike MacArthur's, was on an upward trajectory. His reporting from Korea had earned him a nationwide audience, and the Chicago Daily News Foreign Service meant to make the most of his fame by sending him on a speaking tour. Beech regretted only that news of MacArthur's removal while Beech was in transit meant that he was unable to file a report of his own.

The nature of the war was changing. Eighth Army commander General Walton Walker had been killed in a road accident in December. His replacement, Gen. Matthew Ridgway, assumed much, and then all, of the authority that MacArthur previously had borne. Beech had met Ridgway in Taegu in March and had been impressed. At around the same time he traveled to Taipei, his first visit to the island of Formosa, and stopped off in Hong Kong,

Figure 9. Linda Mangelsdorf Beech with General Van Fleet in Korea at the time of the peace talks. Photo by John Rich, *Korean War in Color* (Seoul Selection, 2010).

a more familiar haunt. In a singularly offbeat dispatch, he reported on a series of basketball games played between teams from Russia and China in Shanghai. The Chinese were accustomed to playing the game by American rules; the Russians, eschewing all artifacts of their imperialist rival, imposed their own version. Unsurprisingly, the Russians (who also supplied the referees) won all their games. Somewhat more surprising was their mercilessness toward their Communist comrades: they won each of their games by more than a hundred points.

Beech's return to the States had a personal as well as professional purpose: he was engaged to be married. The plan was not without complications. For one thing, he was still married to Mildred. For another, there was a good deal of gossip, not just whispered but also in the papers, about his relationship with Marguerite Higgins. But Higgins was not the intended bride. She too, as it happened, was married, the consequence of a youthful romance that came to a practical but not legal conclusion in the earlier war. An equally relevant consideration was that Higgins was no more in love with Beech than he was with her. She had fallen for an air force general who, awkwardly, was married too. Beech, for his part, had been dazzled by a brilliant and accomplished Honolulu-born woman, a university graduate fluent in Japanese who was working as an industrial relations analyst for the occupation.

He first set eyes on Linda Mangelsdorf at the Dai Ichi building before the war began. "Who's da new blonde?" he reportedly asked. The Mangelsdorfs were a prominent family in Hawaii. Linda, who had learned Japanese as a child from their maid, had a degree in Oriental philosophy and might have continued her studies had she not gone to work for SCAP and met Beech. She had been a regular guest at the house he shared with John Rich, and they saw one another whenever he took a break from the war. At some point they became a couple, and when he judged (prematurely) that the war was over, they made plans to make the relationship official. The wedding was to have been celebrated in Hawaii, but first there was the speaking tour and the formality of divorce. And then another distraction emerged. He was in St. Petersburg on May 8 when he got news of the Pulitzer. He was one of a half dozen correspondents to be recognized for their work covering the Korean War. The others were Bigart (his second Pulitzer) and Higgins; his colleague on the *Chicago Daily News*, Fred Sparks; and two correspondents from the Associated Press. To pick up the prize he would have to be in New York at a time that conflicted with his Honolulu wedding. Since the awards ceremony was immutable, the wedding got moved.

A case can be made that both Beech and Bigart, and perhaps the other correspondents cited by the Pulitzer committee as well, all owed their prize in some measure to Higgins. Beech acknowledged how her persistence led him, despite his injured knee, to climb the hill overlooking embattled Seoul in September 1950 lest her story have more color than his. The incident suggests a pattern. He was unstinting in praising her work retrospectively. Other observers never doubted that she set a pace the other correspondents struggled to match. Carl Mydans in his *Life* magazine article quoted Tom Lambert commenting somewhat mordantly, "As soon as Homer kills off Maggie or Maggie kills off Homer the competition will wane and so will coverage of the Korean war." There is no question that Bigart was bothered by Higgins. He disparaged her journalism as unprofessional. He faulted her for putting herself at the center of her stories, for her hero worship of MacArthur, and for her uncritical appreciation of the military command in general. But he also confessed that their competition nearly got him killed by making him take chances he would not otherwise have taken. "No way can I make my behavior toward her appear in a favorable light," he conceded years later. "I wanted her out of there in the worst way but couldn't get her transferred. . . . The desk in New York loved it."

While she made her competitors and colleagues take imprudent risks, it is fair to note that their dispatches, especially Beech's, fully merited the Pulitzer committee's recognition. Beech committed himself fully to covering the war. He shifted from front to front with the action and positioned himself to observe it firsthand. Gifts he had honed over the years, for a sharp lede, revelatory dialogue, and a perspective at once detached and precise, all were in evidence. It was not without reason that the *Chicago Daily News* plastered his name and image on the sides of its delivery vans and positioned his stories on the front page. His dispatches sold papers.

His tour of America was hectic and gratifying. His talks were well attended, and his opinion on the state of the world was sought after. During downtime in New York he took in Broadway plays and cabaret at the Stork Club, El Morocco, and 21. While in St. Petersburg visiting his sister, he enjoyed the sun-drenched beaches at a seaside hotel. In a more practical vein, back in New York, he consulted a high-priced lawyer to find out how he could most expeditiously lay the groundwork for remarriage. Informed that his options were limited, he flew to El Paso and slipped across the border for a quickie divorce. As the ceremony in Honolulu was scotched, the deal was sealed in Connecticut, where Linda had relatives. Her parents flew in from the island. Frank Gibney was his best man.

With his remarkable performance in Korea behind him, the most prestigious prize available to American journalists in his pocket, and the prospect of settling down once more, this time with a woman who embraced life in the Far East, Beech had reached an agreeable midlife plateau. In the memoir that was published later, he looked back on the experiences that had brought him to this point. He had witnessed the collapse of the Chinese Nationalists and the rise of Mao, the reconstruction of Japan in America's image, and the violent collision of Communism and democracy on the Korean peninsula. Now he wondered if it wasn't time for a change. His path had entailed risk. "To cover a war properly you have to get shot at occasionally," he wrote. "According to my calculations it was time the law of averages turned against me." And there was another danger, one that in his estimation had ruined many a good reporter if they survived long enough: that of thinking too much. "But if he persists in this madness," Beech wrote, "he may, if he is lucky, win a Nieman Fellowship at Harvard University. That is what happened to me."

Each year the Nieman Foundation offered a dozen journalists the opportunity to audit classes, collaborate with one another, and participate in events aimed at expanding their horizons beyond the newsrooms that had shaped them. Beech, who had left school at grade eight, didn't hesitate. In September 1952 he and Linda, with a brindle boxer named Tigger, moved into a historic Cape Cod cottage (with historic plumbing to match) situated a five-minute walk from Harvard Yard. They soon were joined by his seven-year-old son, Walter, who had been living with his mother in France, and then in December 1953 by his first child by Linda, William Keyes Beech. They called the new arrival "Kimo" for short.

TRUCE AND CONSEQUENCES

The talks that would lead to the end of active hostilities in Korea dragged on for years. Beech, comfortably ensconced at Harvard, was surely content to be spared the frustration experienced by those who were obliged to be in Kaesong, and later Panmunjom, to cover them. There were days when his colleagues had nothing to report, and there were days when they suspected that items that might have been newsworthy were being kept from them. Staff barred them from military facilities, fed them more or less meaningless scraps of information, and sometimes actively misled them. Higgins, who covered the talks and was hungry as always for a story, was outspoken in her complaints. In desperation, she and a number of her colleagues started picking the brains of their opposite numbers in the Chinese and North Korean delegation. There were two with whom they fraternized: Alan Winnington, an Englishman with a reputation as a surly and doctrinaire ideologue, and Wilfred Burchett.

Burchett was unique among Western journalists: amiable, intelligent, a more-than-competent journalist, and a resolute freethinker whose principles governed his actions. He had been a correspondent with the London *Daily Express* covering the Pacific war and the Far East. He scored a notable coup by being the first Western reporter in Hiroshima after the bomb was dropped. Although never a Communist, he sympathized with Communist regimes, including Stalin's Russia, Mao's China, and Kim Il Sung's North Korea. He was close to Mao's foreign minister, Chou Enlai. The Vietnamese revolutionary leader Ho Chi Minh counted him as a friend. He continued to be employed by British newspapers, whose editors appreciated his ability to separate his role as a reporter from his sympathy for hostile governments. His situation gave him insight unavailable elsewhere.

Among those who regarded Burchett as something other than a friend was a fellow Australian, Denis Warner. Burchett had once filed a dispatch with Warner's paper in what Warner regarded as breach of journalistic ethics. Warner's distaste was amplified by his anti-Communist convictions and by information he got from the Australian Secret Intelligence Service (ASIS), with which he cultivated a relationship and by which, it can be argued, he was used. It's fair to add that anti-Communist hysteria was gripping America and other parts of the world in these years. Senator Joe McCarthy was presiding over congressional investigations aimed at rooting out traitors from government departments. Convicted spies Julius and Ethel Rosenberg were put to death in June 1953. The Army-McCarthy hearings that led eventually to the end of McCarthy's scaremongering took place in '54, but anti-Communist fervor remained a part of public discourse for many more years.

Burchett didn't elevate his standing among Western colleagues when he became involved in the Chinese and North Korean campaign to convince the world that the Americans had employed biological weapons in the war. The charge was first made in 1952 by an official who claimed that UN aircraft had rained "fleas, lice, bugs, ants, grasshoppers and spiders" on the North in order to spread disease. Tape recordings were released in which American pilots who were held as prisoners of war "confessed" to the role they played in implementing the scheme. Beech wrote about the confessions at the time and denounced them accurately as clumsy propaganda. But the charges were repeated and remained in circulation. They confirmed a picture of Communist perfidy and so added impetus to the Cold War.

Beech was present when the truce was signed in July 1954, and he followed the elaborate procedure by which prisoners from both sides were streamed either to the United Nations or Communist reception area. Among the thousands released in Operation Big Switch were a pair of American pilots who had confessed to their part in the biological war campaign. One of the two, Col. Bud Mahurin, told Beech that he felt he had been a traitor to his country. The other, Col. Andrew J. Evans Jr., was mostly silent. They presented a contrast in appearance, Mahurin looking lean but tanned and healthy, while Evans was "thin to the point of emaciation, his skin pale and his mouth twitch[ing] nervously." "You can tell by looking at Andy that he's had a rough time," Mahurin observed. "They were working on him right up until the time he was repatriated."

Mahurin may have been more confident than his companion that his behavior would be excused. As a pilot in Europe in World War II he had shot down twenty German aircraft before being shot down himself. And then, after being transferred to the Pacific, he shot down two Japanese planes. He was a war hero. But both men had signed confessions under duress. And both remembered Alan Winnington and Wilfred Burchett, whom they accused of having crafted and revised the documents to which they signed their names. "I only met him last night," Mahurin told Beech, "and Burchett was very pleasant to me. Very pleasant. No military business at all." Beech never doubted that Burchett had connived in drafting the confessions. He later wrote that Burchett was "always a competent craftsman and a better-than-average writer" and "a friendly, ingratiating type with a fondness for good whiskey and good food." He added, however, that Burchett's professional accomplishments and easy affability made him more dangerous than his repellent colleague, Winnington. Burchett, to his mind, was a Communist propagandist doing valuable work for the other side.

There was a complicated sequel to the story in which Warner wrote scathing articles describing Burchett as a traitor and asking why he retained his status as an Australian citizen. Burchett's passport mysteriously disappeared when he attended the Bandung Conference of African and Asian nations in 1955, and the Australian government declined to replace it. Later, when the government changed hands, Burchett's citizenship was reinstated. In 1972 he sued for defamation an Australian senator who called him out in terms similar to those used by Warner, and Warner took an active part in the senator's defense. Warner appeared to have had access to documents that he couldn't have obtained through regular journalistic practice. And, curiously, Bud Mahurin made an appearance with a story that differed from the one he had told Beech. No longer describing him as "pleasant," "very pleasant," Mahurin now alleged that Burchett had threatened him while staring at him "like a snake staring at a mouse." Burchett's lawsuit failed. The judge agreed that he had been defamed, but the senator had made his allegations in the Australian Senate, where his remarks were privileged. Warner celebrated the outcome as a triumph. Burchett had relied on duff legal advice.

Beech was as opposed to Communism as anyone. Like Warner he cultivated spooks among other government sources, but he also maintained an attitude of amused detachment from the world—and the people—that he was employed to report on. Whether it was Earl Browder being toppled from a platform in Tampa, party apparatchiks signing up for civil defense in Akron, or Harry Bridges joshing with policemen on a picket line in Honolulu, Beech saw the individual as distinct from what they believed in. He certainly believed Burchett was a dyed-in-the-wool Communist. But that didn't stop him from sitting down and sharing a drink with him. Nor did it stop him from listening to what he said.

Beech later suggested that a foreign correspondent without CIA sources wasn't doing his job and went on to cite three stories he broke in Vietnam that depended on them. Obviously, he said, there were risks. But CIA agents weren't, in the end, any different from other government sources: all had interests to promote. "There are times," he said, "when a reporter has to make a value judgment, which is to ask himself, 'Is this s.o.b. telling me the truth?'"

A PRETTY CRUMMY WAR

The slow, remorseless strangulation of the French fortress at Dien Bien Phu in the spring of 1954 had obvious historic significance, and reporters came from all over to witness its agonizing end. The Washington-based columnist Joseph Alsop sensed early on that the eight-year-long struggle between the French occupation army and Ho Chi Minh's guerrillas was reaching a critical stage. He was in

Indochina in February when he learned of the plan, prepared with fanfare by Gen. Henri Navarre, to use the valley stronghold, more than one hundred fifty miles from Hanoi, to cut off Vietminh operations in Laos and, so he hoped, draw the Communists into a pitched battle, which he assumed he would win. Denis Warner also was on the scene at an early stage: he visited French troops on the ground a month or so before the battle began in earnest. He described the broad valley in which the French had built their airfield, bunkers, and artillery emplacements. The position would have been impregnable, he noted, if it weren't for the looming, jungle-shrouded hills that overlooked it. The Vietminh had achieved what the French had thought was impossible, bringing in their own artillery on the backs of porters and situating it on the heights. The French had surrendered the advantage voluntarily, Warner wrote, and "settled down like Christians to await the lions, while the Romans loaded their artillery pieces and prepared to join in the sport from above."

Beech, in anticipation of summer, had rented a beach house on Japan's Sadamisaki Peninsula when he heard that the French were in trouble. He had paid no attention to the conflict in this distant corner of Southeast Asia. It was, he wrote, by all accounts "a pretty crummy war." He had made no attempt to investigate the complicated history that encompassed the transition from the Japanese occupation of Indochina during World War II to the troubled reassertion of French interest in the region. No editor had asked him to go there. The story he missed was in many ways horrifying, as is any long-drawn-out war in which innumerable civilians are the ancillary victims. It also had moments of undoubted drama and gallantry as battles were fought and brave men lost their lives.

Looked at as a sideshow in great-power politics, however, it's possible to view postwar Indochina as a farce, one in which the actors—leads, lovers, character players, and supporting cast—emerge on stage singly, in pairs, and in groups and then disappear, separately and severally, as the plot becomes more convoluted and surprise encounters lead to unexpected twists. The first act opens with the defeated Japanese at center stage. Ho Chi Minh, fresh from Moscow, walks on to lead the resistance and is joined by agents from the OSS, predecessor of the CIA, pistols at the ready and keen to be involved. Then the great powers get together offstage and divide Indochina among themselves. Enter the Nationalist Chinese in the North and the British in the South, sent to sort things out. Some Japanese collude with Ho Chi Minh to resist the Nationalist Chinese, who are more interested in looting than liberating their sector. The OSS agents, assessing the mission as futile, quietly depart. The French, seizing their chance, build up their forces. At first they're willing to deal with Ho Chi Minh and the Vietminh but then lose patience: French warships bombard the port city of Haiphong, killing thousands of civilians, permanently alienating whatever part of the population is not already anti-French. Meanwhile, in the South, the British, whose commanding officer is arrogant and uninterested, connives with the Japanese and then the French before leaving the stage.

There's more intrigue in the wings as the Japanese and Nationalist Chinese take their leave, and the Americans, distracted by matters they regard as weightier, vacillate between distrust of the French, of whose colonial inclinations they disapprove, and fright at the triumph of the Communists in China. The colonial ambitions of the French and the anti-Communist convictions of the Americans come to constitute an uneasy common ground. Some historians have argued that at this point, in choosing anti-Communism over national liberation as its guiding principle, America's future course was irrevocably set. In any event, French Union forces (made up in large part of North African and indigenous Indochinese troops, plus French Foreign Legionnaires) carry on fighting their vicious guerrilla battles until the set-piece engagement at Dien Bien Phu.

Beech was in Saigon on April 23, 1954. Over the next few weeks—through May and early June—he traveled frequently between Saigon and Hanoi, taking the odd break in Hong Kong and Tokyo, gathering what data he could to inform his assessment of the situation. It was too late for him to land at Dien Bien Phu, although French paratroops were still being dropped there. Beech heard directly from Maj. Gen. René Cogny, the officer commanding French forces in the North, just how precarious was Navarre's position.

> "Do you like schematics?" he asked. I said I liked schematics. Cogny took a crayon, red at one end and blue the other, and chuckled: "Red is for Communists and blue is for the French. It is very convenient." He drew a small blue circle for Dien Bien Phu, a larger red circle around it. As he filled in the details the picture he drew became as oppressive as the monsoon heat.

The general explained that supply lines connecting China and the Vietminh at Dien Bien Phu were relatively short and secure. The French supply route was tenuous. "A great many people think that Dien Bien Phu was a tactical error," Beech wrote:

> The enemy commands all the high ground around Dien Bien Phu and his guns literally look down the throats of its defenders. But whether it was a mistake or not is now academic. Cogny pours in more men and more supplies as the drop zone gets smaller and smaller. Everything goes in, nothing and nobody comes out.

A day later Beech boarded an "elderly but durable C-47" whose crew was overseeing the dropping of supplies to the French troops.

> Our altitude was a healthy 10,000 feet—but not healthy enough. Communist anti-aircraft guns below have a range of 15,000 feet. We approached Dien Bien Phu in the soft gray twilight. . . . A lonely captain finished reading—for the third time—a letter from his wife in Paris. Communist anti-aircraft batteries announced

> our arrival. Red tracers cut a pretty pattern in the gathering dusk off our right wing. To our left we could see Flying Boxcars, more formally known as C-119s, disgorging their cargo of supplies. Cargo parachutes blossomed white in the sky. Dien Bien Phu lay directly below, sullen and deadly, a clump of bare earth in the middle of nowhere. A necklace of orange fire outlined the garrison's small perimeter of defense. Outside the perimeter the earth was pocked with bomb craters. . . . [W]e saw nothing move. But flickers of light and bursts of flame signaled that the battle was still on. It was completely dark now and crewmen fastened blackout curtains over the windows. This shut out sight of the tracers and I felt like a child who pulls a sheet over his head to shut out fear of the night. In the blackness a sergeant whistled softly and another member of the crew broke into song. Others curled up on the floor and went to sleep. Up front, a small dark colonel spoke into the radio mouthpiece to direct the jumping of paratroops several thousand feet below us. I pulled back the curtain to watch but saw nothing but leisurely descending flares. It takes a brave man to jump into the night into so small a space and not know whether he will land in friendly or enemy territory. The jump was completed. The colonel said it was a good one but only the men who jumped could be sure.

In Saigon a few days later, Beech stayed at the Majestic hotel and gossiped with the procession of high-ranking American officers whose business brought them to town. That business had mainly to do with the considerable American resources, financial and military, that were being funneled into the war effort. An unnamed general marveled at what he regarded as French inefficiency: "Did you know that they don't even have a logistics planning section?" he asked Beech incredulously. "When they want something, they just call up and want to know why it wasn't there yesterday." From the Majestic's dining room, guests could look out over the Saigon River where, one day, Beech watched "as half a dozen ambulances were drawn up with wounded to be evacuated to France. The following day I watched more wounded being unloaded from a river boat down from the north. These were Vietnamese soldiers. Peddlers, pushcart boys and dock workers crowded around and watched quietly with unreadable faces." French and Asian businessmen, guests at the hotel, observed the scene impassively while eating dinner. Beech was struck by what he described as an atmosphere of "feverish prosperity" in the city, as those who had a stake in the French colony's continued existence worried what would happen after Dien Bien Phu fell. A young French officer told him that Saigon was "like an overripe melon lying in the sun waiting for someone to come along and squash it."

By the beginning of May the end was in sight, and Beech was back at the press camp in Hanoi. On May 4, a grim-faced French press officer posted a notice saying that the Vietminh had mounted what was assumed to be the final assault. The French still had artillery, but artillery played no part at this stage of the battle: what remained would be fought at close quarters, with machine gun, grenade, and bayonet. A correspondent had a question for the briefing officer: "Captain, yesterday you said the situation was serious but not grave. What do you say today?" The officer replied, "I have no adjectives for today."

On the 5th, Beech reported poignantly that Brig. Gen. Christian de Castries, the officer commanding the defense at Dien Bien Phu, was still in telephone contact with Jacqueline, his wife, and she in turn was passing on word of his despair at the failure of high command to send in more reinforcements. No such help was being sent, Beech wrote, for a number of reasons: because the available troops were needed elsewhere, because getting men in and out of the fort was at best perilous, and, not least, because the cause was all but lost. Dien Bien Phu fell on May 7. That evening, de Castries ordered the destruction of radio transmitters, tanks, artillery, and the remaining stores of ammunition, lest they fall into Vietminh hands. The last recorded message came at 5:30 p.m. from the combat engineers. It was brief and to the point: "We're blowing up everything. Adieu."

The French war in Indochina was settled through negotiations in Geneva, which concluded in July 1954. According to the terms of the agreement, Vietnam would be divided provisionally at the 17th parallel. The Vietminh were, unsurprisingly, opposed to the division, which effectively conceded on paper what they had won in the field, but the Chinese prevailed on them to accept it. Ho Chi Minh's forces assumed control of what was called a "regroupment zone" in the North, and a Vietnamese regime put in place by the French (with more or less discreet American involvement) took power in the South. The agreement did not recognize either zone as a nation. Instead, it called for Vietnam to be unified (hence the provisional nature of the dividing line) following national elections that were to be held two years later, in July 1956. It was widely assumed that these elections would result in a Communist win. The point wasn't lost on Ngo Dinh Diem, the newly installed premier of South Vietnam, who made clear that he would not be bound by a document signed by a foreign military power, meaning the French, "in contempt of Vietnamese national interests."

The agreement was unsatisfactory from the point of view of the Vietnamese antagonists, North and South, but as far as most American onlookers were concerned, the issue was settled. Beech, summing up, compared it to Korea:

> The United States position when the Indochina cease fire was signed at Geneva was much the same as Rhee's when the Korean war ended. Rhee . . . would not sign the armistice, but agreed not to obstruct it. That is just about what the United States did at Geneva. Among Asian peoples American prestige probably was never lower. By the same token Red China's prestige was never higher. The Americans bet on a second-rate defeatist colonial power that had stayed too long. It furnished that power with

> billions of dollars worth of modern arms, airplanes and ships. The enemy had no air force and no navy. But still France lost the war.

CARPE DIEM

President Diem had his hands full. South Vietnam was overrun by a number of sects, each combining an armed militia professing some variant of religious dogma with more or less criminal activities. Vietnam's emperor, Bao Dai, a playboy who lived on the French Riviera, had negotiated a deal with the largest of the sects, the Binh Xuyen, that gave its leader, Le Van Vien, exclusive license to run gambling and prostitution in Saigon, plus, crucially, control of the police, in exchange for a cut of the proceeds. This arrangement meant that the city could boast of possessing Asia's biggest brothels and gambling dens, while the emperor enjoyed the life of a sybarite in Cannes. It suited the French to support the sects because the sects were active, and to some extent successful, in suppressing Communist guerrilla activity in the territory over which they competed for influence. Plus, the compromised situation of the emperor gave them leverage over the country's titular, albeit delinquent, leader. The French had no interest in supporting Diem, an incorruptible nationalist whose anti-French credentials were well-known.

So the French were not Diem's ally. Not all the Americans were well disposed toward him either, but some were, notably Edward G. Lansdale, a brilliant advertising executive turned OSS and then CIA agent, who was sent by CIA chief Allen Dulles to insinuate his way into Diem's good graces shortly after Diem took up residence in Norodom Palace in June 1954. Lansdale had previously worked closely with another Southeast Asian leader confronting a Communist insurgency. Ramon Magsaysay, with Lansdale's advice and the CIA's backing, had vanquished the Hukbalahap rebellion in the Philippines, and Lansdale, overlooking some crucial differences, saw no reason why he could not repeat this bravura performance in South Vietnam. Taking a more skeptical view was Eisenhower's special representative, Gen. Lawton Collins. Collins, influenced by the French military commander Gen. Paul Ély, was inclined from the start to view Diem's situation as untenable, a position that hardened over time. By December 1954 he was advocating for the return of Bao Dai (which would have suited the French) or, failing that, a complete American withdrawal from Vietnam. In effect, the American military, the CIA, and the administration were at odds throughout this period, setting a pattern of internal dissension that would continue for years to come.

A French-instigated coup failed, possibly because its leader, Vietnamese Gen. Nguyen Van Hinh, was never really serious. It was only meant to pressure Diem into resigning. Diem shrugged off the threat, and Hinh went into exile in France. More ominous pressure was exerted in spring 1955 when Diem moved to shut down Binh Xuyen gambling operations. The sects responded by forming a coalition and demanding that Diem join them in a union government. Elements in the coalition proved to be susceptible to Lansdale's diplomacy (diplomacy reinforced by CIA cash), and when threats gave way to violence they were no longer acting as one. Nonetheless, on the night of March 29–30, the Binh Xuyen militia shelled Norodom Palace, and in Cholon, the Chinese sector of Saigon, flat-out fighting broke out between the army and the gangsters. Within a few hours it was apparent that the army had the upper hand.

This wasn't headed in a direction that suited the French. Generals Ely and Collins agreed between them that a ceasefire was in order, and French tanks duly took up position at key intersections, thus stymieing Diem's imminent triumph. Troops on both sides remained in the streets but mostly held their fire in the days that followed. Meanwhile in Washington and Saigon, the Dulles brothers—John Foster as secretary of state and Allen as CIA chief—and Lawton Collins, who had the president's confidence, maneuvered to win

Eisenhower over to their almost diametrically opposed points of view. The issue was settled in Collins's favor—a decision to jettison Diem as premier—when a late intervention from Lansdale, by way of a cable to Allen Dulles on April 27, won Diem a reprieve. Diem, Lansdale wrote, was about to score a famous victory over the gangsters. Lansdale then set about making his forecast come true. The army, at Diem's command, renewed its attack on Binh Xuyen strongholds—they had seized the prefecture of police among other buildings—and overwhelmed them, driving them from the streets of Saigon into the far corners of Cholon and beyond. The destruction wrought by the two sides was extensive, as was the loss of life, but the end, after a week of fighting, marked a victory for Diem.

Beech had been in Saigon briefly the previous October when General Hinh appeared to be plotting a coup and Diem appeared to be flailing. Beech, almost certainly influenced by Gen. John W. O'Daniel, head of the American military mission, doubted Diem's ability to sort out the chaos. "The curse of French colonialism lingers on," Beech wrote. "While politicians and generals, cliques and crooks, scrabble for power and profit in Saigon, and Emperor Bao Dai suns himself on the Riviera, the countryside is being lost to the Reds."

With that he turned to other matters. In the new year he traveled to Jakarta, where preparations were being made for the conference that would lead to the establishment of the Southeast Asia Treaty Organization (SEATO). He spent almost all of March and the beginning of April in India, a country that was new to him, seeing the sights, assessing Premier Jawaharlal Nehru, and, memorably, chatting with Nehru's thirty-seven-year-old daughter, Indira Gandhi, at her father's residence in New Delhi, while tiger cubs frolicked untethered in the garden. At the Bandung Conference later that month he witnessed the coming together of some twenty-nine nations, there to formulate a regional response to the Cold War and the end of colonialism. These were momentous developments beside which Diem's troubles must have seemed petty.

Others were on hand to witness what he missed. A Time-Life journalist, John Mecklin, was friends with Lansdale and, through him, one of Lansdale's more flamboyant associates, Maj. Lucien "Three Finger" Conein, an ingenious French-born OSS-CIA agent, who had been in Vietnam back when America was giving support to Ho Chi Minh. At Lansdale's direction, Conein had been sent with a team to Hanoi, landing there on the day the defeated French withdrew their troops from the city and the Vietminh moved in. Conein's assigned task was to sabotage the enemy's takeover through propaganda and dirty tricks (one wheeze involved fouling fuel supplies, another flooding the country with fake ration cards) all dreamed up by former adman Lansdale. But first, on the day Ho's army marched into the capital, Conein fraudulently presented himself as a member of the International Control Commission (ICC), there to supervise the transition to Vietminh rule. With an Australian-style slouch hat on his head and a movie camera in his hand, he drove around Hanoi, stopping where he saw Communist battalions and instructing them to fall in and display their weapons. Amazingly, they complied. He then strolled calmly up and down their ranks filming them. Mecklin and Denis Warner (at Mecklin's invitation) had gone along for the ride—literally: after their singular tour of the city, Conein gave them his Citroen to drive back to Saigon.

Both Mecklin and Warner reported on the street battles that erupted at the end of March and again in April. Warner described Le Van Vien's Cholon headquarters and its sinister menagerie, which included a full-grown leopard that was chained outside his sleeping quarters, a tigress that would pose obligingly for photographs with visitors, and a python in a cage. A day or two later, on the afternoon of April 28, Mecklin, along with Howard Sochurek from *Life*, managed to get himself trapped inside a police station that was being assaulted by the Binh Xuyen. A company of Vietnamese army soldiers, according to Mecklin, was fending off a battalion of gangsters. Heavy machine-gun and rifle fire was being exchanged, and Mecklin, who had a notion that Lansdale might be in a position to intervene, reached him by telephone while taking cover beneath a desk. The enemy was closing in, Mecklin told Lansdale, and if he had any bright ideas on what he and Sochurek should do next, this would be the time to say so. Lansdale had nothing to suggest. Still, Mecklin and the photographer got safely away.

Beech landed in Saigon on May 3, in time to survey the damage. He followed an army patrol through the streets and saw a "scene that compared with Seoul after its first liberation by American forces," where "block after block of brick and concrete buildings were leveled or left with only walls standing." There were Binh Xuyen soldiers—"gangsters in uniform"—holding out in places, and civilians defying stay-at-home orders rummaging through the wreckage for whatever could be saved. His analysis, informed by interviews with officials high and low, was acute. He noted the policy split between the embassy and the military advisory group, correctly identified General Collins as Diem-skeptic, and described the French as secret supporters of the Binh Xuyen, perhaps to the point of supplying them with arms.

In a long piece written two days later, Beech reflected on the continuing tension between Diem's advocates and critics, the former seeing in the premier evidence of the kind of revolutionary nationalism that gave birth to American independence, the latter deploring the methods by which he pursued that goal. "They [his detractors] say Diem is stubborn, narrow-minded, incompetent, autocratic and won't take their advice." Without endorsing this view, Beech goes on to note that "another criticism of Diem was that in nine months in office he never did anything. But in the last eight days he has done so much that his detractors—French and American—are afraid he will do more." The premier whose leadership Beech had recently doubted was about to undergo a rebranding.

By the end of the month, when Beech was back in South Vietnam's capital, the transformation was complete. By routing the country's "weird assortment of racketeers, cutthroats, warlords, ex-river pirates and fanatics," Beech wrote, "Vietnam's stubborn, courageous little premier" had seized control of Saigon. "The key question now is whether Diem can extend that control into the countryside, which is what really counts. The odds against him are great and the time is short, but at least he has made a start."

Beech left Saigon soon after filing this analysis and didn't return for a year. When he was back, he found that the government had "not only managed to survive" but had "held its own against the Communist North and in some respects even seized the political initiative." He gave the "courageous little autocrat," Ngo Dinh Diem, full credit for this achievement, going on to write:

> Today South Vietnam can no longer be taken by subversion. The Vietminh, although active in the south, have been driven underground. Some of them, who were never Communists in the first place but independence fighters against the French, have surrendered. Most significant of all, the peasants who once sheltered and fed the Vietminh out of fear or sympathy, have begun to turn Vietminh agents over to the government.

The guerrillas, Beech concluded, had suffered a disastrous collapse of morale.

He wrote a few more articles before departing again. In one, he described his meeting with Diem's sister-in-law, Madame Ngo Dinh Nhu, a woman who invariably caused American observers to invoke the image of the Dragon Lady, a character drawn from a popular comic strip, *Terry and the Pirates*. Beech's portrait of a "beautiful doll of a woman with skin like old ivory and great liquid brown eyes . . . [who was] up to her shell-like ears in politics" was as much a caricature as any other, and as sexist and racially condescending as most. In another article he made clear that whatever virtues had contributed to Diem's success, a commitment to democracy was not among them. Diem had systematically eliminated political opposition, having handpicked the membership of the constituent assembly and disposed of anything resembling a free press. Beech forgave Diem for his autocratic disposition, however, on the grounds that the difficulties besetting him—a hostile regime in North Vietnam, vestiges of the gangster sects, and Vietminh guerrillas in the South—required harsh measures. This form of government was known locally as "Diemocracy," he reported, and likely to remain in place for some time.

In the news agenda of the day, the defeat of the French at Dien Bien Phu had commanded worldwide attention. The fallout from the Geneva conference that followed was significant in the context of the Cold War. The question for America was whether the Soviet Union was likely to expand its influence in the region following the French collapse. It was Russia, not China, that was seen as a threat, and, on the whole, it seemed to the administration unlikely that Vietnam would be a focus of the Kremlin's expansionism. In the period preceding the Geneva settlement, when a Vietminh victory seemed imminent, there had been talk of sending in American troops. Beech had floated the idea in a speculative column and rejected it. "The French don't want the U.S. in," he wrote. "The Vietnamese don't either. And the U.S. does not want to get in. These would seem to be three excellent reasons for not getting in." His logic was unassailable.

By late spring 1955, President Ngo Dinh Diem—with assistance from Lansdale and the CIA—had consolidated his position. The army, to the surprise of some, had proven loyal. The sects were scattered. And the French, although far from being reconciled to their reduced status, were being compelled to accept it. This was a product of their defeat, the complexities of politics in Paris, and the gradual assertion of American influence in Saigon. The American military mission would remain in place and take an increasing role in the training and orientation of the Vietnamese armed forces. Meanwhile, in the North, Ho Chi Minh was having his own problems. A botched attempt at land reform led to an uprising that was put down by the People's Army with an excess of bloodshed. Jockeying for position within the politburo was a continuing distraction as Ho looked to the elections promised by the Geneva Accords to end the division of Vietnam. Diem declined to honor the accords: the election he held in 1956 was fixed. Guerrilla activity in the South, however, was sporadic and as likely to be caused by criminals as by Communists. There would be scant evidence of an organized guerrilla war in South Vietnam in the next two or three years.

There is an unbroken thread linking American policy in Vietnam from the post–World War II period to the early 1960s, when Viet Cong activity became an immediate threat to the regime's survival. The decisions made in the early years would be hard to unmake later. Most of America was oblivious. After the street fights and excitement that characterized events in Saigon through March, April, and May 1955, the public lost whatever interest it had shown in the region. Beech, for his part, visited Saigon in May 1956, again in December 1957, and not at all in the three years that followed. The implication is unavoidable: whatever was happening in Vietnam after Diem was installed didn't matter much to America. This judgment was conveyed by Beech and other correspondents not only by their absence but also by the nature of their coverage when a few of them did visit. This was characterized, as often as not, by an attitude of cool condescension.

Ngo Dinh Diem, a dictator presiding over a deeply oppressive regime, was routinely described in press reports as portly and short, as if his appearance rather than his actions defined him. His sister-in-law, Madame Nhu, who served as his chatelaine and was a politician in her own right, was compared to a cartoon character.

His brother, Ngo Dinh Nhu, chief of police and the secret service, seems not to have been noticed by Beech in this period, but Joseph Alsop described him, as he would sometimes be described in the future, as an intellectual lightweight with an addiction to opium. He was a bad man, in other words, but not to be taken seriously. Later he would be described in different terms, either as the regime's intellectual or its evil genius.

The French, no less than the Vietnamese, suffered in the estimation of almost all American observers, and for roughly the same reason: they were losers. The French had been fighting the Vietminh for eight years and before that had ruled over Indochina for decades: one might have expected the Americans to draw on their knowledge and experience. They did not. Denis Warner reported that the Americans refused even to look at French intelligence records. Other observers confirmed the impression. "The French haven't won a war since Napoleon," said one American officer. "What can we learn from them?" Whatever lessons they might have shared would have to be learned again.

REVOLUTION IN SUMATRA

Beech and Linda celebrated the arrival of their second child together when Barnaby Carden Beech was born on June 30, 1955. Like the other boys, he was given a nickname: his was "Paki." Their lives took an unexpected turn a couple of years later when Linda, "on a lark," auditioned for a part in a television series. The industry was in its infancy, especially in Japan, although the number of television sets in people's homes was growing exponentially. Most programs were dubbed versions of American originals. A producer looking to change that came up with the idea for a series featuring an American couple living in Tokyo that was loosely modeled on the Hollywood hit *I Love Lucy*. Linda got the part, and *Blue Eyes' Tokyo Diary* became a sensation. Beech wrote about this unexpected development in an article for *The Saturday Evening Post*. He admitted to having some difficulty adjusting to his changed status. "'How does it feel to be the husband of a famous television star?' the fellows ask. The first guy who calls me 'Mr. Linda Beech' gets belted."

Professionally speaking, his stature was undiminished. His memoir of the war, *Tokyo and Points East*, published in 1954, was well received and widely read. *The New York Times* suggested that, despite his year at Harvard, he was "out of his depth when talking about American-Japanese relations." Nevertheless, he

> dramatizes neither himself nor the events and the people he deals with. . . . There are no mock heroics. The approach is that of the professional reporter whose duty is getting the story, getting it out, telling it with the directness of personal reaction. . . . It is the approach of a man who is intelligent but not intellectual, sensitive but not sentimental, irreverent but not brash, moral but not moralizing, skeptical without being cynical.

Newsweek devoted a half page to a laudatory profile in which they described him as "lean, hard and handsome enough," and his character as "at once sardonic and sensitive, bitter and amused, personally unpredictable and professionally stable." In short, *Newsweek* averred, Beech "looks and acts . . . the way correspondents are popularly supposed to look and act." In an era when foreign correspondents had cachet, this was a compliment.

He wrote a handful of articles for *The Saturday Evening Post* about the struggle for power in Indonesia, Syngman Rhee's Korea, and, later, the "neutralization" of Laos. Another, lighter article focused on the making in Japan of *The Barbarian and the Geisha*, a film directed by John Huston starring John Wayne. Wayne and Beech sat down one evening in the hotel bar while the actor knocked back martinis and complained of a cold and about Huston's unorthodox approach to filmmaking. Wayne had considered walking out—"I don't see anything here for the Duke"—but decided to stay and "trust to God and Huston." "You know, although I'm an independent producer," he said:

> "I don't mind working for a director. Usually, however, I enjoy his confidence. But when I go up to Mister Huston's room and say, 'What do we do today?' he just looks out the window and says, 'John, just look at that view. Isn't it magnificent?'" Producer Frenke, hovering nervously about his six-foot-four-inch, 230-pound, $666,666.67 investment, sought to soothe the discontented Duke. "Duke," he said, "this may be the greatest thing you've ever done. The greatest!" "Yeah," said the Duke glumly, "and it may be the worst. . . . Boy, another martini for this cold of mine."

Beech set out in search of a more serious story—and another war—in March 1958. In a roundabout way, he was looking to prove what he had proposed in May 1950. A rebel army in Sumatra, an island in the Indonesian archipelago, had declared its independence in the early spring. Their insurrection was not without geopolitical significance. President Sukarno, whose government was based on the neighboring island of Java, may or may not have been Communist, but his government was deeply indebted to Soviet Russia, and there was reason to think that Indonesia would drift into the Communist camp. It was seen to be in America's interest to support the rebels. As Beech observed, in a line that recalled his earlier lament, the United States for once had the "opportunity to back rather than buck a revolution in Asia." To this end, the CIA was air-dropping weapons to the rebels who, consequently, were amply supplied with M1s, mortars, and recoilless rifles and the ammunition to use them. The utility of this materiel, of course, depended on the rebels. They would have to fight.

It turned out that they weren't that keen. Many of the leaders on both sides were old friends and disinclined to inflict actual harm on one another. It was, as Beech observed later, "the strangest revolution I have ever attended. Both sides took pains to hold casualties to the minimum. When confrontation was unavoidable, each seemed more embarrassed than belligerent."

He wasn't the only correspondent attracted by the prospect of a fight. He was joined by Pepper Martin and a writer for the London *Observer*, Dennis Bloodworth, on an epically uncomfortable, seven-hundred-mile bus journey from the south coast city of Palembang through central Sumatra to the rebel headquarters in Padang. Along the way they passed another bus headed in the opposite direction bearing, among the civilian passengers, Denis Warner and, from *The New York Times*, Greg MacGregor. Warner and MacGregor had entered the country despite having been refused a visa and, having been found out, were heading to Palembang before—they hoped—Indonesian forces barred the road. "You're going the wrong way!" Warner told Beech and his companions. "The government forces are going to land at Padang any minute." Beech was unfazed. "Goody!" he replied. "Then we'll be there in time for the war." "Oh, hell," said the Australian. "I'd stay, too, if I had a visa, but I smuggled myself in without one. I'm headed for Palenbang [*sic*] to try to get out of the goddam country." He did get out, in large part because so many officials were casual in their handling of official papers.

Beech, who had a visa, made it to Padang and waited on developments. The Indonesian army landed and the rebels faded away, leaving a handful of correspondents to greet the new arrivals. They were interviewed by the government commander, a General Jani, who allowed them to carry on, but not without a parting word. "'By the way,' he said, 'when you get back to Bukittinggi, please give my regards to my old friend Colonel Simbolon.'" Simbolon was the rebel commander.

Meanwhile, back in Tokyo, Linda's star continued to rise. She was routinely stopped in the street by fans and autograph seekers. Once a student riot was paused when the rioters formed an admiring crowd around her. Beech confessed that the disruptions her new career were causing to family life were annoying. "This TV business is taking up more time than it's worth," he groused to Linda. "Besides, if I'm going to be a stage-door Johnny I want to get paid for it. For ten per cent I'll be your manager and see if we can't get you a raise." She agreed and they did.

These were in fact good years for the couple. They and their children were flourishing. He had gone looking for a war, but he didn't need one. When yet another war came—when the "pretty crummy war" whose end he had witnessed at Dien Bien Phu erupted again in a new form—he looked on it not like Korea, as an adventure, but rather as a chore. Its reality crept up on him, and on America, gradually.

CHAPTER 6

The American War in Vietnam

BATTLE LINES

When Vietnam first seriously engaged the Kennedy administration's attention, in 1961 and '62, when Communist guerrillas, soon to be known as Viet Cong, stepped up their activities, the Army of South Vietnam (ARVN), with a relatively small number of American advisers attached to it, was doing all the fighting. The Western reporters who were then based in Saigon—Malcolm Browne, David Halberstam, Neil Sheehan, Charles Mohr, Peter Arnett, and a handful of others—went out regularly on military operations. They had been inspired by their predecessors, men like Beech who had made their name in World War II and Korea. The younger cohort saw them as models to be emulated. They also believed in the cause: they had no doubt that Communism had to be defeated. Some of the stories they wrote about the engagements they witnessed reflected their exhilaration. Given the chance, they would have been happy just to be war correspondents too. But they were close enough and smart enough to see that mistakes were being made, big mistakes, that the war was being managed often stupidly and ineffectively. They suspected the war was being lost, and they couldn't help but look for the cause.

They found it in the presidential palace. It was clear that South Vietnam's President Ngo Dinh Diem interfered in operations. His commanding officers were appointed not for their martial prowess but for their loyalty to him. The Vietnamese people, meanwhile, were demoralized by his autocratic, repressive, and corrupt rule. The American mission gave the reporters scant comfort. The reporters judged both the general commanding the American advisory group, Paul D. Harkins, and the ambassador, Frederick Nolting, to be compromised at best and disingenuous at worst. And so they wrote about Diem and corruption and the American mission's evasions. They still covered the war, but they were pushed into writing about politics, whether they wanted to or not.

The younger cohort had Vietnam pretty much to themselves for a couple of years. Homer Bigart, now with *The New York Times*, dropped in for a few months early in 1962. He hated it: the heat, the squalor, the double-dealing. But his appraisal was acute. When Neil Sheehan, working for the United Press International wire service, took at face value the claim made by a South Vietnamese colonel to have presided over a victory in the Mekong Delta in which three hundred Communists were killed, the story appeared over Bigart's less sensational piece in the *Times*. In newspaper jargon, Sheehan had "shirt-tailed" him, and Bigart was not pleased. He called Sheehan up and told him they were going to the Delta, "and there better be three hundred bodies there." There weren't. There were twelve. Sheehan later described Bigart as his "journalism professor." He had an outsize influence on Halberstam as well.

Bigart somehow, presciently, grasped the complicated nature of the war immediately. Sheehan, Halberstam, Browne, and the others who made Saigon their base of operations soon got it too. It was more of a challenge for other outsiders. Beech, as the Asia correspondent for the Chicago Daily News Foreign Service, was in and out of Saigon rather like a fireman called to attend a series of fires. He was there to follow Lyndon Johnson when the vice president was sent to buck up Diem. He was back to cover the fact-finding Taylor-Rostow mission and the buildup of American support that followed. He turned up again when the ARVN appeared to suffer a crushing defeat at Ap Bac. He was a regular visitor throughout 1963, drawn by the Buddhist protests, Diem's subsequent crackdown, and the replacement of Nolting by Henry Cabot Lodge. Then he settled in for a few weeks as relations between Diem and the Americans approached the crisis that ended in the coup. Whenever he was in Saigon, he spent time with the resident reporters, went into the field with them, picked their brains. But he also spent time with the military mission: he was still a Marine at heart, and these were his peers. There is, in consequence, a strain of schizophrenia in his reporting. He respected the Saigon press corps. His own reporting from the field was often like theirs: he was as capable of appraising an operation as they were. At the same time, he could not simply ignore what the American mission told him. He was on their territory. He took seriously what they said. He didn't withhold any of what he knew, but his reporting was splintered. He was skeptical of Diem but deferred to Nolting and Harkins. He reported bad news and good, and it varied from day to day. It was to his credit that he understood the story's implicit duality, that it consisted both of the war with guerrillas and the contentious relations between (and within) governments. Not everyone did.

Other visiting correspondents were notably obtuse: Joseph Alsop regarded Diem as America's only hope if the Communist insurgency was to be defeated. Beech's Korean War buddy Marguerite Higgins concurred. Both Alsop and Higgins now were Washington-based correspondents with access to senior figures in the administration—Higgins having parlayed her Korean War fame into status as a senior political pundit. Alsop regularly welcomed cabinet members, and sometimes the president, to dinner at his Georgetown home. Higgins, now married to her air force general, was close to the Kennedy family. When either Alsop or Higgins visited Vietnam, they were treated not as journalists but as influential dignitaries: if they noticed the difference, they didn't object.

Still others failed to grasp the complexity of the story. Retired Gen. S. L. A. Marshall, for example, wrote articles and books as a military specialist. He railed against the correspondents who spent time in Saigon when, as he saw it, their "real" subject was the fighting. Scripps-Howard correspondent Jim Lucas, who, like Beech, had been a Marine correspondent, similarly stayed away from the cities and instead embedded himself with units in the Mekong Delta fighting the VC. Richard Tregaskis, yet another World War II veteran, famous for his reporting from Guadalcanal, proved incapable of taking the resident journalists seriously. Halberstam, who admired his books, was disappointed by what he saw in the man himself. There was, almost from the beginning, a chasm between the Saigon reporters and most outsiders. Some of it was generational. But mainly there was a difference in attitude dividing those who had been through a world war, and all that the experience implied—a certain hardness, an assumption of worldliness—and those who came to Vietnam with fresh eyes.

Beech, at least, got that politics would play as great a part as the body count in determining the outcome. In these early years, however, he was less exercised than his friends in the Saigon press corps about the evolving Vietnam story. He saw Vietnam, not inaccurately, as a tiny country of no great significance, its ruler as a tinpot dictator, its conflict a "brushfire" affair unlikely to have much impact in the wider world. This was not an eccentric view. In January 1961, Robert Kennedy, newly appointed attorney general by his brother, dismissed Vietnam in conversation with the reporter Stanley Karnow, saying "we've got twenty Vietnams to deal with." It wasn't by any means obvious, even two years later, that his appraisal was wrong.

VIETNAM'S CHURCHILL

Vice President Lyndon Baines Johnson was sent by Kennedy in May 1961 to tour Southeast Asia and report back on what was needed. The president clearly hoped that Vietnam, at least, wouldn't need much. He had flirted with the idea of sending the former CIA operative, now an air force general, Edward Lansdale, to work with Diem, hoping that Lansdale could manage the counterinsurgency campaign more or less under cover, as he had the uprising in the Philippines a few years before. Lansdale was game, but the Pentagon, wary of his unorthodox ways, vetoed the notion. So Johnson's tour was something of a holding action. He was authorized to offer a modest increase in financial support for South Vietnam's military and all the moral support he could bring to bear.

Beech treated the visit as something of a light diversion. He and most other reporters could not help but focus on the contrast between the flamboyant, glad-handing, six-foot-three Texan and the devoutly Catholic, self-contained, and rather stout Vietnamese president, five foot nothing. Johnson, according to Beech, overwhelmed his hosts, "drowned them in torrents of praise for their 'indomitable spirit' . . . lavished praise on the beauty of their women and the model behavior of their children," and, leaving "no cliché unsullied," at least twice described Diem, "the stubby, 60-year-old strongman of South Vietnam," as "the Winston Churchill of his time."

Johnson wrote a thoughtful memo on his return to the States. He argued that both Vietnam and neighboring Thailand needed American support. A decision was required: Diem, he wrote, "is remote from the people, is surrounded by persons less admirable and capable than he. The country can be saved—if we move quickly and wisely. We must decide to support Diem—or let Vietnam fall." Beech wasn't privy to the memo, but a piece he wrote in June echoed its suggestion that without American intervention the Communists would extend their influence throughout the region. Beech called for America to make a stand.

When guerrilla activity intensified over the summer, Diem appeared no more able to deal with it than he had in the spring. Kennedy, still reluctant to make a major commitment, sent two men in whom he had more confidence than either Johnson or the Joint Chiefs of Staff. Retired Gen. Maxwell Taylor was the author of a book critical of the Pentagon's reliance on its nuclear arsenal and advocated instead for an expansion of ground-force capacity. Walt Rostow, an Ivy League academic and an assistant adviser on international security, had written on economic growth in developing countries. Both, Kennedy hoped, would favor restraint.

Beech was again on hand: his three-week stay both preceded and extended beyond the Taylor-Rostow tour. The general was closemouthed about his recommendations, but Beech, conducting his own investigation and tapping sources that doubtless were tapped by Taylor too, came to similar conclusions. The North, Beech wrote, was winning the war by terror and subversion, and Diem unaided was not up to the task of stopping it. The ARVN, armed and trained to fight a conventional war (for which Beech unfairly blamed the French—this had been the American plan too), needed "to learn to live and fight like Communists"—in the lowlands, mountains, and jungles. They would have to do this without the intervention of American troops: a modest increase in the number of advisers was anticipated. The United States would, however, pay for another significant expansion of the Army of South Vietnam.

In December, more of the consequences of the Taylor-Rostow mission became apparent when an aircraft carrier docked a stone's throw from the Majestic hotel on Saigon's waterfront, its cargo of aircraft—thirty-odd helicopters and a half dozen observation planes—plain for all to see. It created a stir among the resident reporters, who were irked when their inquiries were met with blank denials. "I don't see nothing," a press officer told Stanley Karnow when the ship was pointed out to him. Robert Trumbull, writing in *The New York Times*, was inclined to be amused by the military's brazenness. Malcolm Browne fumed.

Kennedy, following up on Taylor's advice, was ramping up the flow of military assistance. Beech tracked the signs. In early February 1962, he noted that Saigon's hotels were filling up with US servicemen. They were sleeping four and five to a room in the Majestic hotel, and the overflow was occupying tents at the airport. At the same time, he found that a $60 million construction program had been launched to build airfields, ammunition dumps, and naval facilities around the country. And in April he reported that American pilots were backing up ARVN ground operations by strafing guerrillas. Beech wondered how they could tell from the air if they were killing peasants or enemy fighters. An air force officer responded curtly, "If they're dead, they're Viet Cong."

This answer, as Beech acknowledged, was grim, but he seems to have been reassured by it. The cavalry had arrived and was sure to turn the war around. If others were alarmed by developments—the influential columnist James Reston wrote a famous piece in *The New York Times* in February accusing the administration of involving America in an undeclared war—Beech was content to let Harkins get on with it. Beech was back in Tokyo in May. He would touch down in Thailand, Hong Kong, Korea, Burma, India, and Pakistan over the summer and fall. He seems to have assumed that the situation in Vietnam was under control. He missed, as a result, a number of changes that roiled the Saigon press corps. Tensions there were on the rise.

AP BAC

A photographer, Horst Faas, and a New Zealand–born reporter, Peter Arnett, turned up together in spring 1962 to bolster the AP office. Both would stay for the duration of the war. Browne handed them a twenty-page memo when they arrived that made clear the assignment would be tough. "Beware . . ." he told them, "of any information at all you get from certain officials who can be counted on to tell bald-faced 180-degree whoppers nearly every time." A list of the liars, some of whom "were in high positions," was available for reference in the AP office and presumably updated from time to time.

The Saigon-based press corps had been tangling with the Diems and the US mission with increasing rancor over the course of the year. They were skeptical of the regime's claims of victory in the field and, especially, of the figures it provided to back them up. They were skeptical, too, of a program the Diems had initiated in imitation of one devised by the British to combat Communist insurgents in Malaya. In the Strategic Hamlet Program, peasants were moved from their homes into fortified villages where, in theory, they were less vulnerable to intimidation, indoctrination, and plunder. Beech expressed some of the same doubts about the program as the resident reporters. Vietnam wasn't Malaya, he noted: there, the Communists were Chinese and more easily distinguished from the Malays, whereas the Vietnamese looked pretty much alike, whether they were Communists or not. Moreover, in Malaya it had been possible to isolate the Communists: they had no sanctuary in which to take refuge nor a contiguous land-based source of supply, whereas the Communists in South Vietnam could take refuge and find support through Laos and in the North. Having made these points, however, Beech still concluded that "the strategic hamlets hold great promise." It was another reflection of his ambivalence as he was whipsawed between the evidence of his own eyes, the testimony of local reporters, and the assurances given by members of the US mission. He was still disposed to take officials at their word.

The officials were more or less hamstrung. Although some in the White House doubted the wisdom of sticking with Diem, officials in Saigon were under orders to back him. John Mecklin, who had covered Vietnam for Time-Life in the period when Diem first assumed power, now was working for the other side, serving as chief public affairs officer for the mission in Saigon. His assessment of Diem makes clear that he wasn't a fan. Diem was honest and courageous, he allowed, but also a "humorless, egotistical, incredibly stubborn perfectionist" who "refused to act on any question, however trivial, without exhaustive meditation and ideal conditions. He was neurotically suspicious of everyone except his family, refused advice, refused to delegate power. He was a Messiah with a persecution complex." This view was shared by most of the Saigon press corps but not by Ambassador Nolting or General Harkins, both of whom took seriously their instructions but, more than that, seemed to have decided that Diem, a nationalist patriot with personal integrity dedicated to the anti-Communist cause, was their only viable choice. Their unspoken mantra, in Bigart's pithy summation, was "sink or swim with Ngo Dinh Diem." Even to contemplate a change of leaders around the US mission, Mecklin reported, was blasphemy. Which meant in practice that the mission was committed to backing the regime's line, and lies.

By significantly expanding the use of helicopters to transport ARVN troops into battle and by providing more in the way of air and logistical support, the Americans combined with the South Vietnamese to throw the guerrillas off balance through much of 1962. By year's end, however, there were indications that the Communists were adapting to the changed tactics. They didn't always scatter or go to ground when helicopters hove into view. They staked out likely landing zones and prepared to defend them. A deadly demonstration of the change occurred in the new year.

Neil Sheehan would make much of Ap Bac in his Pulitzer Prize–winning *A Bright Shining Lie: John Paul Vann and America in Vietnam.* He suggests that the battle revealed almost everything that was wrong with the military campaign: the chronic intelligence failures; the endemic political interference; and the cultural, linguistic, and historical barriers dividing the Vietnamese and their American advisers. Above all, it threw into relief the extent to which American officials struggled to rationalize their association with a losing cause.

The action was initiated on January 1, 1963, by South Vietnamese commanders with input from the Americans. They had information that a company of Viet Cong—about 120 strong, or so they thought—had set up a radio transmitter in a village in the Mekong Delta some thirty miles southwest of Saigon. The allied command devised a plan to annihilate them, bringing to bear all the resources and training that the United States had hoped would transform the ARVN into an effective fighting machine. Two battalions of Rangers from the elite 7th Division, two battalions from the Civil Guard, a company of infantry in amphibious armored personnel carriers (APCs), plus two infantry companies held in reserve, amounting altogether to more than a thousand men, closed in on the village, supported by artillery, troop-carrying H-21 helicopters, and Huey gunships. As conceived, the plan could hardly fail. But it did. It failed because the Viet Cong knew the attack was coming, because there were more of them than expected (though the ARVN still outnumbered them roughly four to one), and because, instead of running, they stood and fought. They were intimidated neither by the artillery, the helicopters, nor the advancing infantry. They understood what was coming and pushed back.

At least as significant in explaining the failure were the mistakes, misapprehensions, and apparent self-sabotage on the government side. Helicopters landed too close to the enemy and were shot up. An advance by infantry was not reinforced when it came under fire. The captain commanding the APCs refused an order to advance and then, when finally prevailed upon to move into position, declined to give the order for troops to disembark and fight. Much later, when the corps commander, Gen. Huynh Van Cao, known to be close to Diem, arrived on the scene, he issued the order that effectively opened an avenue through which the Viet Cong could escape. Cao's chief function as he understood it, and that of the elite 7th Division that fell within his command, was to be on hand in the event that Diem had to fend off a coup. Harkins would describe the result as unfortunate—"mistakes were made"—but Cao's American adviser was convinced he opened the escape route on purpose. Either way, the Viet Cong disappeared.

The ARVN lost eighty men killed in action, the Viet Cong fewer than twenty. Three American officers died. Fourteen helicopters were damaged, five destroyed. It was a devastating defeat in the circumstances, and the Saigon correspondents reported it as such. American officials, under pressure from the White House, demurred.

Beech was in Tokyo when Ap Bac was fought. He didn't land in Saigon until more than a week had passed, and by then new battle lines—this time between the US mission and the Saigon correspondents—had been established. The piece he wrote after consulting friends on both sides reflected his indecision. He acknowledged that it had been "one of the stiffest fights of the war" and "a bad show in which everything went wrong." And he noted that American advisers had been frustrated by the refusal of their Vietnamese counterparts to order their men forward at critical points. At least one adviser, Beech said, had accused the officers of a "lack of aggressiveness." Neither Beech nor the other correspondents wrote that the troops were cowardly, but this was the word Harkins used in his report to the Joint Chiefs of Staff. In effect, Harkins made the argument about the reporters having accused the Vietnamese of cowardice, which was not the case, diverting attention from the actual reasons for the disaster. Beech let him get away with it. He quoted a "top-ranking American commander" who argued that "it's unfair to assess the Vietnamese of cowardice," and pointed to other battles in which "the same Vietnamese officer . . . who refused to advance because his casualties were heavy later recklessly exposed himself to enemy fire."

Beech stayed in South Vietnam for a few more weeks. Throughout that time the US mission, treating him as a friend, fed him material meant to counteract the more downbeat reports of the resident reporters. He was aware that he was being used. Of a document seized from the guerrillas that acknowledged Viet Cong setbacks, he wrote, "It's entirely possible that American officials chose to leak this report to counteract adverse publicity" after the defeat at Ap Bac, but he added, "this doesn't detract from its validity." He went on to cite statistics of the kind that Kennedy's defense secretary, Robert McNamara, was insisting were an accurate measure of progress. These included the "exchange rate," the numbers of enemy combatants killed compared to ARVN losses, which Beech reported were running five to one in favor of the Saigon government. He added that the Strategic Hamlet Program, "with all its admitted imperfections," was beginning to pay dividends. In short, he retailed the government's line.

The resident reporters knew better. Their reporting was based on mid- and low-level military sources rather than the staff officers Beech was talking to. Their captains, lieutenants, and non-coms were frank about what they saw. Both Browne and Halberstam had relationships with well-connected Vietnamese women who gave them insight into Vietnamese politics. Their reporting was accordingly more nuanced and authoritative than his. They knew that leaked documents were cherry-picked because they had seen contradictory evidence. They knew that statistics were misleading because they had checked the facts. And they had come to understand that the Strategic Hamlet Program, whatever its merits in theory (which, in Vietnam, were doubtful), was a disaster when put into practice. Diem's brother, Ngo Dinh Nhu, had made the project his own. With extraordinary temerity, and without anything like the resources to do the job properly, he created by fiat some four thousand fortified hamlets. Villagers were forcibly torn from their homes, rarely given the tools to start over, and the protection supposedly offered by the civil defense forces and ARVN was inadequate where it existed at all. The resident reporters knew this. But they were constrained in what they could tell the world.

For the wire-service reporters like Browne and Sheehan there were two impediments. First were the requirements of the job itself. The job of the agency reporter was to obtain "hard news," that is to say, factual information about developments in the city or country to which they were assigned. In gathering the facts, they were expected to draw on unimpeachable sources, meaning, in practice, highly placed government officials and the functionaries who spoke for them. Whatever else the reporters did, whoever they consulted, the official version had to be accounted for and, more often than not, given pride of place. For the reporters at AP, UPI, and Reuters, time spent on color or think pieces was time subtracted from their central task. This didn't stop them from writing them, but it was limiting. Yet another factor may have mattered more: government sources this early in the war had greater credibility than the Saigon-based correspondents. When the Pentagon pushed back, as it did on the reported disaster of Ap Bac, editors in the home office got skittish. They may have trusted their reporters, but they felt the pressure from the White House, their subscribers, and their readers too. In effect, what Keyes Beech, along with the likes of Alsop and Higgins, wrote had a greater impact than what Browne and company could slip into the inside pages. Plus the war was still so very far away: Vietnam was rarely front-page news.

CARAVELLE CAMARADERIE

Beech was out of the country in spring '63 and so missed some of the events that would lead eventually to the coup that ended Diem's rule. The reporting of these events aroused such controversy that the press itself became controversial. By the end of August the reporters based in Saigon were scrapping with the Diem regime and its secret police, the American Embassy and advisory group, their own publishers and editors, and, eventually, a handful of senior correspondents who concluded, based mostly on misinformation and their own preconceptions, that the Saigon cohort was not up to the task. Almost but not quite forgotten was the war itself.

Was the war being won or lost? Ap Bac set off an acrimonious debate that went unresolved until after Diem fell. Harkins never deviated from the line that the government was on the path to victory. He stopped Col. John Paul Vann, adviser to the ARVN 7th Division, from briefing visiting officials because he knew that Vann held a contrary view. When Vann's superior officer, Col. Daniel Boone Porter, submitted his end-of-tour report that spring, Harkins ordered all copies destroyed. Small wonder. Porter described a campaign that was undermined by a fragmented command structure and communication breakdowns. He said that because of endemic security failures, it was impossible to mount operations that took the enemy by surprise. Invariably, he complained, "someone . . . would inadvertently create some type of disturbance or make some sort of noise that would alert the Viet Cong before they fell into the trap." In general, he said, the government remained committed to a static defense consisting of forts (and latterly the strategic hamlets) that were too easily overrun by the enemy and provided the guerrillas with a ready source of American weapons. Porter, in short, did not endorse Harkins's optimism. But in Washington, Harkins's view prevailed.

The Saigon-based correspondents knew Harkins was wrong but were hard-pressed to gather the data that would substantiate their case. Political developments in the city would keep them tied up for most of the summer. But the AP photographer Horst Faas, who was close to Halberstam (they shared a villa) got tired of photographing demonstrations and spent time instead with ARVN forces. He came to know what Vann and Porter knew: that the Viet Cong were forming in larger units, their battalions sometimes bigger than the ARVN's, and that they were becoming more confident and aggressive. "Everything was wrong," he said later:

> The Americans always looked on the bright side of things and presented a picture that just wasn't correct. I would go out to

> [unclear] province or Camau province near the Cambodian border and wherever I went, there were Viet Cong battalions roaming the countryside and picking off outposts night after night. And putting up ambushes against Vietnamese troops. It was a pretty desperate situation.

Tipped off by Faas, Halberstam and Sheehan agreed to work together to do what neither could do alone in reporting on the fighting. Only Halberstam managed to get his story into print. It appeared in the August 15 issue of *The New York Times* and picked up on all the ideas that Harkins had sought to refute. The White House response was instant and, as official utterances go, furious. On August 17, Secretary of State Dean Rusk gave a press conference in which he "made a point of emphasizing the improvement of the military situation in Vietnam." He went further, claiming that more and more territory was coming under government control and that the Strategic Hamlet Program was an unmitigated success. Everything was rosy. Early in the Korean War Beech had reported that ill-trained American troops were running from the enemy, and the administration had virtually acknowledged that he was right. Halberstam got no such respect.

The Diem regime was a family affair. Another of his brothers, Ngo Dinh Thuc, was the archbishop of the northern city of Hue, and it was there that Thuc provoked a riot. To celebrate his ordination as bishop twenty-five years earlier, he had the city decorated with crosses, flags, and posters, some featuring his own image. The ceremonies, including a parade through the streets, came to an end on Sunday, May 5, three days ahead of the annual observance of Buddha's birthday. Whether from malice, ignorance, or indifference, an order was issued in the interim that required authorities to enforce an ordinance, overlooked throughout the Catholic celebrations, forbidding the public display of religious symbols. When their turn came to march, the Buddhists ignored the edict.

Out of Vietnam's population of some fourteen million, roughly four million were observant Buddhists, but three-quarters acknowledged a nominal connection. Only about two million were Catholic. On May 8, a Buddhist monk, Thich Tri Quang, addressed the crowd outside the pagoda in Hue, denouncing in incendiary terms the government's oppression. When the crowd grew restless, the authorities moved to disperse it. It was unclear precisely how the violence escalated, how rifles were fired and—according to some reports—grenades thrown, but eight members of the crowd were killed in the fracas. And while the government would claim that Buddhists if not the Viet Cong had provoked the violence, there was no doubt that the authorities were responsible.

It's possible that, by showing some humility, Diem could have quelled the unrest that followed. Instead he vacillated. Urged on one side by the Nhus to crush the Buddhists, pressed on the other side by the Americans to show restraint, he first made conciliatory gestures and then negated them. There were Buddhist demonstrations, not just in Hue but also in Saigon and across the country. And then, on June 11, an incident occurred that caught the attention of a world that was still unused to such awful images. An elderly monk stepped out of a car at a busy Saigon intersection, sat down cross-legged on a cushion on the pavement, and allowed a mixture of gasoline and diesel fuel to be poured over him. He struck the match with his own hand. Malcolm Browne, having been tipped off that something of the sort would happen, had with him a camera and the presence of mind to use it. The grisly image caught the world's attention. President Kennedy was appalled.

Beech flew to Saigon from Indonesia to catch up on developments. "If ever there was a man who seemed bent on digging his own political grave, it's Ngo Dinh Diem," he wrote on June 14. He proceeded to summarize the case against the Vietnamese president, noting especially his continuing failure to prosecute the war effectively and his reckless provocation of religious violence. He governed a police state, Beech wrote, as a mandarin "reared in a tradition that equates government with a lower case god. He is also one of the stubbornest men alive." It was "this inflexibility that brought him to power," Beech said, and it was that same trait that "may ultimately destroy him."

Beech stuck around Saigon to the end of June. His dispatches reflected the general atmosphere of crisis as government troops and police put down near-constant Buddhist demonstrations. The Nhus continued to advocate a strong response, Madame Nhu describing the street-corner immolation as a "barbecue" and telling a correspondent that, "if she had her way the Buddhists 'should be beaten ten times more.'" Nhu's police complied. In one protest, a fifteen-year-old boy was killed and hundreds of others injured. In a final dispatch before he left Saigon again, Beech described the "normally pleasant capital" as an "armed camp—all because of Diem's stubborn refusal to make even nominal concessions to the Buddhists."

Ambassador Nolting had gone on holiday near the end of May, leaving instructions with staff to call him if anything happened. No one called. This may have been a more or less deliberate indication that his time in Saigon was coming to an end. In his last meeting with Diem before he went on holiday, Nolting laid out the steps the United States expected Diem to take to resolve the Buddhist crisis. These included taking responsibility for the Hue incident, providing compensation for the victims, and reaffirming the principle of religious equality. Diem was noncommittal. There was no letup in Buddhist agitation in the weeks that followed. Diem dug deeper. Kennedy's position was hardening too.

Nolting's replacement, Henry Cabot Lodge Jr., landed in Saigon on August 22. Beech was among a handful of reporters on the plane with him. He was a last-minute addition to a flight that was itself on a stepped-up schedule. Lodge had planned to spend a few days in Tokyo, but a telegram from the White House alerted him to yet another critical development in the ongoing confrontation between Diem and the Buddhists. On the night of August 20, Diem and Nhu oversaw the declaration of martial law and the launching of a wide-ranging attack on Buddhist pagodas: some fourteen hundred Buddhists were arrested, more than thirty injured, and the pagodas themselves were sealed. Early reports, some soon amplified by the Voice of America, said the army was responsible. Halberstam and Sheehan, who witnessed the operation, knew that the president and his brother had unleashed the police and Special Forces, the latter trained by US advisers for counterinsurgency but employed by Nhu as a praetorian guard. By promoting the fiction that the army had instigated the raids, Diem meant to deflect attention and stifle talk of a coup. The timing, between Nolting's departure and Lodge's arrival, was calculated to present the Americans with an accomplished fact. The situation when Beech and Lodge landed was as confused as Diem could have wanted it to be. But the advantage it might have given him was not to last.

Beech, writing soon after he stepped off the plane, suggested that Diem, whatever forces he had employed, had "won his battle with the Buddhists." Beech was echoing a sentiment that Harkins had expressed to Maxwell Taylor when he said that "the ruthless repression was inevitable if [his] government was to survive." He noted that since June 11, three more monks and a nun had committed suicide by self-immolation. What had begun in May as a religious dispute had spiraled into "a mass disobedience campaign aimed at nothing less than bringing [Diem] down." The United States was snookered, Beech reckoned. It was Diem or defeat by the Communists, a calculus that only the army could change. Beech was saying that it would take a coup to change the government and he didn't see that happening. There were generals who were unhappy with Diem, but none who struck most American observers as a viable leader. This was certainly the way Harkins assessed the situation, and Beech agreed.

In Washington, however, Kennedy's advisers were divided. A faction in the State Department led by an assistant secretary of state, Roger Hilsman, took the view that Diem, by alienating the Buddhists and with them the better part of Vietnam's population, had lost all legitimacy. At a minimum, they argued, Diem had to rid himself of the Nhus, whom they blamed for Diem's recalcitrance. Others, including McNamara and Rusk, cautioned against action that would likely lead to chaos. The Hilsman faction broke the deadlock when they drafted a memorandum that instructed Lodge to let conspiracy-minded generals know they had US support. "Diem," they wrote, "must be given the chance to rid himself of Nhu and his coterie," but if, as they expected, "Diem remains obdurate and refuses, then we must face the possibility that Diem himself cannot be preserved." In other words, the United States would do nothing to stop a coup.

The memorandum was signed off by the principals—including Kennedy, Rusk, and McNamara—on a weekend when none of them was in Washington and in a position to hash it out in person. Later commentators, especially keepers of the Kennedy legacy, have suggested that it was pushed through when the president wasn't giving the issue his full attention. In this interpretation the State Department had pulled off an end run to get their way. The ambassador would be left to implement the policy and, if it came to that, shoulder the blame.

Kennedy's appointment of Lodge was politically adroit. Lodge was a Republican Party grandee. He had been Nixon's running mate in the presidential election that Nixon lost and Kennedy won, and he had his own presidential ambitions. His appointment made Vietnam policy nonpartisan. But it also meant the administration was no longer working with a diplomat who could be counted on to faithfully follow instructions and instead allied itself with a strong-willed politician who could, within limits, hew to his own vision. Lodge, as it happened, had no patience for Diem and his regime. The gist of the memorandum jibed with his own view.

There's some evidence that Kennedy vacillated in endorsing the coup. He had been a friend of Diem. But he could have stepped in to countermand the memo had he wanted to. Instead he sought to put pressure on Diem himself.

On September 2 Kennedy was interviewed by Walter Cronkite on the *CBS Evening News*. Asked about the one "hot war" in which the United States was currently engaged, the president began by emphasizing that only the Vietnamese could vanquish the Communists in their country and that the role of America was simply to offer support and advice. He then segued to the Buddhist crisis, saying that Diem's repression was "very unwise," and he hoped the regime would "take steps to try to bring back popular support" for the war effort. Asked if he thought this was possible, Kennedy said, "I do. With changes in policy and perhaps in personnel. . . . If it does not make those changes, I would think that the chances of winning would not be very good."

Beech had no knowledge of the argument playing out in the White House. He may have been relying on Lodge as his best source, and Lodge was giving nothing away. The ambassador was keeping in touch with the disaffected generals through Lansdale's old colleague, CIA operative, and a sometime source for Mecklin and Warner, Lou Conein. The South Vietnamese generals would go hot and cold in their plotting. They were getting mixed signals: Harkins, pushing back against Lodge and the State Department, was doubtful about the coup's prospects. Weeks would pass before the generals were ready to make their move.

The behind-the-scenes maneuvers had their analogue in the streets. Diem "is at war with his own people," Beech reported on August 26. He had just witnessed a demonstration by students that was brought to a violent end by Nhu's Special Forces. Hundreds of students, some apparently as young as twelve, were roughed up and hauled away in trucks, which, as Beech noted, "bore the familiar clasped hands symbol of the American aid mission." The regime was at war with resident reporters too. Beech knew newsmen who were threatened and harassed by secret police. Two were detained, interrogated for hours, and had their film confiscated. Two others, Beech wrote, "no longer sleep in their homes for fear of midnight arrest." The two correspondents seeking a bolt-hole, Halberstam and Sheehan, had taken refuge in Mecklin's villa, a move not without irony, as they had abused him unmercifully for his role as spokesperson for the mission. His two guests doubtless had reason to be worried, however, what with their contentious relations with Harkins and the bruising tactics adopted by the secret police. As if this weren't enough, rumors were rife that a regime-inspired death list was being circulated. Beech quoted an unnamed American's facetious lament: "It's getting so you don't amount to anything around here unless you're on somebody's assassination list." Mecklin's name reportedly was on one. He shrugged it off. So was that of Denis Warner, who took the threat seriously: he promptly left the country.

Many correspondents, despite their status as noncombatants, were in the habit of carrying a sidearm when they accompanied troops on operations. Beech complained of *Time* magazine reporter Charlie Mohr's getup when they went out together. "You always look like the fucking company commander," he told him. The implication was that Mohr was dangerous to be seen with: to an enemy sniper, officers were an obvious target. "You always have your helmet on, your pack on, your forty-five caliber on. It must be the goddamn Prussian in you." Beech's complaint wasn't entirely fair: there were reasons for correspondents to be armed in the field. As Browne had warned Arnett on his arrival, the Viet Cong made no distinction between soldier and civilian in a shoot-out, and they rarely took prisoners—to the guerrillas they were an encumbrance. Reporters weren't supposed to have guns—it was technically forbidden—but most American officers privately approved. Arnett acquired a

Mauser machine pistol. Sheehan bought a fancy nickel-plated .38. Browne possessed a Schmeisser submachine gun.

The expectation was that their weapons would be used, if at all, against the Viet Cong. But as the summer wore on, as William Prochnau reported in *Once Upon a Distant War*, the Saigon press corps was increasingly beleaguered. They were harassed and sometimes assaulted when they showed up at demonstrations. They were denounced often in threatening terms in the Diems' English-language propaganda sheet, *The Times of Vietnam*. Their relations with MACV (Military Assistance Command, Vietnam) and the embassy were more or less hostile. Lodge expertly flattered and confided in them—individually, so he would know if one leaked—while clamping down on messaging not under his direct control. Harkins was invariably defensive: his reflexive response to the importunities of the press was to curtail access. This infuriated the correspondents. Halberstam once notoriously (and perhaps often, there being more than one version of the story) paused in midsentence while driving past Harkins's residence to announce that he hated the sonofabitch. In July, plainclothes policemen assaulted Arnett, bloodying his face, and would have done worse had not Halberstam—a big man, not shy—intervened, while Browne (putting the interests of the wire service first) found a vantage point from which to snap the confrontation. A day or so later, Browne and Arnett were arrested for assaulting the police who had assaulted them and interrogated for hours. Browne, around the same time, was threatened by secret policemen seeking to interrogate the Vietnamese woman who was soon to be his wife. He scared them off by brandishing his Schmeisser.

The air was thick with rumors. MACV and the embassy were at odds in Saigon, as were the State Department and the Pentagon in Washington. Just about everyone was feeling heat from one direction or another: Diem, the Nhus, the Buddhists and their leaders, the army, and even students—hundreds of whom had been arrested. Not to mention the peasants forced into fortified hamlets, assailed by Communists, abused by Vietnamese troops. And the Saigon press corps taking hits from every direction, some literally taking cover. Into this maelstrom of menace and misunderstanding, fearless as ever and blithely sure of herself, strode Marguerite Higgins.

She wielded less influence than Joseph Alsop, whose Matter of Fact column in the *New York Herald Tribune* was, for a time, the most widely syndicated column in America, but she shared his conservative perspective. If anything, she was more strident: Beech described her to the Saigon correspondents as "a fire-eating quote Commie-hater close quote." He still had a soft spot for her. On an earlier trip to Saigon he wrote to her: "Why don't you come on out and lose some weight? You'll never get anywhere pushing those carts around in the supermarket." She had done her share of globe-trotting, had interviewed presidents and prime ministers, and laid claim to a certain authority when it came to world affairs. She knew Vietnam and had been following press reports with rising choler. In July she decided it was time to straighten the young cohort out.

The Saigon correspondents had struggled for months to get what they regarded as the true story of the war into print. They reacted badly when, after Higgins had spent just four weeks in the country, the *New York Herald Tribune* gave extraordinary prominence to the product of her brief labor. Her series of six long articles, printed over a period of a week, opened each day on the front page under banner headlines. The title of the first, "Viet Nam—Fact and Fiction," made clear the nature of her mission: Higgins would sort out obvious truth and amateur obfuscation.

She had access wherever she wanted it. In the course of a five-hour interview, President Diem assured her that his was a most tolerant administration, that it included many Buddhists in significant positions, and that no other administration facing a lethal external threat would have been as broad-minded as his had been. He had acceded to almost all the Buddhists' demands, and yet they were not satisfied. He was "bitterly convinced" that they "were going for his political jugular" and that the conciliatory policies advocated by the United States were only "making them thirsty for his political blood." Counselor Nhu backed up his brother. "The Americans want us to sit by quietly and let a handful of Buddhist leaders tell lies about us to the world and foment disorders," he told Higgins. "There must be a point where this must stop."

While the Buddhists made trouble, Higgins told her readers, Diem continued to prosecute the war. She quoted General Harkins's assessment: "The Viet Cong are losing because we are steadily decreasing their areas of maneuver and the terrain over which they can move at will." He was sure that "a military breakthrough has begun this summer," and that this early success would be reinforced as new recruits joined the ARVN. As for the strategic hamlets, Higgins reported that no fewer than eight million Vietnamese now were living in 8,500 hamlets—at least twice the number previously advertised—where "more than half the nation has a measure of security from Viet Cong pressure that has never before been available." No mention was made of light or a tunnel, but the implication was clear.

Everything depended on continuing support for Diem and his family. Higgins had only admiration for Madame Nhu. Admittedly, she was "a woman of bad judgement in the sense of insensitivity to the rest of the world," but she was passionate and brave. The American project aimed at having Diem distance himself from Nhu and silence his wife was doomed to fail. "President Diem gave this reporter the impression of trusting and needing his brother," wrote Higgins, "indeed of being extremely proud of him for the strategic hamlet program in which Counselor Nhu has been a driving force."

William Prochnau drew on the reporters' own recollections in describing their furious response to Higgins's intervention. Halberstam, in effect, took over the role of Bigart in their old feud.

Higgins, certainly, was game to carry on with Halberstam where she and Bigart left off. In conversation with her hawkish allies, she pushed the idea that Saigon's "typewriter strategists" rarely went into the field, even hinting that they (and Halberstam in particular) were cowards. The reporters had been beleaguered before. Now their rear was insecure.

And then another big gun—*Time* magazine—was turned against them. The managing editor, Otto Fuerbringer, put a piece in the Press section that took to task the entire Saigon press corps—including the magazine's own reporters. "For all the light" they shed on the war, Fuerbringer wrote, their dispatches "might just as well have been printed in Vietnamese." The problem, he suggested, was their youth, inexperience, and tendency to pool their opinions in the comfort of the eighth-floor bar of Saigon's Caravelle Hotel. "Caravelle Camaraderie" had nurtured a self-reinforcing consensus that Diem was "stubborn and stupid," the Buddhists' complaints were justified, and that the war against the Communists was being lost. When an outsider—unnamed by Fuerbringer but clearly Higgins—had dared to venture a contrasting opinion, "club members were furious. . . . It was the analysis of an outsider and therefore patently wrong." It was an extraordinary piece of work: a major magazine's public dressing down of its own writers. Charles Mohr and his colleague on the Saigon staff, Merton Perry, were already frustrated by changes routinely made to their copy in *Time*'s New York office. Both now resigned. Perry went to *Newsweek*; Mohr to *The New York Times*.

Beech defended them. He called the suggestion put about by Higgins, Fuerbringer, and others that the resident reporters avoided the battlefield "a goddamned lie," adding "and so is the rest of that crap." A seven-hundred-word article he filed with the *Chicago Daily News* was more temperate but no less emphatic. "In 16 years as a correspondent," he wrote, "I have never met more energetic, hard-working, conscientious reporters. They are often accused of being young, which they are. If there is a flaw in their reporting it may be because they are idealists in a most unidealistic setting. If at times personal emotion has crept into their dispatches it's because this is a highly emotional story, in which American principles are deeply involved." They were accused by some of being anti-Diem, Beech wrote:

> But if the press corps is "anti-Diem," so is virtually the entire American community from Ambassador Henry Cabot Lodge down to the lowliest GI. Diem's is the government we must win the war with. But it's not a lovable government and there is nothing in the contract that says we have to love it. It is oppressive, dictatorial and devious.

As for the complaint that reporters had played down government claims of victory, Beech went on:

> Newsmen have justifiably learned to be suspicious of government claims. On more than one occasion Vietnamese commanders have been caught in outright lies. American advisers in the field are reluctant to contradict their Vietnamese counterparts or superiors. Do Saigon correspondents concoct stories in the eighth-floor bar of the Caravelle Hotel? My answer is "No." . . . One thing I do know. A Time magazine story attacking the U.S. press corps in Viet Nam was concocted entirely in New York.

Beech's Vietnam coverage in 1963 was mixed. When it came to the main story, the resident reporters had better sources than he did, and it showed. But he stood by his colleagues.

By the end of September Beech was convinced that pressure on Diem had failed in achieving its intended result. The regime understood that the Americans could not afford to use their only real leverage—the withholding of aid—without undermining their anti-Communist project. As for talk of a coup, it had come to nothing. Lodge himself had complained to Beech that "the trouble is nobody around here has a lust for power except for the people who already have it." Diem, Nhu, and Madame Nhu were immovable, Beech concluded. He left Saigon believing the issue was settled.

This belief remained unchanged a month later when he sat down at his desk in Tokyo. "Americans," he wrote, "aren't any good at overthrowing governments. The latest government we haven't overthrown is the family concern in South Vietnam." No amount of diplomatic pressure had succeeded in getting rid of Diem. And Vietnam's generals weren't about to do it either. "Gradually an awful truth began to dawn on the Americans," Beech wrote. "Nothing was going to happen."

Beech's article was published on October 30. On November 1 the Diem regime was overthrown in an American-backed putsch. Diem and Nhu were murdered. Halberstam, Browne, and Sheehan were among the handful of reporters who knew the coup was coming. Lodge, on whom Beech depended for some of his insights, had done a masterful job of dissembling. The Saigon correspondents, meanwhile, were vindicated. Malcolm Browne took particular pleasure in drawing attention to Beech's disastrous dispatch from the day before, pinning the clipping to the bulletin board in his office as, in his words, "a cautionary reminder." He kept it there for years. Beech returned to Saigon a couple of days after the event, again playing catch-up. In one dispatch he detailed the unfolding of the plotters' plans. In another he described appreciatively the "pleasant rustle of freedom" riffling "the feathery leaves of the tall and gracious tamarind trees that line [Saigon's] broad avenues." The curfew was lifted, censorship abolished. Political prisoners were released from a notorious island prison and joyously welcomed back by family and friends who lined the banks of the Saigon River to greet them. Diem's passing was regretted by few.

Higgins was one of the few. She remained sympathetic to Madame Nhu, who was saved from a grisly fate by her fortuitous absence from Vietnam. She was in the United States on a speaking tour. Higgins had been giving her advice, including "some thoughts how best to phrase, for the benefit of public opinion, the views you are trying to get across." The word "barbecue" was not recommended. Higgins, of course, had opposed talk of Diem's overthrow on a number of grounds, not least because there was no obvious successor.

Beech had a similar concern. "Where the hell do we go from here?" he wondered. He took up the question with colleagues and an Indian diplomat at a table in the Caravelle bar shortly after the coup. "I say," said the diplomat with evident glee. "You Americans are in a pickle now. How do you get yourselves out of this one?" Beech, acting impulsively, picked up a bottle of soda from the table, shook it vigorously, and squirted the diplomat squarely in the face. The answer to the diplomat's question remained unanswered.

A TIME FOR WARRIORS

Horst Faas joined an Eagle Flight taking off from Tan Son Nhut Air Base at around four in the morning of November 22. He rode on the helicopter leading a dozen more, some carrying troops, others offering fire support. Their mission was to flush out, capture, or kill guerrillas in a lightning raid that would end after a couple of hours. These flights "always made great pictures," said Faas. They were circling the targeted village when the pilot, who was listening to the radio, turned to Faas and said, "Did you hear that?" "Yeah," said Faas, "something about Kennedy wounded in Dallas." Then the program—it was the army program made famous by Robin Williams in the film *Good Morning, Vietnam*—went back to playing music, and the pilot and Faas decided that what the disk jockey had said couldn't be true: "This guy is a clown like always." Fifteen minutes later, the news came back on: President Kennedy had been shot and seriously wounded in an assassination attempt. The pilot, stunned by the information, called off the raid. They returned to the airbase. By the time they landed, Kennedy was dead.

The Kennedy assassination dominated the news for a couple of weeks—and the memory of Kennedy's time in office, the golden promise of a latter-day Camelot—lingered. Lyndon Johnson at first sought to reassure the country that the administration was stable. He asked most senior officials to stay and most did. He was acutely conscious that it was Kennedy who had been elected president, not him, and it would be a while before he asserted himself. He would, in any case, have much to contend with: the tumult that marked the mid-1960s at home, including riots in northern cities and civil agitation on several fronts, social upheaval, and an emerging drug culture. And of course the war continued. The Saigon-based correspondents were soon filing stories that confirmed most of what they had claimed before, with the difference that officials, both Vietnamese and American, now felt at liberty to agree with them: the Viet Cong really were forming up in bigger and better equipped units; the Army of the Republic of Vietnam was stymied; and the Strategic Hamlet Program was a failure. Beech, back in Saigon in early 1964, wrote as much. He quoted an American who had been in the country for four years as saying, "I tell you, things are coming unstuck. Aim a No. 5 iron anywhere south of Saigon and you'll hit a Viet Cong."

What the new administration in Washington saw, when it paid attention, was increasing Communist military activity and recurrent political chaos. Buddhist leaders, notably Thich Tri Quang, the firebrand who had ignited the protest in Hue two years earlier, were prominent meddlers in the series of governments that formed and fell after Diem's murder. Americans worried that Buddhist ranks had been infiltrated by the Communists, but this seems not to have been the case, at least not to any great effect. The monks were playing politics for their own reasons, which may or may not have included, as the Americans feared, making peace with the North at the cost of the South's independence. American concern was reinforced by talk coming from the North, as well as from outside observers.

Beech was the conduit for some of this messaging. On a visit to Phnom Penh he sat down with an old acquaintance, the Australian reporter who maintained close relations with the North Vietnamese leadership, Wilfred Burchett. In the previous year Burchett had joined a Viet Cong party traveling on foot and by bicycle down the Ho Chi Minh Trail—an arduous undertaking for a man in his mid-fifties—and written with admiration of the guerrillas' ingenuity and spirit. Now, over whisky by the pool at the Hotel Royale, Burchett passed on the terms that the Communists would find acceptable. While never renouncing the goal of reunification, Burchett said, Hanoi could live with the establishment of a "neutralist government" that brought together the South Vietnamese and the National Liberation Front. Others liked the idea—French President Charles de Gaulle had been actively promoting it—but Johnson, like Eisenhower and Kennedy before him, rejected any compromise with the Communists. As became clear over the course of the year.

In early August a US destroyer operating off the coast of North Vietnam was attacked by torpedo boats, and two days later another destroyer reported that it, too, had been subjected to a seaborne assault. The first attack was real, the second was not. Taut nerves, stormy conditions, or faulty radar gave rise to the latter report, which the ship's captain tried within hours to walk back. Too late. The president ordered retaliatory bombing of targets in North Vietnam and, taking advantage of widespread indignation at the supposed second assault, pushed a resolution through Congress that let him prosecute the war as he saw fit. The Gulf of Tonkin Resolution would have far-reaching effects.

Beech saw the incident as evidence of the North's increased aggressiveness. He described a typical evening in the city, where

Americans enjoying the breeze from the river dined out on hotel patios, the quiet interrupted by the occasional *whomp, whomp* of mortars exploding in the distance. "'I don't know that I like living in the hole of a doughnut,' said the dark-haired woman on my left," Beech wrote. "Unmistakably the war has moved closer to Saigon in the last six weeks. . . . Traffic moves to and from the city. People, Vietnamese and Americans, go about their business as usual. No one has panicked. Yet the mood of Saigon is one of vague unease."

Maxwell Taylor replaced Lodge (who had resigned in order to pursue his own presidential ambitions) in June 1964. In December, baffled and frustrated by their chronic conspiratorial maneuvers, Taylor delivered a frank—verging on insulting—dressing down to a gathering of officers, whom he had invited to dinner. He told them in so many words to stop plotting among themselves and get on with the war. His exhortations were futile. The regime changed hands repeatedly: Gen. Nguyen Khanh, who had overthrown Gen. Duong Van Minh, the leader of the original plotters against Diem, was displaced briefly by a civilian, Tran Van Huong, but returned in January 1965. Both Taylor and the White House had their doubts about Khanh's staying power, and, indeed, he would soon be deposed by another civilian, Phan Huy Quat, who gave way in June to Nguyen Cao Ky, who hung on for a couple of years. Perhaps, Beech suggested, it was time for America to take charge. Taylor thought so. So did Johnson's special assistant for national security, McGeorge Bundy, who had to delay a visit to Vietnam while Khanh was busy overthrowing the government for the second time. Bundy landed in early February 1965.

Some reports have suggested that what he saw in the aftermath of the Viet Cong raid on the Central Highlands base of Pleiku shook Bundy to the core, leading him to push for the start of the bombing campaign that became Operation Rolling Thunder. Beech's reporting suggests that Bundy was indeed shaken. Eight Americans had been killed and more than a hundred wounded in the raid. Six helicopters were destroyed and fourteen damaged. Evidence of a hard-fought battle was visible everywhere. Beech was greeted on arrival by a GI who apologized because his fatigues were smeared with blood. Besides Bundy, both Khanh and Gen. William Westmoreland were on hand. "Bundy blinked in the glare of the sunlight" when he emerged from the meeting, Beech wrote, adding:

> I thought Bundy looked depressed. "A hell of a mess, isn't it?" said Bundy gesturing as he walked among the still warm ruins of a burned out helicopter, bloodstained bunkers and unexploded TNT charges. But Bundy didn't seem to be interested in what the briefing officer had to say during his 10-minute tour. He seemed preoccupied, as if his mind was on other things.

Pleiku was one in a string of military setbacks that the South had been experiencing. In November the previous year there had been a Viet Cong raid against the Bien Hoa Air Base outside Saigon in which the VC had destroyed five B-57 medium-range bombers and three Skyraider fighter-bombers, and damaged several more. There had been a devastating drawn-out battle at Binh Gia, east of the capital, at the start of the year in which for the first time the Viet Cong were seen to be organized in battalion strength. The ARVN had taken heavy losses. Beech saw the aftermath of another defeat, less dramatic in scale but no less indicative of failure, at Ben Cat, where a Special Forces unit was overrun. On all fronts the South Vietnamese appeared to be failing. Bundy later suggested that Pleiku was like a streetcar: one was bound to come along sooner or later, giving the administration the occasion to execute a plan already fully formed. Beech got a hint of this the night before the raid in an off-the-record meeting with Bundy and the deputy ambassador to Vietnam, U. Alexis Johnson. The correspondents who were there asked about the possibility of bombing. We'd never do it, one suggested provocatively, for fear of bringing the Russians into the war. "Oh, they'll rattle their rockets, all right," Bundy replied, "but they won't really do anything." "It's all academic anyway," said another correspondent, implying again that it would never happen, at which Alexis Johnson spoke up, saying with emphasis, "I wouldn't rule out bombing." Bundy may well have been sobered by what he saw the next day, but the escalator leading to full American involvement was moving already.

The bombing campaign over North Vietnam commenced in February and was stepped up a month later. An expeditionary force of US Marines landed at Danang in March. By June the Marines had been augmented by American soldiers, bringing the total of American fighting men in country to 70,000. Westmoreland asked for another 100,000 by the end of the year, and as many more in 1966. The president was minded to give him what he asked for but worried about the domestic response and downplayed the number in public: in a televised speech on July 28 he said just 125,000 American men would be sent to Vietnam by December. He said nothing of adding more later. He definitely made no mention of the half million that might be needed to win the war, a figure that had been put to him in White House meetings and left unchallenged.

The buildup was massive, the logistics complicated. Initial operations by US forces were necessarily tentative. Officers and men needed time to get used to the terrain, to feel out the enemy, and to become accustomed to the inquisitive attentions of correspondents. When, at the beginning of August, the 173rd Airborne Brigade settled in at Bien Hoa, Beech joined them on one of their first patrols. It did not go well in military terms. Nor was it encouraging from the newsman's perspective. "The 173rd is so security conscious," Beech wrote,

> you would think there was a war going on here. The general was in his quarters and not to be disturbed. The operations officer

> was not to be disturbed either. A disturbed captain told us to go away. We asked to see a map and he said he would try to find one without anything on it. He disappeared and came back with a map that didn't have anything on it.

Beech was similarly unimpressed when he took part in Operation Thunderbolt, the prelude to Starlite, a much bigger operation launched later in the month off the coast south of Danang. The official action report presented the engagement as a success. "That isn't the way I remember it," wrote Beech. He described a day in which a girl was killed in the prelanding barrage and more cows and water buffalo gunned down and houses burned than enemy confronted. It was also a day marked by searing 110-degree heat in which scores of Marines were felled by heatstroke. He was with Mike Company when three black-clad figures were seen running along a dike. Two made it to a clump of trees, the third dove behind an embankment. The whole company opened up on the straggler, wrote Beech, but it was a grenadier armed with an M-79 grenade launcher that got him. "The black-clad figure re-appeared, clawed helplessly at the dike, then lay still." Later, Beech asked Colonel Wright how he knew the dead men were VC. "'We don't,' said Wright. 'But we have had two men killed in our platoon and we aren't taking any chances.'"

It was, Beech acknowledged, a dirty war—"the dirtiest war Americans ever had to fight." How dirty was soon demonstrated in the northern coastal region where the 9th Marine Regiment was established. A young CBS correspondent, Morley Safer, was with a team that filmed a platoon shooting up and setting fire to the homes of civilians in what had recently been a strategic hamlet, the village of Cam Ne. According to Safer, his crew intervened to save the lives of an old man, a woman, and two children before the Marines lit up their hut with a flamethrower. The televised report caused a public relations firestorm in the United States.

Beech was not happy to see the Marines' reputation soiled by Safer's broadcast and returned to the scene to get their side of the story. He spoke to the colonel and a number of the men. "When Americans first 'swept' the village July 12," Beech wrote,

> they suffered three killed and five wounded. They took three more casualties when they went back again earlier this week. "When our men were fired on July 12 they naturally fired back," said [Colonel] Garretson. "One of the Viet Cong was a woman with a Thompson sub-machine gun. She died on the way to hospital. Who wants to shoot a woman, but what do you do if women are shooting at you?"

A week later Beech picked up the theme again. "More than 25,000 U.S. marines occupying the coastal strip of central Vietnam are engaged in a two-front war," he wrote. "On one front they are fighting a dirty, tedious campaign against the Viet Cong. On the other, they must defend themselves against Stateside critics for the way they are fighting it." The Americans, Beech wrote, were coming up against a problem that Vietnamese soldiers had dealt with before them: how to tell friend from foe in villages where they sometimes take fire from the enemy. "To complicate matters," he reasoned,

> a Vietnamese house is not always a home. It's often a fortified position. Every Vietnamese home in the countryside is equipped with its air raid trench, which may lead to a system of tunnels that may or may not be used by the Viet Cong. A marine who sticks his head into one of these holes may find women and children cowering there, or he may get a bullet through the head.

The Marines were justified in destroying a village that was repeatedly shown to be occupied by Viet Cong guerrillas, Beech argued. Villages had been razed by Americans in Korea on the same principle. The difference was that "this is a political war and the Communists can be counted on to exploit every incident in which a Vietnamese dies at the hands of an American." By implication, press reports that highlighted civilian deaths played into the hands of the enemy.

Friction between the press and government officials erupted again barely two weeks later. Operation Starlite, the first major American offensive action of the war, was launched in mid-August. It was aimed at trapping the 1st Viet Cong Regiment—an experienced two-thousand-strong unit—on the Van Tuong peninsula south of Danang. A Marine brigade, under the command of Col. Oscar F. Peatross (whom Beech had known on Iwo Jima), brought land- and sea-based guns, helicopters, and fixed-wing aircraft in support of three rifle battalions that, over six days, sought to surround and annihilate the Viet Cong. More than six hundred enemy combatants were killed; Marines killed in action amounted to forty-two. It was widely reported as a victory and a sign of positive things to come.

Beech was quick to celebrate the "smashing first-round victory" in the "first major showdown battle between Americans and their elusive adversaries." In the aftermath of the battle, he found the Marines

> were red-eyed and bone-tired, their stubbled faces streaked with grime and their fatigues stiff with dried sweat. But if anyone thought American boys had gone soft in our affluent society, the Marines proved otherwise. In the test of battle they proved themselves worthy successors to the men who hit the black sand beaches of Iwo Jima twenty years ago or stormed the gates of Seoul five years later. . . . "They were just 18- and 19-year-olds a couple of days ago," said Lt. John D. Steele of Dallas, an elderly 25. "Now they're veterans."

Beech noted the toughness of the Viet Cong soldiers—"fine, well-trained troops" according to one officer—and the stiffness of some of the encounters: "Marine armor was hard hit." But the outcome left him in no doubt that American might had been demonstrated. "American military commanders have a load off their minds," he wrote a day later. "They no longer have to worry about who was going to win the first showdown battle between U.S. troops and the Vietcong."

The AP's Peter Arnett saw it differently. He heard about the operation from a friend on August 18, hitched a ride to the Marine base closest to the action at Chu Lai, and from there climbed aboard another helicopter along with freelance photographer Tim Page that took them directly to the battlefield. He told of a "lost column" consisting of a handful of amtracs loaded with supplies and a couple of tanks meant for their protection. He wrote that the "supply pokes" in the unit "had figured on an easy run," but somehow, despite calling out repeatedly to Marines they saw as they crisscrossed the battlefield, they had been unable to find the battalion they were meant to replenish. And then the enemy found them. Viet Cong soldiers popping up from behind bushes and hillocks started harassing them. Three of the amtracs, struggling to maneuver into an advantageous position, became bogged down. Another was destroyed by the Viet Cong and the tanks rendered helpless. The column, mired in soft sand, the men roasting under a blazing sun and under nearly constant mortar and sniper fire, was helpless. A young corporal, according to a survivor, suddenly shouted to the others, "Okay, men, we're Marines! Let's do the job!" The moment he leaned out of the vehicle, he was shot between the eyes and fell down dead. The others hunkered down. This was where Arnett and Page joined them.

They were rescued by an infantry company later that afternoon. Arnett got back to Saigon and spent the night writing his story. It was widely published, often as a sidebar to a straight report of what was otherwise seen as the triumphant Marine victory. It got the attention not just of the Marine brass but also of the president. Johnson complained of "the flippant attitude taken toward the Marines KIA ('the boys have mothers who will read that article')" and demanded an explanation by the next morning.

To Arnett, the operation was yet another demonstration of an argument he and some of his fellow correspondents had been making for a couple of years: that the American approach to the war, heavy on armor, technology, and firepower, was inappropriate to the conditions in Vietnam. The amtracs "flopped from one rice paddy to another," he wrote, while their adversary, comfortable in the terrain, picked them off and then withdrew at will. When the officer at the "five o'clock follies" (the name by which the daily military briefing came to be known) presented Starlite as a famous victory, Arnett stood up and challenged him. The uproar that followed led the officer to end the meeting. Beech later alluded (rather gently) to Arnett's report in a Stateside interview:

> Sometimes reporters—good ones—become so narrow in their reporting that they miss the big picture. For example, a top correspondent reported an important recent battle a disaster. He was with a small unit of 100 men who were "chewed up with crossfire"—to use his quote, and he got some good ones, riding out with the wounded in medical 'copters—but he didn't mention that this unit was a small part of a 5,000-man force and the battle was considered a major victory in Saigon.

As far as Beech could tell, the war was going well for the Americans and their Vietnamese ally. The 1st Cavalry Division, riding helicopters instead of horses, was demonstrating the blossoming of a theory whose seeds had been planted earlier: how helicopter-borne troops, trained for the task, could swoop in on the enemy, taking it by surprise and cutting off its retreat. It was a theory given practical application in the Ia Drang Valley in mid-November when American forces confronted some twenty-five hundred North Vietnamese troops and killed nearly half of them, taking a quarter the number of casualties themselves. For Beech this was evidence of progress, progress that also was made obvious in the almost-instant transformation of a seaside village into one of the biggest ports in Southeast Asia. Beech accompanied a congressman on a flight over Cam Ranh Bay. They saw seventeen ships in the harbor, LSTs on the beach, "acres of PSP (perforated steel planking) . . . warehouses going up . . . trucks churning their way through yellow sand . . . acres of tents." It looked to Beech like any big Pacific supply base in World War II. Army engineers had effected the transformation in just six months, and already the port was supplying both the Cavalry and the 101st Airborne Division in Central Vietnam.

The North was building up its forces too, apparently determined to match whatever America brought to the fight. This was unfortunate, as Beech saw it. He quoted an American official saying, "we could save a lot of bloodshed on both sides. We know they can't win, but they don't know it . . . and even if they did, I'm not sure it would make any difference." "It would be most agreeable to write that peace lies just over the horizon," Beech wrote a few days later, "but it's not the case. The time is not ripe for the peace seekers. It's a time for warriors. . . . Each side is committed to the point of no return."

Nineteen sixty-six would see the realization of this grim forecast: the war got bigger and both sides became more entrenched. Losses grew with the buildup, and so did the voices raised in opposition. Beech, in Honolulu over Christmas, reacted irritably to the rising discontent. Reports from Saigon sometimes were characterized by "a sort of confused honesty," he wrote, but some eminent pundits based in Washington were even more wrongheaded. He especially objected to what he had read by the columnist Walter Lippmann, "who has never set foot in the Far East and thinks Hanoi is a seaport. Lippmann's argument, when stripped to its bare bones, is that we should rid ourselves of the Vietnam problem by giving it and the rest of Southeast Asia to the Communists." This view was shared by others (Beech mentioned the political scientist Hans Morgenthau) who had lately "discovered from afar that war is hell. It is." But this was no reason to abandon Vietnam, or Southeast Asia. To do so was folly, in Beech's view. "True, these are dangerous times. But the United States is in fact stronger in Asia today, simply because of its presence in Vietnam, than at any time since the Korean war. For that matter, so is non-Communist Asia. Conversely, the Communists are weaker."

Other nations were well aware of the importance of the stand America had taken in Vietnam. Korea, Australia, and New Zealand all had committed troops to the war. Thailand was providing bases for American bombers. To those who argued that good works rather than guns would better serve the cause of freedom, Beech replied that good works doubtless were necessary, and that America had done more than it was given credit for, but, as Mao had observed, "power comes from the mouth of a gun."

While he remained based in Saigon throughout 1966, Beech traveled a good deal. In January he talked to the pilots flying B-29s from Andersen Air Force Base in Guam. In February he played poker with Prime Minister Nguyen Cao Ky and members of the US mission on the flight from Saigon to Honolulu for the impromptu conference called by President Johnson. (Ky "displayed an insatiable curiosity to see the next hand, regardless of whether his hand justified the curiosity." Ky lost $8—doing better than Beech, who lost more than $80.) When not playing cards on the flight, Ky crafted his speech with help from the American officials: in it he stressed his, or perhaps the officials', commitment to democracy and freedom. Johnson was pleased. "Boy," he told Ky, "you speak just like an American."

In February Beech accompanied Vice President Hubert Humphrey on a tour that took them to Canberra, Manila, and

Seoul. (His Australian hosts marveled at Humphrey's oratory: "so overcome by his own eloquence" was the VP, Beech wrote, "that great big tears rolled down his cheeks.") At the end of May, Beech was at the Bandung Conference of nonaligned states that brought together representatives from twenty-nine countries, ranging from Asia and the subcontinent to Africa and the Far East: "Colonialism was their theme," Beech observed, "and they were against it." Before the year was out, he would be back in Bangkok, Tokyo, and Manila. He ended the year as he had begun it, in Honolulu.

As usual, what he had to report when he was in Vietnam was split between politics and war. Both had their complications. Ky presided over a government whose stability depended on balancing the ambitions of a handful of generals who, when left alone, behaved as regional warlords. Ky upset the balance early in the year when he fired Gen. Nguyen Chanh Thi, who commanded ARVN forces in Tactical Zone I based in Hue. Thi was allied with the Buddhist association, and his ouster riled the Buddhists, who were led, in part, by a familiar figure, Thich Quang Tri. The disturbances that followed erupted off and on through the spring and included, at one point, a standoff between military units that had to be quelled by the Americans. Ky finally brought the insurrection to an end by sending in a ruthless enforcer, Gen. Nguyen Ngoc Loan. The means he employed were bloody but effective.

At the end of June Beech spent time with the 1st Infantry Division in one of the most intensely contested parts of the country, north of Saigon, not far from the Cambodia border. His guide was Maj. Gen. William E. DePuy, "a small, hard-driving man full of restless energy," who was doing his best to make a success of his command. From the air he showed Beech how he was dealing with the elusiveness of the enemy. He had instructed his engineers to cut the jungle into squares so that when his troops pushed through the bush, the guerrillas would be driven into open fire lanes where they could be cut down expeditiously. On the ground they spoke to a battalion commander who said he had called in air support after a firefight in which nine of his men were wounded. The bombs, thousand-pounders, had opened up several tunnels and underground bunkers. He said, "It looks like something pretty big." This, again, was America fighting the war on its terms, using the technology at its disposal. But because this also was a war being fought for the hearts and minds of the people, it had another side.

In a nearby village, Beech saw what pacification looked like. Adult males were moved to an assembly area where they were interrogated. "So far," said DePuy, "we have the local VC chief, the security chief, the political commissar, 29 VC suspects and 60 draft dodgers already in the army." Women and children, meanwhile, were gathered for what DePuy described as a "festival." An army doctor, soaked in sweat, was examining a ten-year-old girl with an open sore on her leg. "They have everything, you name it," the doctor said. An army dentist was pulling teeth. "Worst teeth I ever saw." And army cooks were dishing out meals consisting of potato salad, hot dogs, and a can of milk. "They'd rather have rice," DePuy admitted, "but we aren't quite ready for that yet." The villagers were okay with the potato salad, Beech noted, but suspicious of the hot dogs. As they ate, the children sat in the shade of rubber trees and listened to a military brass band. "A funny way to fight a war," Beech said. "Yes," said DePuy, "but then it's a funny war."

Still, Beech was sure that the Americans were headed to victory. If nothing else, the overwhelming numbers of men they were putting into the field pointed in this direction. In July, he reported, there were "now over 270,000 men [in the country] . . . scheduled to reach 400,000 by the end of the year." Combined with ARVN, there would be "more than 1,000,000 men under arms by the end of the year." The most generous estimates suggested the enemy force was 280,000. "Hard-hitting, highly mobile American forces are already slaughtering the Communists at a rate no enemy, no matter how dedicated or callous of human life, can long sustain," he wrote. "As more American troops arrive, the enemy will be punished even more severely."

Beech remained optimistic through to the end of the year, notwithstanding his own admonition that, in Vietnam, "the casualty rate among optimists is high." If he worried, it was that America's resolve would be undermined by doubters and critics. An interview with a defector in December reinforced his concern. The defector, a North Vietnamese lieutenant colonel, agreed that America was too strong to be defeated militarily. Then how does the North expect to win? Beech asked. "By prolonging the war and spreading disunity in the United States and among your allies abroad," the officer answered. "Also by exploiting contradictions within South Vietnam and the formation of political struggle groups in the cities." This was prescient.

Beech was aware of the student protests disrupting campuses in the United States. He would have known that a student leader, Tom Hayden, had joined a group of Western observers invited to Hanoi the previous year, their visit timed to coincide with the suspension of bombing over Christmas. Others who visited the North included a British journalist, James Cameron, and an American historian, Staughton Lynd. Their reports on their return, while not uncritical (especially in the case of Cameron), still put a human face on what had been until then a faceless, and therefore sinister, enemy. And even as Beech was quizzing an NVA defector a year later, another journalist was on his way north. Harrison Salisbury, well known and justly admired for his work as a Moscow correspondent for *The New York Times*, was taking a roundabout route (Paris–Tirana–Cairo–Karachi–Phnom Penh–Vientiane) to Hanoi. Salisbury's dispatches from the North, which trashed American claims that the bombing spared civilian targets, were particularly damaging to President Johnson's standing. The anti-war movement was gaining adherents.

Beech returned to the US mainland, after a three-year absence, in April 1967. While he was away there had been a cultural revolution.

Bob Dylan had gone electric. The Beatles were more popular than Jesus. It was fashionable to indulge in illicit drugs. The Pill was upending sexual mores. Young men presented an appearance that a few years earlier would have provoked scandal: jeans, sandals, tie-dyed T-shirts, and hair down to their shoulders and below. Suits and ties were gone, along with horn-rimmed glasses and crew cuts. The women, to an older man's eyes, presented a spectacle no less shocking. Beech, flying in from Saigon, had the feeling that he had landed in the wrong country. The time must have seemed desperately out of joint.

A few weeks earlier he had been shadowing Westmoreland in the region northwest of Saigon known as the Iron Triangle. The general was presiding over yet another operation, Cedar Falls, bigger as always than all the others before. Five hundred Viet Cong had been killed at the time of Beech's visit, and three thousand tons of rice had been seized. The two men flew to a camp where a Special Forces unit was sending patrols to the Cambodia border. They were briefed by a first lieutenant, weary and unshaven, who reported that his party had killed another two Viet Cong. Then Beech and the general set out to investigate an initiative called Arc Light, in which B-52s dropped World War II–era incendiary bombs on patches of jungle where the VC were thought to have their hideouts. So far, Westmoreland said, the experiment had failed because the jungle was too wet. Their aircraft described lazy circles around the area while "invisible B-52s" dropped sticks of bombs in orderly rows "as if planting corn." A soft gray cloud of smoke rose up. "'I don't see any fire down there,' Westmoreland said. 'Do you?'" Beech didn't either. They returned to Saigon.

From the Iron Triangle to the streets of San Francisco was a journey that could hardly be measured in miles. This was the "gay and elegant" city where twenty years earlier, Beech recalled, soldiers from another war with another country had returned to be greeted with open arms. Today, he wrote, "there is no reason for the returning soldier . . . to linger here and every reason to move on. The atmosphere here is not favorable to warriors. The town is full of hippies and teeny boppers who want peace." He watched the march in which, the local paper estimated, three-quarters of participants were under twenty-five years old. "They were—bless their dirty little necks, matted beards and stringy hair—too young to know anything about war. But they were against it. That's for sure." Fifty thousand attended the rally that followed at Kezar Stadium, where the speakers assured them that the war was being fought for big business and war profiteers. "There was something drearily familiar about that," Beech wrote:

> It took me back to the days of the Nazi-Soviet pact before Hitler let loose his armies against Russia. But of course nobody remembers that any more. Courteous, soft-spoken young Negroes circulated through the crowd hawking "the little red book that can free you from oppressors. Seven hundred million Chinese can't be wrong." Fascinated, I handed over 15 cents for Mao Tse-tung's thoughts. And I thought: "The old boy isn't getting a cent of royalties for this."

Beech had returned to the United States in April with the announced intention of taking a sabbatical to write a book. The writing project was genuine, although the book wouldn't see the light of day for another four years. But he had another motive: his marriage was in trouble. When he moved his base of operations to Saigon in the fall of '65, Linda moved to Honolulu to pursue a PhD in psychology at the University of Hawaii. She indicated at the time that she planned after graduation to return to Tokyo to practice her profession, but the move suggests she saw no reason to remain—so often alone—in Tokyo. Beech, as always, was utterly absorbed in his work: neither Linda nor the boys saw much of him as he covered the war and traversed the region. He made a point of spending Christmas in Honolulu after she moved there, in 1965 and '66, but these flying visits were not enough. By the fall of '67 they were in trouble: there came a day when Beech moved out of the house into a garage down the street. His drinking was almost certainly a factor in driving them apart. If he had intended by his return to Honolulu to put new life into their relationship—just as he had on a similar mission to Mildred years before—it wasn't going well. Things had changed. The fire had died.

He kept his eye on the war while on sabbatical. He remained consistent in his defense of the American intervention. He took the view that the war would wind down of its own accord as the Communists came to realize that winning was impossible. "North Vietnamese troops will filter back to the north. Part-time guerrillas will become full-time farmers. That's the way other Communist insurgencies ended," he wrote.

But Beech also worried that Americans would lose heart. It wasn't just "the hippies and the teeny boppers, the weirdies and the beardies, the long-haired boys and short-haired girls, the draft card burners and flag destroyers" who were troubled by the war. The "great mass of American people, good people, intelligent people" were worried too. They needed to be shown how necessary the war was. Beech wanted to see the president "stand before a map of East Asia with a pointer and explain, country by country, how a 'new Asia' is emerging. . . . Our national obsession with Vietnam has blinded us to the fact that after more than 20 years of war and revolution, non-Communist Asia was shaping up." America was on the verge of presiding over a newly prosperous, more nearly free, or at least better governed Far East, fixed in its opposition to Communist expansion. It would be folly to let go too easily what had been with such enormous effort achieved.

He took his message to the White House in May. In an off-the-record meeting, he asked the president if he would sanction the bombing of Haiphong as others had suggested. "I'm not going to say whether I will or whether I won't," Johnson told him. "An awful lot of good people come in here and tell me what I ought to do. But sure as hell if I did, one of our pilots would drop a bomb down the smokestack of one of those Russian ships out there in the harbor. And the next morning, after Russia had declared war, all those good people who wanted me to bomb Haiphong would come in and say: 'Mr. President, that ain't what we meant at all.'"

"WAR ISN'T FUN ANY MORE"

Linda filed for divorce in January 1968. Beech, setting aside the book project, resumed his rounds in the Far East: Tokyo, Bangkok, Phnom Penh. He was back in Tokyo when the Communists launched the great offensive in South Vietnam that was meant to ignite a mass uprising against the American occupiers and their puppets. The Tet (Vietnamese New Year) Offensive was, in its way, as decisive a turning point in the war as the fall of Diem had been. The coup had precipitated the beginning of the American war in Vietnam. Tet presaged its eventual end.

There had been significant developments in the previous year. The number of American troops in the country had topped out at close to half a million as Westmoreland pressed on with his big-unit war. He continued to report progress, even hinting on a visit to Washington in April that victory was achievable within one or two years. Not everyone was convinced. Thousands and then tens of thousands of protesters were taking to the streets to demand an immediate end to the bloodletting. Thirty-five thousand (the official estimate) massed outside the Pentagon in October, their chants ("Hey, hey, LBJ! How many kids did you kill today?") clearly audible to the men and women inside. Among those watching from inside was the defense secretary. The certainty with which Robert McNamara had prosecuted the war had given way to doubt. Months earlier he had floated a peace proposal that was turned down by Hanoi. In November he resigned.

Johnson badly needed a palpable indication of progress. What he got wasn't that. On the night of January 31, North Vietnamese troops and Viet Cong guerrillas launched a simultaneous attack on more than thirty cities and provincial capitals in South Vietnam. In Saigon, a commando unit succeeded in breaching the outer wall and blowing up the main door of the US Embassy: they held out for more than six hours. Other units engaged American and ARVN troops around the palace, in Cholon, and at Tan Son Nhut Air Base, where the fighting went on for days. In Hue, the Communists seized parts of the city and, crucially, the thick-walled citadel, which they defended tenaciously for a month. In the North, the American base at Khe Sanh, established to watch over the Demilitarized Zone, was threatened as NVA troops massed on the other side.

Westmoreland later claimed that he knew the attack was coming. There was some intelligence to this effect, but no real steps were taken to act on it. Just one of his generals, Frederick C. Weyand, who had responsibility for the Saigon region, took seriously a report that seemed to indicate imminent action by the Communists, and moved additional forces into the city. It was a good thing that he did. At least half the South Vietnamese army was on leave to celebrate the holiday. Most senior American officials were celebrating that night too. They mistook the first explosions they heard for firecrackers. The fact that some seventy thousand enemy troops filtered into the South under American and Vietnamese noses was in itself an extraordinary achievement. The surprise with which the offensive was launched was complete.

Civilian flights into the city having been canceled, Beech flew in from Thailand in an Air Force C-130, along with a score of other correspondents. At the airport they were led to a bus by a bluff military policeman for the ride into town. "There are still snipers around," he warned them, adding, "Anybody on the streets after 5 p.m. gets shot." "Except correspondents," said someone. "That's your privilege, sir," said the MP. The journey to the Caravelle Hotel took less than half the usual time: there was no one on the streets "except for a few children and military vehicles loaded with gun-toting men." Beech hoped the hotel manager, Mr. Dang, remembered the two bottles of whisky Beech had given him three years earlier for his daughter's wedding. He did. "For you, Mr. Beech," he said, "I have a room." From the hotel, Beech walked down the street to the home of his *Daily News* colleague, Ray Coffey, and found that he was ill. He had been covering the story while suffering from a bronchial infection. He was running a temperature of 102. "Westmoreland keeps saying things are great," Coffey told him. "I'm glad they're not bad."

Westmoreland never wavered in his declaration that the "well-laid plans" of the Communists "went afoul." He uttered these words to incredulous reporters in front of the embassy on the morning after the attack, even as corpses still lay on the ground around them. He stuck with the same line through succeeding days as, at considerable cost in lives lost and damaged property, the Communists were repulsed. In a sense, he was justified: the popular uprising Hanoi had hoped for never happened, and the losses they took were huge. But the notion that the Americans had scored a victory was hard to sustain. The gruesome photograph taken by AP's Eddie Adams of General Loan executing a Viet Cong prisoner with a pistol, an image that appeared in numberless American newspapers the next day, looked more like desperation than victory. And the sheer scale of the North's achievement in attacking cities and towns from one end of the country to the other was no less shocking. To those at home who were weary of the carnage and increasingly cynical, Tet looked like defeat.

Beech's initial reports that February echoed the official narrative, that the enemy had overreached and his forces were being decimated. They had dropped their hit-and-hide tactics and come out in the open. Tet, seen in this light, was an opportunity to rout them once and for all. "Things are not so bad as they might seem," he wrote on February 8. "This could be the long-awaited turning point of the war in favor of the United States and its allies. . . . During the nine-day period ended Wednesday, they lost 24,000 men, including some of their best troops. . . . Even allowing for a certain amount of exaggeration, that is a lot of dead Communists." A few days later he quoted an old friend, now a Marine major general, Raymond Murray, saying of the Communists, "They actually persuaded themselves that they could knock out our airfields, capture our artillery and with the aid of 'general uprisings' by the local population, seize the cities. . . . They failed on all counts."

Westmoreland suspected that the Tet Offensive was a trap. He saw the attacks on Saigon and Hue and the other southern and central urban centers as a feint intended to draw American resources away from the North. Hanoi's real objective, he was certain, was Khe Sanh. Westmoreland guessed that the isolated fortress on the edge of no-man's-land was meant by Vo Nguyen Giap—the military genius who had outfoxed the French—to be the American Dien Bien Phu. Westmoreland made plans, accordingly, to shift more of his forces to meet them. President Johnson, as obsessed by the prospect of a crushing defeat like Dien Bien Phu as Westmoreland was, had a scale model of the base set up in the White House situation room. Staff were startled to find him leaning over it at all hours of the day and night. Propelled in part by Westmoreland's certainty, and always happy to spend time with the Marines, Beech made the trek to see for himself what the siege looked like.

> Commercial airline companies could learn a lot about speeding up arrivals and departures by observing air traffic at this Marine base. There are no formalities upon arrival. You just jump off the plane and run like hell for the nearest cover, hoping you don't get hit by mortar or artillery fire. There is no waiting for baggage. You are carrying it on your back—and the less the better.

He found the base commander and his men confident of their ability to withstand the Communist onslaught. The defensive posture, however, was a change: they had been obliged to give up their original mission of blocking enemy infiltration by frequent patrols. They didn't have to go looking for the enemy anymore: the enemy was everywhere. Their only supplies came in by air.

Beech found leaving every bit as harrowing as his arrival had been:

> I waited behind a sandbagged bunker at the airstrip parking apron for the next U.S. Air Force C-123 to come in. Others with more pressing reasons for getting out also were waiting. Among them were a dozen or so marine and Vietnamese medevac cases. We were halfway across the parking apron when a mortar shell splattered the concrete not more than 20 yards away. "Get back, get back," somebody screamed. I took cover behind a bulldozer along with a tiny bloodstained Vietnamese ranger who looked at me with hurt, puzzled eyes. We heard the C-123's engines roar and I assumed it was getting out of there without us. But the pilot, a gutsy man whoever he was, only moved his plane about 50 yards in case the hidden Communist gunners had zeroed in on his original parking place. I was running as fast I could, legs churning, when I discovered to my horror that I wasn't getting any place. I was caught in the prop wash from the C-123's engines. It was like breasting a hurricane. I twisted to the right, out of the windstream, and made a final desperate lunge for the C-123's tail gate just as it was being raised. "Here, hold this," said somebody who turned out to be a Special Forces medic. I found myself holding a plastic bag of plasma and a bottle of anti-shock solution. Slender yellow rubber tubes led down to a wounded marine, one of four stretcher cases. Another shell smacked into the concrete, closer than the first, but by this time the plane was in motion, swiftly gathering speed. Suddenly, with a powerful wrench, it was off the ground. The stretchers, none too secure in the first place,

> slid backward and I fell forward with my bottle and plasma so my wounded man's lifeline wouldn't snap. His head slid off the stretcher and hit the metal deck with a sickening crack. He made no sound. He was beyond caring. But in the blur of motion I saw another wounded marine's face twist in agony. He was the lucky one. He could still feel pain. Now the plane's engines settled to a steady hum as we cruised above the clouds. The sun cast rays through the rounded ports. Men began to sit up and relax and light cigarets. We felt safe.

From Khe Sanh, Beech traveled south to Danang and on to Hue. He found people were starting to question whether the base he'd just left—"a remote patch of earth tucked away in the northwest corner" of the country—was really the prize the enemy wanted and, even if it was, was it worth saving? At least one senior Marine officer said it was only "because Westy says so" that the Americans were there. It had become a symbol, and the decision to defend it had been made at the highest level. "To hell with fighting for symbols," said the officer. "Khe Sanh isn't worth the candle." There was nothing novel in a Marine being critical of an Army project, but to criticize Westmoreland to a correspondent suggested that a threshold was being crossed. "Westmoreland's whole military future," Beech observed, "as well as the outcome of this war can rise or fall with Khe Sanh."

He visited Hue on the twenty-fifth day of the battle to retake the city, in time to be told that an earlier order to avoid damaging buildings had been discarded. The 108-mm guns they'd been using were insufficient to penetrate the citadel's ten-foot-thick walls. They were bringing in 155-mm howitzers to do the job. A day later, Beech wrote, it was only fitting to speak of Hue in the past tense. It had been "the cultural and political heart of Vietnam, a center of learning, a repository for national treasures." Now it looked "like a page torn from World War II." "It's a pity," said a Marine sergeant.

"This used to be a right pretty town."

His northern swing left Beech depressed. Hanoi's strategy of eroding America's willingness to carry on was working. For all the casualties inflicted on the NVA and Viet Cong, there was no sign that the Communists were giving up. But the signs on the American side were discouraging:

> Westmoreland's conduct of the war has been severely shaken. More Americans have been killed than during any comparable period of the war. The pacification program has been shot to shreds. . . . Mass destruction has saddled the Saigon government and the United States with tens of thousands of refugees. . . . Despite 500,000 American troops, the enemy still has the initiative, at least psychologically. . . . U.S. headquarters in Saigon is mesmerized by Khe Sanh. . . . At the same time it fears another wave of attacks.

Beech's downbeat mood may have been inspired by the off-the-record portion of the conversation he'd had with Ray Murray. Beech waited until he was back in Saigon before quoting without attribution what Murray had said. "War isn't fun any more," he had told Beech:

> "It's centralized, computerized and automated. Those aren't my troops out there. They belong to the Pentagon. Remember Inchon? Remember when we went into Seoul? I lost a lot of men going into Seoul, and they gave me a Silver Star. I lost a lot more men in the Chosin Reservoir, and they gave me another medal and finally promoted me to full colonel. The other day we took 48 casualties and now I've got an investigation." The general laughed ironically. "I'll tell you something else," he said. "When I first came out here, I was full of enthusiasm about this war. Now that I've been here for a while, I'm beginning to wonder. . . . I

> can't help wondering what kind of country we are going to leave behind when this thing is over? Will the sacrifices we have made be worthwhile? I don't know."

Murray would write in his memoir that he had opposed the intervention in Vietnam in the early sixties. He may not have said so to Beech, but he may not have needed to: his disillusion was shared, Beech wrote, by all conscientious Americans, whether military or civilian, in post-Tet Vietnam. He had never seen anything like it. "There has been more personal soul-searching about Vietnam . . . during the last six or seven weeks than during the previous six or seven years." A piece Beech wrote in early March was grim:

> From the mist-shrouded northern highlands to the swamps of the Ca Mau Peninsula, the news is bad—all bad. Militarily, politically and psychologically the Communists have the initiative. Any statement to the contrary, regardless of whether it comes from Saigon or Washington is sheer nonsense. So is the argument over whether we killed 40,000 or 30,000 or 20,000 of the enemy during the recent offensive. No doubt we killed lots of them. But the number is irrelevant. There are plenty more where they came from. Nor does Ho Chi Minh have to account for casualties. The situation is not desperate. We are in no danger of being run out of the country. The formidable American fighting machine is intact. But to try to pretend that the enemy's Tet offensive was a minor defeat for him is absurd.

There was soul-searching in the White House too. Clark Clifford, a Washington lawyer and longtime political insider, had replaced McNamara as defense secretary. He was recruited by Johnson because he was a hawk who could be counted on to bring new vigor to the prosecution of the war. Clark, however, soon shed his hawkishness. He asked questions about the American war effort—What would it take to win? How many more troops? For how long?—that elicited answers that were either vague or unsatisfactory. It wasn't clear what victory would look like or what would be left when it was achieved. These findings constituted an implicit but damning indictment of Westmoreland's strategy, one that the Joint Chiefs of Staff had backed to the hilt. Westmoreland would presently be appointed Army Chief of Staff, a move announced before Tet but one inevitably perceived as a professional rebuke. He was replaced as MACV commander in July by Gen. Creighton Abrams. Clark, meanwhile, determined that it was time to get out.

Johnson came round reluctantly to the same view. The divisions in America had reached a point where the normal operations of government—never mind the creation of the "Great Society" that had been his project—had become unmanageable. On March 31 he gave a solemn televised address in which he proposed unilaterally to suspend bombing of the North and de-escalate military operations in the South in the hope that Hanoi would reciprocate. He was sending a senior diplomat, W. Averell Harriman, to represent him in Paris. An end to the war was attainable if both sides began bargaining in earnest. These remarks, shocking in themselves after all that had gone before, were overshadowed by Johnson's concluding sentence. He would neither seek nor accept, he said, his party's nomination to run for another term as president.

The war ground on, but Johnson's announcement altered its context. Attention was increasingly focused on the talks in Paris.

Beech remained in Saigon. He wrote a friendly profile of Marshal Nguyen Cao Ky, now out of a job following an American-managed election in which he had been replaced by Nguyen Van Thieu. Ky had no desire to undermine Thieu, he told Beech. Americans, he said, were always trying to create the impression that Vietnamese politicians devoted all their energy to plotting against one another. "They speak of Ky and Thieu factions," he said. "There wouldn't be any factions if the Communists took over." Still, Ky was bitter about the American presence. He believed that if it wasn't for their influence he would still be president. He also shared the feeling, current among his countrymen, that the Americans were ready to sell out Vietnam in order to extricate themselves from the war.

Beech was weary. One day in June he saw a column of smoke rising from another section of the city and hired a car to take him to its source. He found a handful of military police pulled up beside a monument in a square and people running past them. It wasn't clear, at first, what was causing the commotion, but then shooting broke out. It seemed to be coming from a power plant across the way. Some of the MPs and the Vietnamese soldiers who were with them threw themselves to the ground. Beech took cover behind a jeep, all the while muttering to himself that he was old enough to know better than to get into this kind of mess. The MPs started blazing away blindly with their M-16s. It was a fine weapon, Beech observed, if you knew what you're shooting at. He wished he was wearing a helmet and flak jacket instead of a pale pink sport shirt. He wished he were somewhere else.

A big MP was on the radio saying they were under fire and asking for help. How many VC are you up against? a voice asked. The MP guessed there were two. There are four of you, the voice said. Deal with it. "But sir . . . ," said the MP. Meanwhile, a man in a white shirt was running across the square. He was unarmed, Beech noted, but he shouldn't have been running. There were too many men there with rifles in their hands and itchy fingers. He saw a Vietnamese soldier raise his rifle. His eyes turned again to the man in the white shirt, and he thought for a moment that he'd make it. He had almost crossed the square and rounded a corner when he leapt into the air and came down kicking. It reminded Beech of a time in Tennessee when he shot a rabbit with a .22-caliber rifle. He was sorry when he shot the rabbit, but by then it was too late.

He heard a man shout, "Stop it! Stop it!" A Vietnamese marine lieutenant was walking toward the cluster of MPs. He was, Beech said, "a very cool lieutenant." "Stop shooting at the electricity," said the lieutenant mildly, pointing to the power plant. "ARVN is in there. Friendlies." The MPs stood up and looked at one another. One of them checked out the man in the white shirt. Blood was pouring from his chest. He was screaming. An MP and a Vietnamese soldier tried to help him. Another MP climbed into his jeep and raced the motor. "We're getting out of here," he said. Beech decided to get out of there too. He found his driver waiting for him, drinking coffee. When he got back to the hotel he took a couple of aspirins. "All that shooting," he said, "had given me a headache."

His reports over the summer varied in tone. Some allowed that progress was being made, others not. In either case, he observed that the state of the war, the advances and setbacks, would surely be reflected in the state of the peace talks, with each side seeking to negotiate from a position of strength. And then, as summer gave way to fall, another factor emerged. "Both on the battlefield and in the conference room," Beech wrote, "the Communists seem to be marking time, waiting for the breaks, perhaps with an eye on the November Presidential election." Would Hanoi reap an advantage if the Republican candidate, Richard Nixon, triumphed over the Democrat, Hubert Humphrey? Both had pledged to stick with their Vietnamese ally. In theory it should have made no difference who won. The reality, however, was that Johnson wanted credit for the peace—he had given up the presidency to achieve it—which meant reaching an agreement before his term ended. The candidates also had a stake in the negotiations: Humphrey stood to gain if the war ceased to be an issue. Nixon, by the same logic, would lose traction.

The negotiations were complicated. Johnson pressed his negotiators to find solutions both he and his Vietnamese ally could live with. His negotiators, in turn, leaned on their Vietnamese counterparts. An especially heavy burden fell on Ellsworth Bunker, who had replaced Lodge (who had replaced Taylor) as ambassador to Saigon. His task was to extract agreement from President Thieu to proposals hashed out in Paris. Thieu balked.

Beech by this time had solid sources, not just in the military but also in Vietnamese politics and society. He was close to now-Vice President Nguyen Cao Ky, a relationship he had been cultivating ever since losing to him in their long-ago airborne poker game. The occasional sympathetic profile doubtless helped too. Now, as the US election loomed ever larger, Beech got rare insight into a relationship that was rapidly deteriorating.

Beech's exclusive story about the "often bitter, tension-packed negotiations" between Bunker and Thieu in the days leading up to the November 5 election caused consternation at the embassy when Beech, before going to press, asked for official comment. Bunker responded by calling an off-the-record press conference through which he hoped to head off flak by placing events in a more "balanced" perspective. But nothing Bunker said contradicted Beech's narrative in any significant detail. The facts, as Beech reported them, implied bad faith in America's dealings with its ally.

The facts were that Bunker in a series of meetings between October 16 and 31 pushed Thieu hard to go along with an agreement that Harriman had thrashed out in Paris. In essence, Johnson, through Harriman, was prepared to concede points that were patently unacceptable to the South Vietnamese: a unilateral bombing halt with no explicit reciprocal de-escalation by Hanoi, and acceptance of the National Liberation Front's separate status in the negotiations. Bunker tried a variety of strategies to force Thieu's hand. He tried bluster, supposedly waving a draft agreement in the air and insisting that it be signed immediately. When this went nowhere, he tried circumventing Thieu, approaching Ky and other Vietnamese politicians, hoping they would see sense in the American position. Ky reportedly upbraided the ambassador, asking how many times had the Americans told him to support the president. "It was at this point," Beech noted sardonically, "that Ky began to have visions of something that South Vietnam has never known—national unity."

And then, in a meeting near the end of the month, Bunker produced a communiqué that Thieu was almost certain to sign. It stated that Hanoi would, after all, agree to de-escalate the war and that the NLF would be sidelined. Thieu delayed signing in order, he said, to consult with his security council. He called Bunker back in the small hours of the morning and asked casually if Hanoi had, indeed, agreed to the terms outlined in the communiqué. Bunker said yes. Thieu then produced a cable from his own man in Paris, Pham Dang Lam, there as an observer. According to Lam, Harriman had told him unequivocally that Hanoi would never accede to those conditions. Bunker retreated to the embassy.

A few hours later, Bunker produced a letter from President Johnson denying what Harriman had told Lam, but Thieu still declined to sign. The Americans did, after all, stop bombing the North on November 1 without conditions. The move was deeply resented in the South, and Thieu, a man previously not noted for charisma, became for a time "the most popular leader in his nation's brief and checkered history." "His defiance of the United States," Beech wrote, "gladdened the hearts of Vietnamese with long-festering resentments against the overwhelming American presence—the rich, towering GIs who had seduced their women, the American advisers who tell them how to do their jobs, the huge, coughing Army trucks that sometimes crush fragile Vietnamese bodies beneath their wheels." Vice President Ky was so moved by a speech Thieu made to the National Assembly that he decided to de-escalate his war of nerves with the president. He quit landing his helicopter on the palace roof, above President Thieu's bedroom, and instead landed in the garden.

There was a subtext to all these meetings. "At no time during the negotiations did either side mention the American elections," a Vietnamese source told Beech. "Yet an awareness of the elections hung over every meeting." Thieu and his colleagues understood perfectly how badly Johnson wanted to end the war. They also believed, according to Beech, that while both Humphrey and Nixon were committed to their support, Humphrey was "soft" on Vietnam and Nixon a "hardliner," and therefore the latter was to be preferred. Neither Beech nor any other reporter at the time knew for sure that Nixon had sought through back channels to influence Thieu. The information came out much later that he had used an influential Washington socialite to tell Saigon's ambassador in Washington that Thieu would get a better deal if he hung tough until after the votes were counted in the United States. Nixon's interference—unscrupulous and likely illegal as it was—hardly mattered. Johnson had little chance of securing anything that looked like progress in Paris given Hanoi's caginess, Thieu's objections, and Vietnamese suspicion that the Americans were selling them out. Johnson's last desperate attempt to secure a kind of absolution for the war by ending it fizzled into nothing. Now it would be Nixon's turn.

WE LEARNED NOT TO RUN

Beech was often frustrated by what he saw as a double standard in judging the morality of the enemy's and his own side's actions. He complained that certain congressional critics (specifically Senators George McGovern and J. William Fulbright) were outraged when there was a spike in American casualties but silent with respect to what caused them. Rather than condemn the Communists for stepping up the fighting, they apologized for American provocation. Similarly, they had nothing to say when—as happened all the time—the Viet Cong lobbed five-inch rockets indiscriminately into Danang or Saigon, but loudly deplored the dropping of a few bombs on Hanoi or Haiphong.

To some extent the critics reflected what they saw and read. There were correspondents on hand to expose American or South Vietnamese excesses, but Viet Cong depredations were mostly out of sight. The handful of American dissidents who traveled to Hanoi tended to show the enemy as more or less reasonable people, patriots who wanted nothing more than to free their country from foreign oppression. There were rumors of atrocities, peasants accused of collaboration who were tortured and recalcitrant village leaders murdered in the night, but there were no reliable witnesses to confirm them. ARVN transgressions were well known. The other side got a pass.

This changed in spring 1969. It had long been whispered that the North Vietnamese had rounded up and killed scores of residents in Hue when they occupied the city. It was said that they had gone door-to-door with lists of suspected bourgeois elements and traitors to the cause. It was only much later, when a farmer tugged at a strand of wire poking above the earth in a field outside the city, that the scale of the rampage was understood. The wire was attached to the remains of a hand. The hand was attached to a human skeleton. The discovery set in motion a search that revealed hundreds and eventually more than three thousand corpses.

Beech interviewed survivors and witnesses in November. He was told that some of the victims had rags stuffed into their mouths to muffle their screams. Some of the bodies were mutilated. There were twenty different grave sites. "In nearly all cases the pattern was the same. The victims were tied together in groups of 10 to 20, sometimes with wire, sometimes with bamboo fiber." Local residents were forced to dig the graves while those who were about to die looked on. The victims then were lined up along the trenches. Many were mowed down by machine-gun fire. Others were bludgeoned to death.

The news from Hue might have had a greater impact if not for the nearly simultaneous revelation of the My Lai massacre.

Beech filed a couple of reports from My Lai, the first from a refugee center, the second from what was left of the village. Neither made comfortable reading.

Beech reckoned that between three and four hundred villagers were murdered by a platoon of soldiers from the US Army's

Americal Division. The lieutenant in command of the platoon, William L. Calley, was charged with murdering "no fewer than 109" civilians. Most of the dead were women and children. "They were the only ones left to kill," Beech wrote. "Their able-bodied Viet Cong husbands and fathers ran away." Women were raped in the midst of the mayhem. A rice farmer said a woman was raped after her children were shot. Another said a thirteen-year-old girl was raped and then murdered. Yet another said a woman was spared only because her six-year-old son, riddled with bullets, fell on top of her. A thirty-nine-year-old farmer who claimed once to have been Viet Cong reported being puzzled as well as shocked. He said they were used to Americans handing out canned goods, candy, cigarettes, and soap. "Regardless of our feelings, we learned to smile at them. . . . But these Americans were different. They started shooting."

Beech bribed four members of the regional defense force to take him to the village. The path was sodden—it was the rainy season—and they had to slosh their way across two muddy streams. The soldiers reminded him more than once to watch out for booby traps. Of the village there remained only a few ruined houses and overgrown rice paddies. A man in blue shorts and a white shirt emerged from nowhere. He identified himself as Nguyen Khoa, and it was apparent that he was the local authority on what had happened. "They [the Americans] were sweating and breathing very hard," Khoa told him. "Their faces were very red. They were very frightening." He pointed to an empty space that once had been the village square and said that sixty people had died there. He pointed in another direction to indicate where another two hundred had been murdered. People were killed when they tried to run away, Khoa said. "So I did not run. I walked to the road with one of my sons. My ox was there. We walked slowly down the road with my ox. Nobody shot us. We have learned not to run."

Beech was in Washington in April 1971, around the time Calley was convicted in a military court of murdering twenty-two

Vietnamese civilians. The sentence was controversial: many onlookers, including prominent Republican politicians, felt that Calley was scapegoated. Beech didn't share that view:

> Before somebody proposes erecting a national monument to William L. Calley Jr., there are a few things that ought to be said. . . . First, Calley got a fair trial, the longest in US military history. On the basis of the evidence, the court had no choice but to find him guilty. . . . Second, to portray Calley as an innocent victim of the system, a typical young American sent to Vietnam to "fight for his country," and then be crucified for it, is a gross distortion of the facts. More than that, it is an insult to the honorable and decent young officers and enlisted men who did not do what Calley did even in the heat of combat. There was no combat at My Lai that day. There was only mass murder.

Beech went on to point to the racism implicit in the position of those who argued that Calley should be let off: "the Calley verdict is a forceful reminder that Vietnamese are people. And it is ironic that those who object to the Vietnam war on moral grounds should react so violently to what was a real reaffirmation of American morality." As for the notion that the verdict raised questions about the morality of the war itself, such questions were legitimate, but neither General Westmoreland, nor Lyndon Johnson, nor Richard Nixon was on trial. "Calley was."

MY IMMUNITY FAILED ME

Nixon's first year in office was marked by mixed signals regarding Vietnam: tough speeches offset by troop withdrawals, continued bombing, and the promise of Vietnamization. He was, in effect, as much confounded by conflicting priorities as his predecessor had been, committed both to the preservation of non-Communist South Vietnam and to negotiation (and an implicit promise of concessions) with Hanoi. The success of this approach depended on Hanoi's willingness to offer a face-saving way out—a way to avoid America being revealed, as Nixon would say on April 30, 1970, as "a pitiful, helpless giant." No such path was found. And so Nixon, assailed on one side by liberal critics and reassured on the other side by conservative allies, continued on an erratic course: pursuing Vietnamization and withdrawing American forces, while at the same time launching invading armies first into Cambodia in 1970, and then a year later into Laos. Both invasions were controversial, provoking massive demonstrations in the United States and a backlash that led, in one tragic instance, to the murder of four students by National Guardsmen at Kent State University. For Nixon supporters, the incursions were a welcome reversal of the long-standing policy that had left Communist sanctuaries (at least officially) unmolested. For opponents, they amounted to war crimes.

Vietnam—its people, culture, and environment—suffered grievously over the course of the war. So did its neighbors. Both Laos and Cambodia were enmeshed in ways that threatened their existence as secure and independent nations. Both were the unwilling host of alien armies: the Viet Cong and North Vietnamese used them as a highway through which they funneled troops and supplies into South Vietnam. They also used them as a refuge to which they could retreat and as a depot in which to store arms and food. The North Vietnamese had expansionist ambitions as well: they had their proxies in both countries, the Pathet Lao in Laos, the Khmer Rouge in Cambodia. The dexterity with which Laotian and Cambodian leaders managed either to resist or accommodate these interlopers according to changing circumstance made their politics extraordinarily complicated. Both professed to be neutral.

Hanoi and Washington were nominally committed by the Geneva Accords to respect that neutrality. Neither did, but they tried not to be obvious about it. The NVA could certainly have taken all of Laos had it chosen to do so. Instead it settled for protecting its sanctuary and supply route. There were elements in the Laotian armed forces that were effective, notably the irregular units fielded by the Meo people, whose guerrilla attacks against the Communists were supported by the CIA, but in general the Laotians were no match for the disciplined and battle-hardened Vietnamese. The US commitment to noninterference, meanwhile, had not stopped it from conducting a bombing campaign aimed at the Ho Chi Minh Trail—in Beech's words, "the most heavily bombed piece of real estate in Southeast Asia"—while keeping mum about American advisers attached to the Laotian army.

Word of all this activity was bound to leak out: charges that a "secret war" was underway riled an already aroused anti-war movement to the point where President Nixon and security adviser Henry Kissinger issued a carefully crafted announcement admitting to increased American "air activity" over Laos but denying the presence of American troops on the ground. Press reports soon unearthed evidence contradicting the claim, leading the White House to respond with grudging and still-evasive corrections. Nixon's credibility took a hit. Beech was one of many foreign correspondents, spurred by the controversy, who set out to investigate. His report from Vientiane on March 6 suggested that at least on the surface nothing untoward was happening: "It looks like just another Laotian crisis. Rotary met as usual Thursday night at the Lane Hotel on the bank of the Mekong. Top-ranking officers of the Laotian army were observed playing tennis. Nobody seems excited except some 60 correspondents in search of a fact." The rest of the piece was given over to speculation: perhaps Hanoi was ready to up the ante in the region, perhaps not. A few days later, he flew to Phnom Penh, paid $4.30 for a tourist visa because journalists were officially barred, and found himself the only American correspondent on hand after the sacking of the North Vietnamese and Viet Cong embassies:

> Pedicab boys tried to peddle half-burned $100 bills to astonished American tourists in the aftermath of organized rioting that left two Communist Vietnamese embassies in ruins and could signal [a] turning point in the Vietnam War. . . . The bills were sifted from the charred remnants of what was once the contents of the North Vietnamese Embassy. . . . There was no resistance at the Viet Cong embassy as secret papers, books, newspapers, film and other items flew out its windows. The attack climaxed months of steadily mounting indignation over the continued presence of an estimated 40,000 North Vietnamese and Viet Cong troops in Cambodian territory.

For nearly three decades Prince Norodom Sihanouk, Cambodia's head of state, had preserved his country's independence by alternately accommodating and resisting pressure from outsiders—French, Vietnamese, and American—all the while keeping internal rivals at bay. Beech was not alone in holding his survival skills in high regard. So high, indeed, that even though Sihanouk was on holiday in the south of France at the time, Beech still assumed that the prince was behind the riots. This was undoubtedly a mistake. In any event, a couple of days later Beech had moved on to Thailand to report on the fate of a freighter that, while under charter to the US government, had been hijacked in the South China Sea. As a result he missed the coup.

An AP reporter, T. Jeff Williams, had taken Beech's place as the only American correspondent in the Cambodian capital when, on March 18, the legislature voted to oust Sihanouk. His replacement was Sihanouk's prime minister, Lon Nol. What Lon Nol hoped to achieve was unclear. Although he demanded that the Communists pull back from Cambodian territory, it's possible that he was angling to bargain with them. For his part, Sihanouk announced his intention to come home, but chose an indirect route, landing first in Moscow and then in Peking—where he stopped.

What followed over the next four months was first a civil war, messy, sanguinary, and cruel, in which internal divisions between ethnic

Cambodians and Vietnamese were exploited and made worse by outsiders—the North Vietnamese and Viet Cong, Norodom Sihanouk making trouble from Peking, the army of South Vietnam, and the United States through its armed forces and the CIA. Beech was viscerally affected by what he saw. "If you attend enough wars—and this is my fourth," he wrote later, "—you develop a kind of immunity to death and destruction. Otherwise you would go out of your mind. But my immunity failed me in Cambodia." It was a rare admission for a man who had witnessed more than his share of battlefield butchery. He was more saddened by it than anything he had experienced before.

At first, however, it was war as usual. Beech was on the Vietnamese side of the border the day after the coup, his way barred by Cambodian border guards, as "huge columns of smoke—apparently from American strikes—rose in the distance." At this stage only ARVN, not American, troops set foot across the border. The CIA, however, was charged with supplying military aid—hundreds of "man packs" of weapons—to the Cambodian army. American helicopter gunships were also deployed.

A week later Beech was in Cambodia, on a tourist visa again, in time to get a sense of the violence that Lon Nol had unleashed. Anti-government riots, Beech reported, were breaking out "like measles" across the country. From Kampong Cham, he wrote:

> This lovely little town on the bank of the Mekong River was tense but quiet Saturday after a bloody clash between Cambodian Army troops and peasant supporters of ousted Prince Norodom Sihanouk. Province Chief Tian Kim Chieng said 27 civilians were killed and 62 wounded Friday when the Army opened fire after the enraged peasants murdered two national assemblymen and sacked three public buildings.

Sihanouk, long regarded as a god-king by much of the rural population, could be heard on nightly broadcasts from Peking urging his peasant supporters to revolt against the new regime. They took up the cause with enthusiasm. Armed often with scythes and machetes, sometimes with Chinese-made AK-47s, they attacked the institutions associated with the usurpers, which meant, in this instance, two officials who had come to explain the change. "The peasants," the province chief told reporters regretfully, "do not have a 'clear understanding' of why Sihanouk was ousted." He blamed Communist agitators for the unrest and claimed he had three in custody but was unable to produce them when asked.

Beech moved around a good deal as he tried to get a handle on what was happening. To reach one trouble spot, Kampong Trabek, twenty miles from the South Vietnamese border, he and three other reporters first crossed the Mekong by boat and then traveled the rest of the way by motorcycle. Their wanderings were not without incident.

> At least half a dozen times in three days foreign newsmen, including me, have faced the prospect of being hacked to death by angry peasants armed with knives, machetes and scythes. I am convinced these people are not kidding. They are in no mood for explanations or arguments. Four correspondents, including me, were turned back by angry crowds yesterday 40 miles south of the capital on the road to Takeo. The crowd carried large pictures of Sihanouk and brandished a variety of weapons. . . . It was the third demonstration in that same area during the day. Several people were reported killed.

The Lon Nol government would have liked reporters to believe that they were fighting the Communists rather than their own people. A government source claimed at one point that three columns of NVA troops were marching on the capital. The marchers were Sihanouk supporters. The fight with Communists, however, would begin soon enough. Beech was in Chiphou in early April when he described an upsurge in NVA activity:

Figure 10. Beech with ARVN soldiers at the time of the Cambodia incursion, 1970. Courtesy of Barnaby Beech.

Casually, almost contemptuously, as if swatting a troublesome fly, the Vietnamese Communists have served notice on the Cambodian government to keep hands off their border sanctuary.

> It is clear that the military situation in Cambodia's border provinces with South Vietnam has deteriorated sharply during the last few days. Communist soldiers . . . came into this pleasant little district capital, which sits astride Route 1, and shot it up four nights ago. . . . Their objective apparently is limited to clearing the border area of trespassers, including newsmen, to preserve intact their Cambodian sanctuary. However, they have the capability to do a great deal more.

While Sihanouk was pushing Cambodian peasants to take on the upstart government of Lon Nol, Lon Nol was pushing Cambodians to see the Vietnamese—all of them, not just the NVA and Viet Cong—as their enemy. There were an estimated four to six hundred thousand Vietnamese living in Cambodia, not all of them sympathetic to the Communists. Some had been brought into the country by the French, who valued their enterprise and administrative skills. All, however, were resented by the Cambodians. When state-controlled media was used to vilify a population many viewed as alien, the Cambodians' resentment of the Vietnamese turned to hatred and their hatred led to bloodshed.

"Nearly 100 Vietnamese civilians, including women and children, apparently have been massacred by Cambodian soldiers during a Viet Cong attack on this crossroads town six miles from the South Vietnamese border," Beech wrote from Prasaut on April 11. This, at least, was the explanation given by a Cambodian officer, who said that the civilians had been caught in a cross fire with the Communists.

> But there were few if any bullet holes in the buildings outside of which the bodies lay. Nor was there any other evidence, except for three or four bodies presumed to be Viet Cong, that a battle had taken place where the bodies were found.

Beech spoke to some of the remaining Vietnamese:

> Half a dozen survivors told the same story through Vietnamese-speaking interpreters. They said that about 300 of them had been rounded up and taken to the co-op compound for "security reasons." When the Viet Cong attacked at about 10 p.m., they said, the Cambodian troops opened fire on them. . . . "Please don't ask us any more questions," pleaded an old Vietnamese woman. "If you do they will kill the rest of us when you are gone."

A few days later, Beech found evidence at Neak Loeung that the massacres were widespread:

> The slaughter of Vietnamese civilians continues as smiling, happy Cambodian peasants wind up their lunar New Year's celebration. At this Mekong River ferry crossing, 36 miles southeast of Phnom Penh, I counted more than 50 swollen bodies floating toward the sea. After that I got tired of counting. "Those are Vietnamese," said a khaki-clad Cambodian ticket-collector, and spat over the side into the muddy Mekong. The ferry got under way and plowed through the bodies. Cambodian passengers watched impassively or talked in low voices. A French Catholic priest a couple of miles down the river told us he counted 40 bodies yesterday. He said they were headless. Those we saw today had their heads.

Other reporters counted many more waterborne corpses. An AP report at about the same time said that four hundred bodies floated past Neak Loeung in a single morning. Later estimates suggested the total tossed into Mekong's slow current may have been a thousand or more. No one knew for sure. "But what leaves the stomachs of Western correspondents a little queasy," Beech wrote on April 18, is the "casual indifference of the Cambodian soldiers as they go about the killing." He was in Takeo, a provincial capital south of Phnom Penh, the site of another massacre.

> This time the scene was an outdoor theater in a high school yard less than a quarter mile from the province chief's mansion. About 75 survivors, including two dozen wounded, huddled in clusters on the concrete floor. The floor was slippery with blood, and you had to be careful to avoid skidding. . . . Flies buzzed and settled on the wounded, some of whom bore wounds that could have been inflicted only by bayonets. Nothing, absolutely nothing, was being done for the wounded.

While elements of the Cambodian army were busy killing Vietnamese civilians, North Vietnamese troops were moving out from their border sanctuaries into the interior of the country. On April 21 Beech reported that they were blocking roads and blowing up bridges that connected Phnom Penh to its port, Sihanoukville, and to South Vietnam. They were meeting with little resistance. Beech was with a group of correspondents looking for a way to Khbal Pou when they encountered fifteen wounded Cambodian soldiers. They sent three of the most severely wounded back to the hospital at Takeo in their car. Farther on, they came to a ruined bridge:

> Half a dozen trucks and buses were drawn up at each end of the 100-foot bridge, part of a causeway spanning a shallow, muddy lake and the only road into Khbal Pou. The soldiers didn't seem to know what to do next. . . . We watched while two Cambodian Air Force MIG-15s and two U.S. T-28s strafed Khbal Pou. The whole scene—the ruined bridge, the wounded soldiers, the sight and sound of the strafing planes—was a wrenching reminder that the war in Vietnam has now come to Cambodia.

If some Cambodian soldiers seemed unsure what to do, others knew where their preference lay. Beech spoke to Capt. Saut Nim at his command post near Prasaut. The town had been taken over by the enemy. "So long as they don't bother me, I'm not bothering them," he told Beech. "My mission is to hold, not attack." The captain's complacency struck Beech as ill-advised: the other side had seized the initiative. "During the last few weeks," he reported, the Communists "have quietly, but effectively, sometimes without firing a shot, vastly expanded their Cambodian real estate holdings. Often the mere presence of Viet Cong troops was enough to cause Cambodian police, soldiers and civil servants to abandon their posts." The capital was in danger of being overrun.

On the 29th, Beech wrote a piece from Bangkok in which he speculated on the likelihood of Sihanouk returning to Phnom Penh a conquering hero at the head of a North Vietnamese army. It would be a strange irony, he wrote, for the prince, who had for so long struggled to keep Communists from taking over his country, to rely on them to restore him to power. But this was not to be. On the 30th, President Nixon announced in a television address his decision to send American troops into Cambodia. He was aware that the move would be seen by many as provocative. To head off his critics, he promised that the operation would be time-limited and that American soldiers would go no more than twenty miles into Cambodian territory. He called it an "incursion" rather than an invasion. The war's opponents were not mollified. Protests, some violent, erupted at universities across the United States.

Beech was at a Buddhist temple-turned-command post on Route 7 in early May when he interviewed a young Cambodian captain. "'Before the Americans came to our rescue,' he said without conscious irony, 'we lived in quiet and peace. But now that you're here all our people know is terror and bloodshed.'" The captain told what he knew of what was happening a few miles to the east:

> "Everybody who can flee is fleeing," he said. According to the captain . . . there were four battalions of Cambodian troops deployed on the road ahead. But it seemed clear they were in no hurry to go anyplace. And it seemed equally clear that there was little or no coordination between the Cambodians and the attacking Americans. There was not even radio contact between the two.

It was an American show put on, not for the benefit of Cambodians, but for Americans, and to demonstrate toughness in their negotiations with Peking and Hanoi. Beech left it for others to track the fighting. For the most part he watched from the sidelines, either from Bangkok or Saigon. He was unimpressed by the way it was conducted, calling it a "furtive, un-American war," with no obvious end in sight. He acknowledged that it had hurt the Communists badly—but "it seems to have hurt the United States more." He was aware of the protests at home.

When, at the end of June, American forces were pulled back, Beech wrote a long meditation on the damage the invasion had done and the sadness it had given rise to. The "melancholy lingers on," he said. "It is the unwritten story of what happened in Cambodia and how it affected all of us who were there." For more than a month, he said, he had been trying to figure out why this particular war affected him and others—correspondents, soldiers, and diplomats—so deeply.

> Among people I know the feeling was universal. And that includes American GIs who, upon crossing the border into Cambodia looked around in wonderment and said: "What a beautiful country. This must be what Vietnam looked like before we cratered it." That omission has since been corrected by U.S. air strikes. Give the Air Force time, and Cambodia may come to resemble a moonscape like Vietnam.

He added that this was unfair to the air force, which was only doing its job. But he still wondered what it was that made Cambodia seem different. In the end he concluded that it was the devastation of a beautiful country, one that reporters too had sometimes used as a refuge, one that had somehow remained intact despite what was going on next door. Now it was lost.

> I think all of us were aware that while Vietnam would survive the war, Cambodia probably would not, that this last remnant of an empire that once stretched from the South China Sea to the Bay of Bengal was doomed. And this brought to mind some words that Sihanouk spoke one sultry day long, long ago. Turning to a group of journalists he said gloomily: "We are all going to die." When the newspapermen protested that nobody wanted to see Cambodia die, Sihanouk said, almost angrily: "But you don't understand. We must die."

The Laotian incursion the following spring was meant to serve as proof yet again of American resolve and of South Vietnam's readiness to take over the fighting. Beech was in Khe Sanh in early February, reporting on the buildup of forces and speculating on what would come next. There was some deliberate misdirection by the military, which allowed or encouraged correspondents to infer that the troop movements were a ruse to fool the Communists. And then the invasion began, twenty thousand South Vietnamese soldiers, some of their best, backed by American air power, aimed at cutting off or at least severely disrupting traffic on the Ho Chi Minh Trail. The absence of American troops on the ground was a point emphasized in official communiqués, but Beech, talking to the helicopter pilots who were ferrying ARVN units into battle, told a different story. "'It's as though they were saying you can't be shot unless you're on the ground,' a 21-year-old helicopter pilot said, after counting 13 bullet holes in his aircraft." The air crews were taking heavy losses. "The flak there is so thick you can walk on it," observed another.

Later in the month, Beech was in Ban Son, Laos, where he reported on the desperation of the Meo tribesmen who, with CIA and special forces backing, had for years been harassing the Communists. The Meo now were being battered by the NVA, squeezed into a smaller and smaller area, in what officials interpreted as a calculated response to the allied incursion. "After a decade of bitter fighting and nearly 10,000 dead," Beech wrote, "the Meo are discouraged and dispirited." "We are running out of places to hide," a Meo chief told him, adding, "We are also running out of sons." There were roughly two hundred thousand refugees in Ban Son, a village in a valley sixty miles from the capital, Vientiane, half of them Meos. Their number was growing.

It was by no means clear that the Laotian adventure was achieving its aims, and Beech did not rush to declare victory. There were obvious setbacks and some unpleasant surprises. At Hill 31 in late February, for example, nearly one hundred paratroopers were killed or captured when their command post was overrun by Communist infantry spearheaded by tanks. The Vietnamese soldiers weren't prepared for the tanks. "Our intelligence was lousy," said one officer. Their anti-tank rockets were useless against the enemy's armor, but then they hadn't expected to use them. The Americans were getting beaten up too. In early March, Beech reported that fifty-two helicopters had been destroyed, thirty-three Americans killed, twenty-nine reported missing in action. The pilots believed that most of those listed as missing were dead. He dutifully repeated official claims: for example, that seven thousand enemy soldiers had been killed or captured, and that six enemy regiments had lost one or more battalions. But he was skeptical, or at least careful, when he wrote that the most telling fact of all "—if it is a fact—" was the claim that troop and supply movements on the trail were down by 80 percent. Official credibility had worn thin.

Beech needed a change. Back in '68, after the breakup with Linda, he had embarked on an on-again, off-again affair with another *Daily News* correspondent, Georgie Anne "Gee Gee" Geyer. She contrived to join him for a time in Saigon, but it didn't last. Their relationship was renewed in August 1970 when he took a stretch of leave back in the States. Together he and Geyer wrote a series of articles exploring territory unfamiliar to the grizzled war correspondent. Its subject: the baneful, radicalizing influence of Fidel Castro's Cuba on disaffected American youth. The tenor of the series accurately reflected the rancor that infected American politics at the time. "Buildings are blown up. Policemen are killed. Violence from America's revolutionary left continues to grow," wrote the editors introducing the series. "To gain insight into the young radicals and the origins of their violent philosophy, veteran reporters [Geyer and Beech] were assigned to dig into the story. Their findings: Cuba has become a revolutionary factory for the processing and refining of American radicals."

The eleven long articles published over the month that followed were as alarming as the advance publicity said they would be. Geyer later claimed that she was more moderate in her politics than Beech was, and it may be that being back in the States, where so much was in turmoil, threw Beech off-balance. But for whatever reason, the series lacked his wry wit and dispassionate outlook. In December he was back in Saigon dealing with material he was more comfortable with. The war, he wrote—revisiting a familiar theme—was close to being won, if only American troops weren't withdrawn in too much of a hurry.

He visited the States in April '71 in part to promote the book he had begun four years earlier. In *Not Without the Americans* he mounted a stout defense of America's Far East policies. He argued that America's power, diplomacy, and example had succeeded much more than credited in transforming the region into a Western-facing, democracy-friendly (if not democratic) bulwark against Soviet and

Chinese communism. The writing, as always, was entertaining, and the thesis was taken seriously by reviewers. "Casual, sometimes cynical, but never dull," wrote East Asia specialist Maj. Harry Summers Jr. John P. Roche, who had served in the Johnson administration, dismissed the charge of cynicism: "To be without illusions is not to be disillusioned; to be skeptical and sardonic is not to be cynical and despairing. Beech has what David Riesman once called 'the nerve of failure,' the willingness to go forward in the world without any IOUs on the cosmos." This was a generous assessment and an accurate reflection on the book: Beech's take on the bailiwick he'd patrolled for so long was cool and considered. He mostly avoided writing about Vietnam, but it was in the background, and it nagged at him. Curiously—at a time when American troops were still fighting and dying there—he wrote about it in a sort of conditional past tense. "We had not won the war," he wrote,

> but neither had we lost it. The principal losers were the Vietnamese, both North and South. But those who said nobody was going to win it were wrong. Hanoi was either going to get South Vietnam, or it was not. My own conviction was that it would not.
>
> It was fashionable to say that we had failed in Vietnam, and we had. But it was a failure of ignorance and stupidity rather than American power. There was nothing wrong with our commitment in Vietnam; what was wrong was the way we executed that commitment. We tried too long to fight World War II and Korea all over again. By the time we learned how to fight the war nobody cared.

The substance of these two passages, printed cheek by jowl, reflects Beech's conflicting sentiments: he professed faith that America would succeed while admitting that it had failed. The ambivalence with which he had been afflicted from the beginning of America's war in Vietnam never left him.

He would continue to write sometimes that America was winning the war, and he never abandoned the conviction that it should have won. But he had come to understand that its loss was possible and perhaps even likely. There was no single event, no epiphany, but there was a change of mood. Tet, of course, shook all observers. Beech was prepared at first to believe that Hanoi had made a mistake. The Communists had failed to ignite an uprising and took countless casualties in making the attempt. He bought briefly into Westmoreland's assurance that America's moment of triumph had at last arrived and the Communists would be crushed. But that's not what happened. Instead, Johnson announced his abdication and Westy went home in unacknowledged disgrace.

And then there was Ray Murray's lament. Murray, beside whom Beech had fought on Tarawa, with whom he had marched into Seoul and shed tears at the Chosin Reservoir, was for the first time in his life doubtful and despairing of the American project, asking plaintively, "what kind of country are we going to leave behind?" And then there was the stupid incident on a Saigon square, the senseless shooting of a man in a white shirt that reminded him of a time in Tennessee when he shot a rabbit. And then the bad faith and double-dealing that marked the treatment of Thieu and Ky and the Vietnamese people as Johnson tried one last time to bring about peace.

Beech had, he said, built an immunity to death and destruction. It had been tested by the discovery of the massacres at Hue and My Lai. There had been massacres in Korea too, but nothing like what Calley did. He was aware that American morale was deteriorating. His visits home were not encouraging. He was baffled by the long-haired hippies and dirty-necked peaceniks. And there was something about the civil war in Cambodia, the murder of innocents in a realm that had remained mostly untouched while Vietnam was cratered. He was deeply affected by the thought that the last vestige of this ancient empire was about to be annihilated.

There was no single moment when his mind was changed, but the "nerve of failure" with which the reviewer had credited him faltered. His immunity broke.

He had thought about leaving. The interlude he spent with Gee Gee Geyer in Los Angeles was, if the articles they wrote together are any indication, more unsettling than not. He chose at the time not to stay. After covering the Laotian incursion and then his promotional tour to the States in spring '71, he returned to Saigon to carry on doing the work he'd been doing for a quarter century. He pursued a story in late summer and fall that showed the Nixon administration was just as capable as Johnson's of bad faith interference in Vietnamese affairs. Duong Van Minh, a perennial aspirant to political office—he had briefly succeeded Diem after the 1963 coup—presented Ambassador Ellsworth Bunker with documents showing that Thieu had been giving instructions to province chiefs on how to rig the upcoming presidential election. Thieu had the votes sewn up. Minh and Ky, both of whom had planned to campaign against Thieu, announced their decision to withdraw. They were leaned on by Bunker and the CIA to stand anyway. Thieu got involved, first by using the courts to disqualify them, and then, under pressure himself, rescinding the order. And Bunker reportedly offered bribes to Minh and Ky to persuade them to stand despite the certainty of losing, "in order to make the election look more democratic." In the end, Thieu's name stood alone on the ballot. He took 91.5 percent of the vote in a result that, as Beech reported, "would have done credit to his communist neighbors."

Beech had had enough. On October 30, 1971, he announced that he was relocating from Saigon to Hong Kong. This time it stuck.

The dispatch he wrote on parting, more than a thousand words long, was reminiscent of the Sky Room piece he wrote in the aftermath of Iwo Jima: naked in its eloquence and not entirely coherent. A sympathetic (and maybe oversensitive) reader might detect symptoms of post-traumatic stress in his alternating attempts to make light of the preceding decade and his frankly grim observations. He had often been asked, he wrote, why he had stayed so long. One reason, he supposed, was a desire to see how the war turned out. Now he wasn't sure that he would live that long. He quoted others on the war, including an Australian who said, "I don't want to talk to anybody about Vietnam who doesn't know what I'm going to say before I say it," and Herman Kahn of the RAND Corporation, who countered the suggestion that Hanoi had been beaten in the aftermath of Tet, saying, "Any military operation that results in the abdication of the president of the United States can hardly be called a failure." Beech still badly wanted to believe that American arms had triumphed. After Tet, he said, the enemy no longer had the initiative—"we were the hunters." Overwhelming American firepower had wrought its terrible effect: "We slaughtered them by the tens of thousands." He acknowledged, however, that Americans had never understood their enemy:

> So we fought the only kind of war we knew how, which was largely World War II all over again. We stomped him to death. We ran him over in our bulldozers. We plowed him under. We rained destruction on him from our invisible high-altitude B-52s. We mowed him down with artillery and gunships. There was nothing noble about this, but it was effective.

Beech was at his most provocative when he referred to Maj. Gen. Nguyen Ngoc Loan, the ARVN officer notoriously caught on camera in the act of shooting a Viet Cong prisoner at the height of Tet, who was dismissive of the American mission to spread democracy. "We know Vietnam isn't ready for democracy," he once told Beech. "But we have to talk about it to keep you interested." Loan had been unfairly vilified. "He's a nice guy," Beech said, "when you get to know him."

As for lessons from the war, Beech wrote, the most obvious was not to get involved in another one: "If that sounds cynical or smart-alecky, I don't mean it that way. But I would like to think that Vietnam has taught us a lesson in humility. Never has as small and primitive a country turned such a powerful nation on its ear." The achievement demanded respect. "In closing I would like to offer this salute to that skinny little Viet Cong somewhere out there in the jungle shivering in the monsoon rains. He is one hell of a fighting man."

GI GO BYE-BYE

Beech was still the Chicago paper's East Asia correspondent, responsible for news from countries besides Vietnam. Soon after moving to Hong Kong he set out to make up for his neglect of the others. In November he was in Thailand, in December in East Pakistan (Bangladesh) and India. In the first two months of 1972 he was writing about the Nixon-initiated rapprochement with China from Hong Kong before traveling again, this time to Taiwan and then Korea. In May he was in the States: in Chicago, from which vantage point he described Nixon's blockade of North Vietnam as the "act of an angry and desperate man"; and then in Washington, DC, and St. Petersburg. In June, in Hawaii, he interviewed Gen. Creighton Abrams and compared his record with Westmoreland's: Westy suffered in the comparison. In July, in Tokyo, he had a positive take on Nixon's diplomacy respecting China and Russia. And then, because of widespread concern about the ubiquity of addiction in the armed forces, he investigated the drug trade in northern Thailand and Laos. In the fall he touched down in the Philippines, before returning, finally, to Saigon amid rumors—triggered by an optimistic statement by Henry Kissinger—that a peace deal was about to be signed.

The rumors were premature by a couple of months. The Saigon government remained an obstacle, as Thieu sought—and obtained—promises from Kissinger and Nixon of continued support in the event that Hanoi violated the ceasefire. Those promises would be broken, but Nixon, determined to demonstrate strength of purpose, ordered in mid-December a renewed aerial assault on the North that even Beech was moved to describe as "the most savage bombing in the history of the world," adding that "you don't have to be a Communist or a pacifist to sympathize with a small country that is being bombed to pieces by the most powerful nation on earth, especially when the justification for that bombing is, to put it mildly, unclear." The assault was suspended again at the end of December, but little reason for either its start or ending was forthcoming from the White House. Beech speculated that Moscow and Peking, both with an interest in furthering rapprochement with the West, were leaning on Hanoi to make concessions. In the event, a ceasefire agreement was signed in Paris in January 1973.

The agreement brought a sense of relief to many Americans, and jubilation to some. Beech, however, was grim. "It was a most unhappy war," he wrote in another long piece that summed up his reflections on the conflict more coherently than the one he had written the year before. "It was a war without heroes, only Medal of Honor winners; without humor, except of the blackest kind. The American GI's sardonic 'Sorry about that,' was both its slogan and its epitaph." He went on: "It left no man who touched it unscarred. It corrupted and degraded both Americans and Vietnamese. It made liars out of honest men. It made hawks into doves and doves into hawks, until finally there was nobody left except people who wanted out." He picked up on a thought that had occurred to him long ago, when the French were departing and the Americans were taking their place, that America's antagonists were the true revolutionaries and America had backed the wrong side. A sad observation to make after ten years of war. Now Kissinger had announced that peace was at hand: "But peace for whom? The Americans, yes. But it's the Vietnamese who live here. 'When will there be peace?' I asked a Vietnamese over coffee at Givral's. 'When all Vietnamese are dead,' he said." The reply was flippant, but Beech had no better answer. He had given up looking for meaning. "Let the historians tidy it up," he wrote.

If the Americans were relieved to be going, Beech found the mood among some Vietnamese to be bitter. "GI go bye-bye," said a taxi driver, "GI fini." His gleeful smile showed off a gold tooth that GIs likely helped pay for. "We Vietnamese got along before you Americans came," said a prostitute. "We still get along." "The vast sea of sweating, green-clad Americans that washed over this tiny country in the '60s has receded," Beech wrote, "leaving in its wake abandoned air strips, empty billets, broken down air conditioners and refrigerators, forlorn bar girls smiling bravely from darkened doorways, [and] hundreds if not thousands of mixed-blood children." The return of American prisoners of war, mainly pilots, should have been a more cheerful story, but the accounts they shared with Beech at Clark Air Base in the Philippines struck a sour note too. Many had suffered abuse, some had been tortured, and all had been kept in poor conditions. Beech provoked a minor controversy by bringing up the allegations of torture in a report published before all returning fliers had landed, leading some to complain that the prisoners who remained would be held back or suffer worse abuse. To Beech, given what he remembered from Korea, the notion that Communists might have employed torture was unremarkable. The controversy subsided. The charges were true.

At the end of July, Keyes Beech married for the third time in Tokyo. Yuko Horiguchi, a graduate of Bryn Mawr, had been editor of a Tokyo newspaper and Beech's sometime translator. They would have one child together, a girl, whom they named Hannah Keyes.

For most of the rest of the year, Beech watched from a distance as the North built up its conventional forces and expanded its infrastructure in the South—including all-season roads and oil pipelines—to support them. Neither side had paid more than lip service to the ceasefire agreement. The year since it had been signed had been as bloody as any that preceded it: Beech reported that a total on both sides of about fifty thousand had died in the interim. He did not bother to underline the irony when he observed that Khe Sanh, by December 1973, had become a Communist supply depot and air base "so thick with anti-aircraft weapons . . . that South Vietnamese warplanes prudently avoid the place."

The following spring the South Vietnamese army under President Thieu's direction succeeded in retaking some territory from the enemy, but in the process was stretched dangerously thin. Beech mostly left it to others to report on this and on Hanoi's methodical response: their continued buildup of forces, the probes and engagements with which they tested the South's defenses, and the moves they made to push the Army of South Vietnam from successive defensive positions until, by the end of the year, they were within striking distance of Saigon. Thieu's cause was not helped by President Nixon's Watergate-enforced resignation in August and the subsequent decision by Congress to reduce military aid to the country. Beech, noting this development, reported that the former ranking military officer in South Vietnam, Maj. Gen. John E. Murray, was roundly rebuked by Pentagon spokesmen for accusing the government of "sacrificing blood for lack of ammunition." An anonymous officer was more plainspoken, calling the authors of the cuts "fiscal whores."

"So much for peace with honor," Beech wrote in April 1975 when it was clear that the end was imminent. The last few weeks had been ugly. When Danang was abandoned, Vietnamese soldiers had been seen trampling women and children to be first on the last plane out. But then, the spectacle of Congress going on Easter break after refusing to authorize additional aid—despite pleas from Kissinger and Nixon's successor as president, Gerald Ford—wasn't pretty either. "There ought to have been a less shabby end to perhaps the most inglorious chapter in American history," Beech wrote, than to see congressional representatives bickering over inconsequential sums of money as their ally was destroyed.

A few days later, having returned to Saigon, he described the unraveling of Thieu's defensive strategy. Panic had set in, Beech said, when the Communists seized Ban Me Thuot in the Central Highlands. The panic got worse when Thieu first ordered his forces withdrawn from the region and then sent them back in with orders that the town be retaken. Thieu's overmatched 23rd Division was battered from all sides. It no longer possessed the air mobility to manage an airborne extraction. The ravaged division disintegrated. "Thus began the exodus to the sea," Beech wrote, "a movement of Biblical proportions over an unused road that turned into a nightmare column of 3,000 vehicles and 100,000 refugees and soldiers who stripped off their uniforms and fought civilians for food and water." The Communists attacked and harassed them to such brutal effect that just twenty of eighty-six tanks that started the journey reached the coast. Meanwhile, in South Vietnam's northernmost military region, Thieu's vacillation—first ordering the abandonment and then the defense of Hue, where two ARVN divisions faced three of the enemy's—led to a similarly catastrophic collapse. "It was then that the whole show came apart," an American official told Beech. The result of the conflicting orders was chaos.

Thousands, perhaps tens of thousands, of Vietnamese trapped in the North boarded boats, junks, and barges to escape the Communist advance. Not all survived. On April 12 Beech reported from Vung Tau, a resort town south of Saigon, where some of the survivors washed up:

> Some obviously would have been better off if they had stayed behind. A motorized barge arrived two days ago with 49 dead, many of them children. They died of thirst, starvation and exposure to the blazing sun. Estimates on the number joining the seaborne exodus from Da Nang, Qui Nhon and other coastal

> cities during the last 10 days vary wildly from 50,000 to 300,000. The truth is nobody knows. But a U.S. aid official guessed that 50,000 is close to the actual figure. The Saigon government insists on a total of one million refugees. U.S. officials estimate 400,000.

Beech worked hard in the three weeks that would end with the comic-opera travesty that was the evacuation of the US Embassy in Saigon. He took a few final opportunities to cover the fighting, going out with Denis Warner to find the enemy. They found him when they were shot at and nearly rocketed near Bien Hoa before beating a tactical retreat. Beech "liked to be where the action was," observed Warner later. "North Vietnamese forces were tightening their noose around the capital," Beech reported. His CIA and military sources told him that the final assault was likely to come within days. "Things are moving so fast we're having a hard time keeping track and the worst is yet to come." Three days later, Thieu announced his resignation. Tran Van Huong, an old and sick man, half-blind and given to memory lapses, briefly took over before Gen. Duong Van (Big) Minh—the same Big Minh who had been in on the coup to overthrow Diem more than a decade before—showed courage by stepping in, president at last.

Away from the front Beech took on the task of covering the chaos that was enveloping the capital. Ambassador Graham Martin, an aging, frail, and prickly diplomat, delayed initiating the evacuation of American citizens and those Vietnamese who had supported them. Martin's hesitancy had to do with bureaucratic inertia: he was reluctant to okay sending home more than a hundred IBM employees because they were responsible for the payroll. He also suffered from the misguided belief—delusion really—that more time could be purchased either through continued fighting or adroit negotiation. Beech had no such illusions: he described what was happening as precisely as a scientist might, laying out in plain prose the evidence of Vietnam's fatal corruption and America's humiliation.

"The final American bugout from Vietnam is not a pretty thing to see," he wrote on April 23. A long, ragged line had formed at the processing center at Tan Son Nhut Air Base. There were Americans, of course, sweating and clutching their passports, but also their Vietnamese wives, mistresses, and children.

> A gold-toothed bar girl tapped an elderly, white-haired American on the shoulder and said accusingly: "You take me. You promise to take me." "I told you for the last time I can't take you," he said embarrassed and trying to keep his voice low. "You goddam sunbitch," she shrieked, snatching off a jade bracelet and hurling it at him.

An embassy spokesman told Beech that only about fifteen hundred Americans had been evacuated so far, a figure that included missionaries, businessmen, doctors, reporters, and close to five hundred State Department personnel. The official said they had reckoned on processing a total of about six thousand Americans, but then another sixteen hundred had turned up. Some were deserters, but there was no way to sort them out. Stateside officials would have to deal with them. In apparent confirmation that delinquents were among the would-be evacuees, a number of men in the line declined to give Beech their names. "Not interested," they said.

There were no customers at the Post Exchange, although it was still fully stocked with everything from women's wear to air conditioners. The Stop'n'Shop next door was also deserted. Beech asked the pretty Vietnamese clerk when they planned to close. "No idea," she said, and then added mischievously, "Say, papa-san, how about you take me to America?"

Two days later the number who sought a way out was mounting. There was a near-riot at the airport as thousands of Vietnamese tried to force their way into the processing center. There was a strange incident the following morning when two planes with

South Vietnamese Air Force markings dropped four five-hundred-pound bombs on the base. The situation was under control, but barely. The air force had run twenty-eight flights out the previous day. An estimated five thousand men, women, and children were waiting for the next ones. "If the airlift continues long enough," a Vietnamese newsman told Beech, "you Americans will clean out every bar in town."

Beech was standing by the window in his room at the Caravelle Hotel on April 29 watching smoke rise from a nearby square. He had been taking calls all morning from Vietnamese friends asking when they would be able to board a plane to the States. He told them the truth, that they probably wouldn't. When the phone rang again, it was his *Daily News* colleague Robert Tamarkin, saying that the embassy had ordered a full-scale evacuation of correspondents. Buses would pick them up at a prearranged collection point to take them to the airport. Beech had already decided to leave. It wasn't that he was afraid he'd be shot if he stayed: he doubted that there would be shooting, at least not right away. He wanted to make sure he got his story out, but there was another reason: he had no desire to see the Communists take power. He picked up his typewriter and made for the door.

His account of his departure from Saigon would become something of a classic, the one article of his that the editors saw fit to include in the Library of America two-volume anthology of Vietnam war reportage. It's some 1,200 words long, and unsparing.

Beech made his way to the collection point as instructed. When three buses pulled up, the crowd of correspondents and their Vietnamese staffers surged forward in an unseemly mass. Beech and some others stood back from the rush, choosing dignity amid panic, a decision they would have reason to regret and would soon abandon. Those three buses made it to Tan Son Nhut in time for their passengers to catch one of the last planes out of the city. But when Beech boarded a fourth bus, news reached them that the security situation had deteriorated and the base was closed. Their driver headed there anyway, there being no other plan, and the bus was turned away by guards not just once but also on a second approach. The sound of explosions and machine-gun fire vividly underlined the nearness of the enemy. It was 2:00 p.m., and it was apparent that whatever plans had been laid for the evacuation were kaput.

"Nobody on the bus will ever forget the next few hours," Beech wrote, "while our security escorts tried to figure out what to do with us. We were a busload of fools piloted by a man who had to wire the ignition when it stalled because the Vietnamese driver had run away with the keys." Other buses joined theirs, apparently in the vain belief that their driver knew where he was going. Together the caravan careened through the streets, "knocking over sidewalk vendors, sideswiping passing vehicles and sending Vietnamese scattering like leaves in the wind." Whenever they stopped, Vietnamese would "beat on the doors and windows pleading to be let inside." Every time they opened the door, they had to beat people back. Eventually they stopped at the port, a tough part of town, where the crowds were even uglier than elsewhere. Police had to fire their guns into the air to clear a passage for the bus to reach the dock. Beech spoke to an embassy official he knew who had no answer to his question as to what was to be done. "There are ships," said the official, gesturing vaguely to some Vietnamese vessels alongside the dock. "I looked around at the gathering crowd," Beech wrote. "Small boys were snatching typewriters and bags of film. I didn't know how or whether I was going to get out of Saigon, but I damned well knew I wasn't going to stay here."

The other correspondents who had joined him on the dock felt the same way. They had to fight their way back onto the bus:

> Ed Bradley of CBS, a giant of a man, was pushing, kicking, shoving, his face sad. I found myself pushing the middle-aged Vietnamese woman who had been sitting beside me on the bus

> and who had asked me to look after her because she worked for the Americans and the Viet Cong would cut her throat. That's what they all said, and maybe they were right. . . . But she fought her way back to my side. "Why did you push me?" she asked. I had no answer.

Their driver decided that their next best bet was to drive to the embassy. When they got there, Beech's seatmate decided she'd had enough.

> "I have worked for the United States government for 10 years, [she told him] but you do not trust me and I don't trust you. Even if we do get to Tan Son Nhut, they wouldn't let me on the plane." She was right of course. "I am going home and poison myself," she said. I didn't say anything because there was nothing to say.

There was no way the bus could enter the embassy grounds. All gates were closed. And all around it was a seething, angry, agitated mob. Beech again stepped down from the bus, found a phone, and was able to reach an embassy friend who, after the situation was described to him, left the line briefly and then returned with instructions: they were to make their way to a nearby police post where they'd be told what to do. "'They know you're coming,' said the friend. 'They will help you over the wall.'" Beech did as told and led his flock across the street, past police barricades to the station, and identified himself to the officers. They had never heard of him or his colleagues and wanted nothing to do with them, a point they emphasized by firing their guns over the correspondents' heads.

The last scene in this daylong drama, the riot at the foot of the embassy wall, where Beech at last found safety by pushing his way past so many to whom safety would be denied, was as wretched as memory has it.

> Once we moved into that seething mass we ceased to be correspondents. We were only men fighting for our lives, scratching, clawing, pushing ever closer to that wall. We were like animals. Now I thought, I know what it's like to be a Vietnamese. I am one of them. But if I could get over that wall I would be an American again. My samsonite attache case accidentally struck a boy in its mother's arms and its father beat at me with his fists. I tried to apologize as he kept beating me while his wife pleaded with me to take the baby. Somebody grabbed my sleeve and wouldn't let go. I turned my head and looked into the face of a Vietnamese youth. "You adopt me and take me with you and I'll help you," he screamed. "If you don't you don't go." I said I'd adopt him. I'd have said anything. Could this be happening to me? Suddenly my arm was free and I edged closer to the wall. There were a pair of Marines on the wall. They were trying to help me up. They were trying to help us up and kick the Vietnamese down. One of them looked down at me. "Help me," I pleaded. "Please help me." The Marine helped me. He reached down with his long muscular arm and pulled me up as if I were a helpless child. I lay on the tin roof gasping for breath like a landed fish, then dropped to the ground. God bless the Marines.

At 6:30 p.m., more than seven hours after leaving the Caravelle Hotel, Beech climbed into a helicopter on the US Embassy roof and was flown to the aircraft carrier *Hancock*. A little later, when he and others were shifted to the carrier *Blue Ridge*, he had a brief encounter with Ambassador Graham Martin. Martin, who had delayed the start of the evacuation for so long, took a seat in a cabin aboard the ship where the correspondents were gathered. Beech took a seat beside him. "I was on your side most of the time, Graham," he told the diplomat. "You know that. And the one thing I want to know from you is why the fuck I had to fight my way over that wall on Tuesday." The diplomat didn't answer.

CHAPTER 7

After the War

Beech once said that he'd seen a lot of Japanese before he went to Japan, but almost all of them were dead. This was, if anything, an understatement. Between Tarawa and Iwo Jima he saw hundreds of corpses, not just Japanese but American as well. So many that he would say later that he had acquired an immunity to death, that if he hadn't, he would have gone mad. And yet he went to wars.

He said that he was sometimes accused of being a war lover. He denied the charge, writing in *Not Without the Americans* that he abhorred violence, and adding that he couldn't be held responsible for the wars he had attended. "War," he wrote, "has been part of the Asian scene for the past two decades—as it was for decades before that—and so I have gone to wars. You may hope that they'll go out of fashion, but you can't just ignore them."

This was a bit of dodge: He chose to go to Korea when war broke out there, and to move to Saigon when the Marines went in. As he wrote himself, when recalling an incident on the road from Inchon to Seoul, he didn't have to be there. He could go where he pleased and do what he pleased:

> Well, if that was the case, what was I doing here? Did it please me to be lying here in this ditch? It did not. Then what was I here for? For money? They don't pay that kind of money. Newspapers especially don't pay that kind of money.
>
> I turned over on my back and lit a cigarette. Maybe I was here because I liked it.

He wasn't unique in liking it. Men and women before and after him have been fascinated by war. Among them, of course, are those who find a vocation in the military. But journalists too have succumbed to its allure. Beech wasn't the only one who, having covered World War II, went on to report from both Korea and Vietnam. Jim Lucas, who like Beech had been a Marine correspondent on Tarawa, later reported for Scripps-Howard from Indochina and, later still, covered the fighting in the Mekong Delta. The Australian Denis Warner, the *Los Angeles Times*'s Jack Foisie, and Homer Bigart, latterly of *The New York Times*, also reported from all three wars, though Bigart detested Vietnam and got out as soon as he could. There may have been others. But no one stayed as long or paid as close attention to them as Beech did.

We can only infer what made Beech want so badly to be, as Warner said, where the action was. When he was still writing about Korea, Beech mentioned how glad he and his companions had been to put wives, children, "refrigerators, responsibility, and respectability" behind them. He was separated from Millie at the time and would soon take up with Higgins. Romance, danger, adventure—and freedom from the routine of everyday life—lay ahead. Putting aside whether this was an admirable ambition, and the effect it had on his own life and the lives of those close to him, he acted with a determination that commanded attention, a determination that led, among other things, to a Pulitzer Prize.

That trait had been evident in the earlier war too. The general commanding the 5th Marine Division wrote Beech a citation when he returned to civilian life that took note of his conduct on Iwo. "Technical Sergeant Beech continued to expose himself to enemy fire in order to cover properly the story of his regiment's part in the operation. He refused to leave the front lines for the comparative safety of rear areas to prepare his stories for release," wrote the general, concluding that his "conduct was in keeping with the highest traditions of the United States Naval Service."

There was something about war that attracted Beech. There was especially something about the earlier wars, in the Pacific and Korea, that made a commitment to following them compelling. There was no doubt about the rightness of the cause—in the first instance fighting Japan's aggression, in the second repelling the invasion of South Korea. There was almost no domestic dissension in the first case; not much in the second (although it helped that the heaviest fighting was over relatively soon). Both wars were run competently. The names of generals who played a part in World War II's winning campaigns are famous: Patton, Bradley, Marshall, MacArthur, Eisenhower. MacArthur merits less credit for Korea than Walker and, after him, Ridgway, but for the most part America could take pride in its commanders' exceptional ability. And the presidents who presided throughout—Roosevelt, Truman, and Eisenhower—did not waver in prosecuting the wars on their watch.

There were no doubts, in other words, about the reason men were being asked to fight. There was no question that the enemy had to be defeated and that the resources to ensure victory would be provided. So when Beech went to cover these wars, he did so knowing that he and his country were as one. His experience, everything that had shaped him as a man and as a reporter, had equipped him for the task. He had trained and served as a Marine. He knew how to handle himself in a fight. He had seen men deal with death and had dealt with it himself when he saw friends die. He had found peace and a kind of acceptance when life was elemental, when simple choices had simple consequences, when the decision to turn a corner or climb a hill could be fatal: the beautiful simplicity of war.

Vietnam wasn't simple.

Years before intervention was seen as an option, Beech had lamented America's tendency to buck rather than back a revolution. He was sometimes reminded that Ho Chi Minh was a revolutionary leader seeking to liberate his country from colonial rule. After the French were defeated at Dien Bien Phu, he mooted the question of American involvement. "The French don't want the U.S. in," he wrote. "The Vietnamese don't either. And the U.S. does not want to get in. These would seem to be three excellent reasons for not getting in." His reasoning was impeccable.

And yet America went in for reasons Beech chose to accept. He ignored the argument often made by opponents that the conflict was a civil war from which outsiders had nothing to profit. He saw the war in its regional context—he was after all the *Chicago Daily News* Far East correspondent—as part of the larger struggle between democracy and Communism, a struggle being played out in countries throughout the region, from Japan to Korea, the Philippines, Indonesia, Malaya, and Thailand. He believed that America had to set an example, to make a stand. He made this argument the theme of *Not Without the Americans* and stuck with it. He never accepted the dissidents' view that the war was immoral. Morality wasn't at issue as far as he was concerned. He had long known that war is hell.

It was at this juncture, when he accepted his government's decision to send American troops into Vietnam, that Beech's war got complicated.

He still spoke for many Americans, for a majority for much of the war, for people like him who believed in America, in what it represented. There was a reason why newspapers across the country continued to feature Beech's articles on the front page. These were newspapers served by the Chicago Daily News Foreign Service that were mainly in the hinterland, rather than on the coast, whose readers knew nothing of Halberstam, Browne, Arnett, and Sheehan. They viewed the anti-war movement as subversive. The culture wars of the 1960s worried them. They were men and women of Beech's generation, most of them, people who like him remembered the Depression and America's rise to glory in World War II. It was their children who were drafted, more or less willingly, and who put their lives at risk.

But opposition to the war was heard almost as soon as American advisers attached to the ARVN first took casualties. Senators voiced concern. Correspondents wrote dispatches, and photographers captured images—of civilians killed, Buddhists bonzes on fire, and enemy soldiers tortured—that made Americans uncomfortable. A student movement first stirred by the demand for civil rights added the war to its critique of America, seeing racist oppression at home and colonial oppression abroad. Even the administration was divided. In the end, first Johnson and then Nixon wanted nothing so much as to get out.

The war's opponents were on to something that Beech had known but chose to ignore: that the government in Saigon was barely legitimate, created on paper at Geneva and never intended to last. It was an autocracy, far from being democratic, and thoroughly corrupt. Americans—acting in good faith—devoted years and uncounted billions of dollars to propping up Vietnam's government and armed forces in a futile effort to make them self-sustaining, capable of standing alone. As often as they tried, they acknowledged that they were failing. And the gap between the hope and the reality explained, at least in part, the lies.

In the early years, when Beech was just visiting, the reporters based in Saigon had better sources than he did. They knew the mission was led by incompetents, that official utterances were unreliable when they weren't deliberately misleading. They operated on the assumption that nothing could be believed that they had not seen themselves. The best of them, Halberstam, Browne, Arnett, and Sheehan, knew the coup was coming when Beech had no idea. It wasn't just that they were in the field more: he went out with them, he saw what they saw, and his reports were as accurate as theirs were. He was always a good reporter. But the resident reporters were there all the time. They had no ties to the people who staffed the American mission, and no reason to trust them. When their own experience collided with the official story, they went with what they knew. For Beech, this was harder.

It was harder because the staff officers were his peers: their backgrounds were similar; they were much the same age. He didn't believe they would mislead him. And it was harder because he had implicit faith in America, its military and industrial might and what it represented. The Communists had to be defeated. The job would get done.

And so he was conflicted, and his dispatches reflected both his own confusion and the dissension at home. By reporting accurately what he saw while staying true to what he believed, he often seemed to be making the case for both sides. He wrote that American pilots were strafing Viet Cong fighters, but there was no way to tell Viet Cong fighters from farmers. He wrote that the Strategic Hamlet Program was working but also that it probably wouldn't work. After the battle at Ap Bac he wrote that American advisers "charged Vietnamese officers with refusing to order men into battle," and that American officials denied it, saying "it was a defeat only in the sense that government forces failed to come to grips with the enemy." (Which sounds a lot like defeat.) He wrote repeatedly that it was a dirty war, an implicit recognition that the means by which it was fought were counterproductive at best, and probably immoral. He reported official statistics but learned in time to doubt them. He believed Westmoreland was running the war effectively, until he didn't. He called Nixon's Cambodia incursion "furtive and un-American." And when Nixon broke the Christmas truce in 1972, he wrote that you didn't have to be a Communist "to sympathize with a small country that is being bombed to pieces by the most powerful nation on earth," especially, he added, when the justification was "to put it mildly, unclear."

War wasn't simple anymore. America was divided—and so, in a way, was he. Beech understood that America had failed, that it had lost the will to go on, but he never accepted that this was the way it had to be. This put him at odds with the many reporters and that part of the public that had long deplored America's conduct of the war. The war's opponents were vindicated and even pleased in the end, while he experienced the defeat as a personal humiliation. It was fury that infused his last dispatches with their force.

Some critics blamed the media for stoking dissent at home by publishing downbeat stories. Beech wasn't one of them—not while the war lasted—although he was sometimes critical of his colleagues. He never forgave Morley Safer, whose report from Cam Ne traduced the Marines. He had chided Arnett for his "Lost Column" article, saying he'd been so caught up in the story that he lost perspective. They remained friends. "The reporting from Saigon may at times leave a good deal to be desired," he told an interviewer, but "it has a sort of confused honesty compared to the dreary tripe" uttered by some of the nation's leading intellectuals. He detested the pontificating academics back home. He regularly disparaged young reporters in general for their lack of experience, for not knowing, as their older colleagues did, that war is hell. He wasn't alone in this. Over the course of the war, thousands of journalists were accredited by the military mission. There were six hundred in Saigon after Tet in 1968. Many were novices. As a matter of course, senior reporters who were present at the start of the war moved on, making room, in historian William Hammond's words, for younger men "who often were less sympathetic to the official point of view." Their bias may or may not have skewed their reporting, but Beech was not alone in viewing them with disdain.

It was only much later, when he retired and was back in the States, as William Prochnau observed, "that Beech became angry and joined the national search for scapegoats." Denis Warner was one of the instigators of that search. In a book describing Hanoi's road to victory, Warner quoted an unnamed intellectual saying that "this is the only war ever lost in the columns of the *New York Times*." Whatever the identity of his source, Warner clearly shared the opinion. He went further, suggesting that the newspapers' anti-war posture was at least partly the product of "the most skilfully handled wartime propaganda campaign that the world has ever seen." It wasn't just, as Beech had reported, that Hanoi was counting on America to become exhausted by the loss of American lives and the endless unfulfilled promises of victory. In Warner's telling, the Communists mounted a concerted and ultimately successful campaign to fund, befriend, and influence the anti-war movement. The media, by implication, was manipulated into serving the enemy's purpose.

Another of Beech's correspondent friends, Robert Elegant, writing in the pages of *Encounter* magazine, took a slightly different tack in making the same argument. "For the first time in modern history," he wrote, "the outcome of a war was determined not on the battlefield, but on the printed page and, above all, on the television screen." The charge that the "television war" in particular turned the American public around was to become its own subgenre in the debate over press and media influence. It was a line especially favored by the generals glad to escape blame.

"I don't think I'd go quite that far," wrote Beech in January '83, in a belated response to Elegant's article published two years earlier, "but the media helped lose the war. Oh yes, it did, not because of any massive conspiracy but because of the way the war was reported." Like others who could not let go of the fact that the mightiest nation on earth had been defeated by a tiny faraway country that possessed barely a fraction of its resources, he fell back on a proposition that would often be repeated in the years that followed: that "the war was lost in the U.S., not in Vietnam. American troops never lost a battle; but they never won the war."

The statement does him no credit. America's military failed in Vietnam. The only general who emerged from the war with an undamaged reputation was Creighton Abrams, whose task it was to manage the withdrawal.

Beech was still based in Hong Kong when the war ended. He remained the Far East correspondent for the *Chicago Daily News* and continued to travel around the region. He was nearly sixty-three, however, nearing retirement age and with his third wife, Yuko, and infant daughter, Hannah, to consider. In the summer of '76, he left them with Yuko's mother in Tokyo while he took a trip to the States. His purpose, he told his oldest son, Walter, was "to finally make up my mind where I want to settle and what I want to do when I turn in my trench coat, which I anticipate will be some time next year." The paper, he said, wanted him to serve out his last two years in the Far East, but he was thinking of retiring early.

The paper changed its mind. The *Daily News* was running at a loss. In December it recalled its foreign staff and sent Beech to Washington. Beech bought a house in Bethesda, Maryland. He'd be covering the political scene again, the one he'd left years earlier, before he made the leap from Washington to Hawaii. His sojourn in the capital was brief: in March 1978 the *Daily News* closed its doors for good and Beech hit the road again. He stopped to visit family in Tennessee and his sister in Florida. He saw colleagues in Ohio and friends in New Mexico. And then he drove to California where both his first and second wives were living at the time, along with two of his three sons. Thinking his future lay on the West Coast, he bought a house in Poway, near San Diego. He lived there for a while but confessed to son Barnaby that he knew only one of his neighbors and was at a loss for something to do. He told friends at the *Beacon Journal* that he wasn't sure that he was ready for retirement.

He wasn't. He accepted an offer from the *Los Angeles Times* to serve as their Southeast Asia correspondent based in Bangkok. He took over the position from his old friend George McArthur and wrote his first piece for the *Times* in January 1979. There were no wars to cover, but he still had an eye for a colorful incident and an ear for a telling phrase, and his pieces found their way regularly into the pages of the paper. He finally, really retired in spring 1982, returning with Yuko and Hannah to a comfortable house in Sumner, a suburb of Bethesda. Here, he slowed down at last, becoming an attentive husband and father, in a neighborhood where sometimes the sound of a lawnmower or backfiring car disturbed the peace.

Vietnam continued to dog him. He gave occasional interviews and attended colloquia devoted to the war. At a seminar he had a run-in with Morley Safer. He called him "one of that new breed of super-slick TV hit men," to which Safer responded by calling Beech an "old hack." He was present at a rowdy reunion of Vietnam War correspondents in New York that brought some four hundred newsmen and women together eleven years after the war had ended. There were rumors that General Westmoreland, Walter Cronkite, and Dan Rather would address them, but they didn't show, and the lectern was turned over to Robin Moore, author of *The Green Berets*, whose remarks, according to Tim Page, took a "neo-colonialist" turn that caused the audience to mutter its displeasure until George McArthur finally bellowed that Moore was an asshole and demanded that he sit down, which he did.

Eddie Adams made a presentation in which he showed images taken by photographers who died in Vietnam and Cambodia. This brought on a moment of silence. And later Beech stood up to deliver a toast "to all the Asians who died in the war." Some of his colleagues, he said, had reported that the Vietnamese didn't fight, but 254,000 were killed between 1960 and 1974. And, he added, "I don't think they were all shot in the back." The assembled correspondents rose, raised their glasses, and once again were silent.

The wars had left their mark. Barnaby was with his father one time when they took the car through a car wash and a fracas broke out on the pavement outside: a woman and a man were screaming at each other, and then the woman pulled out a knife and thrust it at her assailant's throat. Barnaby was shocked. His father laughed. Another time, Barnaby and Walter were with their father at a restaurant when Beech fell silent. Their family gatherings were rarely silent. Minutes passed before Barnaby finally asked what he was thinking. Beech said he was remembering a time when he was in a plane over Vietnam and there was flak all around. They were well within range of the anti-aircraft guns below, and they stayed there for a long time. On another occasion, when Barnaby was visiting, Beech paused as he was shaving and said, "I've seen so many people die, it doesn't bother me anymore. And that bothers me."

McArthur and Beech remained close. They shared memories of good times and bad, and an appreciation of attractive women. (Beech, in his seventies, once sent Barnaby a postcard that pictured a bikini-clad woman on a beach and invited his son to join him for a week in Fort Lauderdale. Barnaby, who had just graduated from college and started a new job, regretted having to say no.)

The years of smoking and hard living finally had their effect, and Beech developed emphysema. Friends rallied to his side when he was hospitalized. McArthur was a regular visitor. Barnaby recalls seeing his father on oxygen, having difficulty breathing, his voice raspy. McArthur finally said, "Goddammit Keyes, you're making me nervous. I gotta go have a cigarette." McArthur had told Barnaby that he "had a slot in the longest running poker game in town" and was anxious to get back to it. Beech knew it too. "Okay, George," he said. “You go have your cigarette.”

Keyes Beech passed away in Sibley Memorial Hospital, Washington, DC, on February 15, 1990. He was buried in Arlington Cemetery.

Notes on Sources

The spelling of proper names, especially locations in Southeast Asian countries, varies with time and source. Contemporary readers may be unfamiliar with China's capital being called Peking rather than Beijing, for example. The transliteration of Korean place-names has similarly changed. In general, I have stuck with the spellings used by Beech and other writers at the time. A few choices are necessarily arbitrary. Dien Bien Phu was sometimes rendered as Dienbienphu, Vietnam as Viet Nam, and Viet Cong as Vietcong. To be consistent is one thing, to be up to date, another. I've tried for consistency.

Abbreviations used in the notes that follow:

- KB *TAPE*: Keyes Beech, *Tokyo and Points East*. New York: Doubleday, 1954.
- KB *NWTA*: Keyes Beech, *Not Without the Americans*. New York: Doubleday, 1971.
- *Akron BJ*: *Akron Beacon Journal*
- *CDN*: *Chicago Daily News*
- *Hon SB*: *Honolulu Star-Bulletin*
- NARA: National Archives and Records Administration
- *PP*: *Pentagon Papers*, Gravel edition. Boston: Beacon Press, 1971.
- *St. Pete EI*: *St. Petersburg Evening Independent*

CHAPTER 1: BEFORE THE WAR

Pulaski

Background Sources

Information about Beech family history has been drawn from reports in the *St. Petersburg Times*, *Tampa Sunday Tribune*, and *St. Petersburg Evening Independent*; the US Census for 1920 and 1930; the Florida State Census, 1935; the St. Petersburg city directory; and *TAPE*.

- "a stringbean of a youngster": Don Whitehead, Don Whitehead Reports, *Knoxville News-Sentinel*, August 14, 1960, 69.

Green Park Benches

Background Sources

St. Petersburg Museum of History; Will Michaels, *The Making of St. Petersburg* (Charleston, SC: History Press, 2012).

- "Lee Davis, a two-gated gambolier": KB, "Local Lad Goes Down Under Fire," *St. Pete EI*, September 20, 1933, 6.
- "I can't see why all this fuss": KB, "Seeking Utopia," *St. Pete EI*, February 6, 1935, 1.
- "That can wait": KB, "Career to Come First," *St. Pete EI*, March 10, 1935, 9.
- "their blue-clad ranks": KB, "Thinning G.A.R. Ranks," *St. Pete EI*, April 16, 1935, 1.
- "cadaverous and hopeless informant": KB, Beech Combings, *St. Pete EI*, April 13, 1935, 2.
- "middle-aged urge for youthful company": KB, Beech Combings, *St. Pete EI*, January 18, 1936, 2.
- "Browder, short, middle-aged": KB, "Mob Assaults Browder," *St. Pete EI*, October 26, 1936, 1.
- "Eccentric Noel A. Mitchell": KB, "Mitchell Nabbed Asleep," *St. Pete EI*, April 29, 1936, 2; "Noel A. Mitchell Found Asleep," *St. Petersburg Times*, April 29, 1936, 1; "Mitchell Allowed Delay," *St. Petersburg Times*, April 30, 1936, 16.

- "Mitchell fought the charge": KB, "Mitchell Found Not Guilty," *St. Pete EI*, May 1, 1936, 5; AP, "Green Bench Giver," *Tampa Bay Tribune*, May 1, 1936, 13.

Hell Wagons

- "During the three-hour drive to Columbus": KB, "Tried to Strangle Garber," *Akron BJ*, February 2, 1938, 1, 6; KB, "Bravado Fades," *Akron BJ*, February 3, 1938, 6.
- Wellsburg "marriage racket"; "He brought the blackjack down": KB, "Minister Uncovers Racket," *Akron BJ*, June 16, 1940, 1, 8; KB, "Marriage Mill Keeps Pastor in Bondage," *Akron BJ*, June 17, 1940, 1, 7.
- "Harlem Hal": KB, "Not for Speculation, But," *Akron BJ*, January 14, 1940, 17.
- "Old Sgt. Pat Raleigh"; "Raleigh and party started": KB, Biography in Brief, *Akron BJ*, November 12, 1939, 10.
- "His only concession to judicial dignity"; "the dean of Summit county": KB, Biography in Brief, *Akron BJ*, October 29, 1939, 8.
- "a nightmare of sour faced": KB, "Informal Business," *Akron BJ*, October 25, 1938, 11; KB, "Code of the Open Road," *Akron BJ*, October 26, 1938, 7; KB, "Drunk Drivers, Inspectors," *Akron BJ*, October 27, 1938, 17; KB, "Haulers Aren't at All Fond of New York City Helpers," *Akron BJ*, October 28, 1938, 37.
- "The roaring sound": KB, "Turnpike Becomes War Road," *Akron BJ*, September 6, 1942, 1, 5.
- "All day long, all night long": KB, "Turnpike Becomes War Road," *Akron BJ*, September 6, 1942, 1.
- "Occasionally, someone passed through town": KB, "2 Scars Remind Akron Man of Liner 'Hoover' Bombing," *Akron BJ*, September 20, 1937, 1.
- "As martial music echoed": KB, "Akron Peace Forum Hears Keep-Out-Of-War Ways," *Akron BJ*, November 12, 1937, 6.
- "At 5:15 a.m. an A.P. bulletin": KB, "Wait for War," *Akron BJ*,

September 4, 1939, 13.

- "Some unruly fellow": KB, "Russia Is Utopia," *Akron BJ*, March 15, 1938, 17.
- "Useless but well-meaning citizen": KB, "Communist Leaders Register for Defense," *Akron BJ*, December 21, 1941, 12.
- "Beech traveled to Detroit on his union's behalf": Robert H. Stopher, "Behind the Front Page," *Akron BJ*, June 22, 1941, 46; KB, "How to Lose a War: A Response from an Old Asia Hand," in Harrison E. Salisbury, ed., *Vietnam Reconsidered: Lessons from a War* (New York: Harper Torchbooks, 1984), 151–52. See also James S. Pooler, "Leaders Ask for Unity," *Detroit Free Press*, June 24, 1941, 3.
- "He was in his attic apartment": KB, *TAPE*, 105.
- "You don't give a damn": KB, "Did You Ever Ride," *Akron BJ*, May 15, 1941, 1, 2.

CHAPTER 2: WAR IN THE PACIFIC

The Birds on Betio

Background Sources

Joseph H. Alexander, *Utmost Savagery: The Three Days of Tarawa* (Annapolis, MD: Naval Institute Press, 1995); Maj. David N. Bruckner, *A Brief History of the 10th Marines* (Washington, DC: History and Museums Division USMC, 1981), 65; Harry A. Gailey, *The War in the Pacific* (Novato, CA: Presidio, 1995), 254–62; Charles T. Gregg, *Tarawa* (New York: Stein and Day, 1984); Robert Sherrod, *Tarawa: The Story of a Battle* (New York: Duell Sloan and Pearce, 1944); Earl J. Wilson et al., *Betio Beachhead: U.S. Marines' Own Story of the Battle for Tarawa* (New York: Putnam, 1945).

Extracts from KB's dispatches from his time with the 2nd Marines on Tarawa: National Archives and Records Administration (NARA), National Archives, College Park, MD. RG 0127, US Marine Corps Division of Public Administration. Entry #A1 1004, Story Files of

Former Public Information Division, Enlisted Personnel (Inactive), 12/1942–10/1946, box #3, Beech, Tarawa.

- "It was their job": George McMillan et al., *Uncommon Valor: Marine Divisions in Action* (Washington, DC: Infantry Journal Press, 1946), 18.
- "Mr. Murphy could": KB dispatch, September 10, 1943, NARA.
- "I suppose men have been saying": James Jackson, Behind the Front Page, *Akron BJ*, August 15, 1943, 45.
- "When the batteries in our rear": KB dispatch, September 10, 1943, NARA.
- "We chortled": KB dispatch, November 20, 1943, NARA.
- "I didn't get ashore"; "That night the Japs launched"; "The next morning": Staff, "Tarawa's Sky Like Portage Country Club on July 4—Beech," *Akron BJ*, January 2, 1944, 33.
- "A bird flew in": KB dispatch, November 24, 1944, NARA.
- Siwash: Picture of the Week, *Life*, January 17, 1944, 21. See also Douglas M. Allen Jr., "Siwash's Snub Leaves Keyes Beech Bitter," *Akron BJ*, June 30, 1947, 8.
- "It was like any new camp": KB dispatch, December 16, 1943, NARA.

The Flag

Background Sources (General)

Robert S. Burrell, *The Ghosts of Iwo Jima* (College Station: Texas A&M University Press, 2006); Harry A. Gailey, *The War in the Pacific* (Novato, CA: Presidio 1995), 408–21; Captain Raymond Henri et al., *The U.S. Marines on Iwo Jima* (Washington, DC: Infantry Journal Press, 1945); George McMillan et al., *Uncommon Valor: Marine Divisions in Action* (Washington, DC: Infantry Journal Press, 1946); Gordon L. Rottman, *World War II Pacific Island Guide: A Geo-Military Study* (Westport, CT: Greenwood Press, 2002), 420–26.

Background Sources (The Flag)
James Bradley, with Ron Powers, *Flags of Our Fathers* (New York: Bantam, 2000); Daniel L. Bronson, "The Picture That Will Live Forever," *Us* magazine, February 25, 1985, 24–29; Albert Hemingway, *Ira Hayes: Pima Marine* (Lanham, MD: University Press of America, 1988); William Bradford Huie, *The Hero of Iwo Jima* (New York: Signet, 1962); Karal Ann Marling and John Wetenhall, *Iwo Jima: Monuments, Memories, and the American Hero* (Cambridge, MA: Harvard University Press, 1991); Tedd Thomey, *Immortal Images: A Personal History of Two Photographers and the Flag-Raising on Iwo Jima* (Annapolis, MD: Naval Institute Press, 1946); Derrick Wright, *The Battle for Iwo Jima, 1945* (Thrupp, UK: Sutton, 1999).

Background Sources (The Flag Raisers)
Robert S. Burrell, *The Ghosts of Iwo Jima* (College Station: Texas A&M University Press, 2006), 81; Matthew Hansen, "New Mystery Arises from Iconic Iwo Jima Image," *Omaha World Herald*, November 23, 2014, http://www.5thmarinedivision.com/flag-raisers.html; Michael S. Schmidt, "Man in Iwo Jima Flag Photo Was Misidentified Marine Corps Says," *New York Times*, June 23, 2016, https://www.nytimes.com/2016/06/24/us/politics/marines-iwo-jima-flag-photo-mistaken-identity.html; and https://www.stripes.com/news/us/marine-corps-flag-raiser-in-iconic-iwo-jima-photo-was-harold-keller-not-rene-gagnon-1.603396/keller-1.603471.

Extracts from KB's dispatches from his time with the 5th Marines on Iwo Jima: National Archives and Records Administration (NARA), National Archives, College Park, MD. RG 0127, US Marine Corps Division of Public Administration. Entry #A1 1004, Story Files of Former Public Information Division, Enlisted Personnel (Inactive), 12/1942–10/1946, box #3, Beech 1945.

- "There was a day when": Jim Schlemmer, "Marine Tells Gobs," *Akron BJ*, April 26, 1944, 15.
- "Up all hands!": KB, McMillan, *Uncommon Valor*, 163–64.
- "Everybody drops into this hole": KB dispatch, February 19, 1945, NARA.
- "The first of the walking wounded": KB dispatch, February 20, 1945, NARA.
- "If you will excuse the first person": KB, "Beech Pens Tribute," *Akron BJ*, April 15, 1945, 5.
- "At Iwo Jima, when my best friend was killed": KB, *TAPE*, 33–34.
- "On Iwo, where men lived with death": KB, "Suribachi," in Henri, *The U.S. Marines on Iwo Jima*, 97–98.
- "Out of countless tales of heroism": KB dispatch, February 22, 1945, NARA.
- "In the four-day battle": KB dispatch, February 24, 1945, NARA.
- "Marine Platoon Sergeant Ernest I. Thomas": KB dispatch, February 25, 1945, NARA.
- "Fox company's command post": KB dispatch, March 2, 1945, NARA.
- "Except for a couple of days' rest": KB dispatch, March 12, 1945, NARA.
- "There was a humming sound": KB dispatch, March 13, 1945, NARA.
- "You know these Jap grenades": KB dispatch, March 12, 1945, NARA.
- "The bodies of Marine dead": KB dispatch, March 24, 1945, NARA.
- "We were up on a sort of ridge": KB dispatch, March 30, 1945, NARA.

The Sky Room

- "Did they tell you it was a small world?": KB dispatch, March 27, 1945, NARA.

- "Keyes was a big drinker": Bradley, *Flags of Our Fathers*, 284.
- "Our fighting men 'get sore as hell'": "Talk of Jap War End Ires Yanks Says Beech," *Akron BJ*, May 18, 1945, 43.
- "I [knew] if anyone tried to take it": Hemingway, *Ira Hayes*, 131–33.
- "the War Bond drive is show business"; "I was sweating blood": Huie, *Hero of Iwo Jima*, 38–44.
- "That evening . . . Beech watched as Ira Hayes": Hemingway, *Ira Hayes*, 131–33.
- "It was a circus": Bronson, "Picture That Will Live Forever," 24–29.
- On postwar life of Bradley, Gagnon, and Hayes, see Bradley, *Flags of Our Fathers*, 3–5 and 331–37; Hemingway, *Ira Hayes*, 46–63.

CHAPTER 3: BETWEEN WARS I

The Bomb

- "still a little dizzy about it all": Charles C. Miller, "Keyes Beech's Saga of Death on Bloody Iwo," *Akron BJ*, March 31, 1945, 1, 11.
- "Testimony Before the Mead Committee": KB, "Thefts at P.H. Revealed," *Hon SB*, October 25, 1945, 1.
- "Native teams have defeated navy players": KB, "Majuro Natives Beat Navy Teams at Baseball," *Hon SB*, November 4, 1946, 10.
- "The most spectacular sight": KB, "Explosion Most Spectacular Yet Seen by Man," *Hon SB*, July 25, 1946, 4.
- "I looked at him and thought": KB, "This Little World," *Hon SB*, August 29, 1946, 6.

MacArthur's Japan

- "It is inconceivable that a man": KB, "Unpleasant Facts Kept from MacArthur," *Akron BJ*, August 7, 1947, 9.
- "My mistake was to beat the general": KB, "Journey to Peiping—With a Chinese General," *Hon SB*, December 27, 1947, 8.
- "I wanted absolutes to cling to": KB, *TAPE*, 33.
- "the people of Chicago are not interested": KB, "Correspondents

Still Being Curbed in Tokyo," *Akron BJ*, June 27, 1948, 10.

- "he accused Beech of 'professional incompetence'": KB, "Gen. Casey Calls Beech," *Hon SB*, July 10, 1948, 8; KB, *TAPE*, 50–51.

Two Hundred Communists

- "One candidate . . . established campaign headquarters": KB, "In the Orient," *Hon SB*, January 19, 1949, 8.
- "a refugee-swollen city": KB, "Seoul Seems Drab to Foreigners," *Hon SB*, April 18, 1949, 2.
- "The Chinese peasants": "Keyes Beech Sees Communists Scoring Gains," *St. Petersburg Times*, July 23, 1949, 13.
- "two hundred 'known Communists' in Hawaii": KB, "Stainback Keeps List of 'Reds' in His Desk Says Keyes Beech," *Hon SB*, August 22, 1949, 3.
- "It doesn't really matter"; "One reason we have failed": KB, "Wants U.S. to Start Backing Revolutions," *Akron BJ*, May 5, 1950, 41.
- "From Tokyo we hear": "Mainly About People," *Hon SB*, April 8, 1950, 15.

CHAPTER 4: WAR IN KOREA

The Beautiful Simplicity of War

- "None of the men said so": KB, *TAPE*, 108.
- "I hate to say this": KB, *TAPE*, 120.
- "Now I didn't have to get up": KB, *TAPE*, 163.

Higgins

Background Sources

Marguerite Higgins, *News Is a Singular Thing* (Garden City, NY: Doubleday, 1955); Toni Howard, *Shriek with Pleasure* (New York: Signet, 1950); Richard Kluger, *The Paper: The Life and Death of the* New York Herald Tribune (New York: Knopf, 1986); Antoinette May, *Witness to War: A Biography of Marguerite Higgins* (New York:

Beaufort Books, 1983).

- "blonde, 23-year-old war correspondent": Peter Furst, "Dachau Cheers Its Liberation from Horror and Death," *Stars and Stripes*, May 2, 1945.

Escape from Seoul

Background Sources

KB, *TAPE*, 112–22; KB, "'I Have Feeling It's Start of World War III' Says Keyes Beech Under Fire," *Herald-News* (Passaic, NJ), June 29, 1950, 1, 2; Burton Crane, "South Koreans Kill Own Troops by Dynamiting a Bridge Too Soon," *New York Times*, June 29, 1950, 3; Frank Gibney, in Michelle Ferrari, ed., *Reporting America at War: An Oral History*, large print ed. (Waterville, ME: Thorndike Press, 2004), 102–16; Marguerite Higgins, *War in Korea* (New York: Doubleday, 1951), 18–30; May, *Witness to War*, 136–41; John Toland, *In Mortal Combat: Korea, 1950–1953* (New York: William Morrow, 1991).

- "The poor fools didn't know": Toland, *In Mortal Combat*, 50.
- "'a rather jazzy blue and white' number": Gibney, in *Reporting America at War*, 106.
- "The American planes will come tomorrow": KB, *TAPE*, 116.
- "Out of the cloudless sky came six": Crane, "South Koreans Kill Own Troops," 3.
- "Maggie was mad about losing the dress": May, *Witness to War*, 140–41.
- "no place for a woman": KB, *TAPE*, 166.
- "General, I'm glad to see you here": Toland, *In Mortal Combat*, 60.
- "dramatically buoyed the defenders' morale": Marguerite Higgins, "South Korean Panic Gone Following General's Visit," *Boston Globe*, June 30, 1950, 4.
- "Do they really think this handful of men": Higgins, *War in*

Korea, 43.

- "we'll fight the Russkies too"; "The miscellaneous group of 232 American officers": KB, "U.S. Troops Ready to Fight Russians in Korea—Gen Church," *Boston Globe*, July 1, 1950, 1, 3.

The Defense of Taejon

Background Sources

Roy E. Appleman, *South to the Naktong, North to the Yalu* (Washington, DC: Center of Military History, United States Army, 1961); Toland, *In Mortal Combat*; Betsy Wade, ed., *Forward Positions: The War Correspondence of Homer Bigart* (Fayetteville: University of Arkansas Press, 1992).

- "What a place to die!": Marguerite Higgins, "Death of the First Infantryman," *New York Herald Tribune*, July 5, 1950, 1, 2.
- The agencies "have whole companies of men": KB, "War Correspondent in Korea—Lots of Work for Little Results," *Herald-News* (Passaic, NJ), August 4, 1950, 8.
- "Why are Homer and Maggie beating our asses": Kluger, *The Paper*, 446.
- "'inconceivable' that the North could stand against": KB, "A Primitive Foe," *Kansas City Star*, July 3, 1950, 5.
- "American and Australian fighter planes": KB, "Troop Morale Rises," *Washington Evening Star*, July 10, 1950, 1.
- "As the Americans came down": KB, "Enemy Suddenly Descends on U.S. Troops in Village," *CDN*, July 9, 1950, 1, 5.
- "we have been getting our teeth kicked in": KB, "Yanks Back Up from Tanks They Can't Stop," *Akron BJ*, July 8, 1950, 1, 2.
- "Russian-managed Oriental peasants": KB, "Beech Tells Why U.S. Is Taking a Drubbing," *CDN*, July 15, 1950, 1. Beech tells a modified version of the story in *Tokyo and Points East*, where the regimental commander is identified as Colonel Richard W. Stephens, 24th Battalion, 8th Army.

- "My men won't fight": KB, "Lack of Know-How, Leadership," *Tampa Tribune*, July 27, 1950, 2; KB, *TAPE*, 147.
- "It would be difficult to find a parallel": Appleman, *South to the Naktong*, 164.
- "a number of soldiers who fled": Homer Bigart, "Weary GIs Give Accounts," *Morning Call* (Allentown, PA), July 21, 1950, 1, 21.
- "The United States Army suffered": KB, "Yank Trucks of Taejon Wounded," *St. Louis Post-Dispatch*, July 20, 1950, 7.
- "Kimba, 'a fast man on the draw'": KB, "Yank Trucks of Taejon Wounded," 7; Denis Warner, *Wake Me If There's Trouble* (Ringwood, Victoria, Australia: Penguin, 1995), 150–51; Homer Bigart, "Weary GIs Give Accounts," *Morning Call* (Allentown, PA), July 21, 1950, 1, 21.

"I Should Have Been Blown Up"

- "I saw one first lieutenant": KB, "Lack of Know-How, Leadership," 2; KB, *TAPE*, 157–58.
- "The officers . . . fresh from service in Europe": Frank Gibney, "The First Three Months of War: A Journalist's Reminiscences of Korea," *Journal of East-Asian Relations* 2, no. 1 (Spring 1993): 101–10.
- "We drove one mile to the deserted village": KB, "Yanks Too Green to Mine Roads," *St. Louis Post-Dispatch*, July 24, 1950, 2.
- "Communications have improved greatly": "Had to Use What We Had," *Boston Globe*, July 28, 1950, 5.

The Pusan Perimeter

- "machine-gun bullets ripped": KB, "Coffee Pot Explosion Signaled Red Attack," *St. Louis Post-Dispatch*, August 3, 1950, 7.
- "one correspondent learned how": Marguerite Higgins, "Woman Reporter Pinned by Fire," *Morning Call* (Allentown, PA), August 4, 1950, 1, 13.
- Higgins "saved the lives of many": letter to the editor of the

New York Herald Tribune, reprinted in *Boston Globe*, September 15, 1950, 9.

- "The hill is nameless but not the Marines": KB, "Glimpses of the Korean War," *Boston Globe*, August 9, 1950, 3.
- "The Marines went up the hill"; "Men were falling like flies": KB, "Glimpses of the Korean War," *Boston Globe*, August 9, 1950, 3.
- "The Marines ran into their toughest fight"; "I watched through binoculars"; "An aging gunner sergeant": KB, "Marines Reach Goal But Pay," *St. Louis Post-Dispatch*, August 17, 1950, 2.
- "Washington's apparent refusal": KB, "Length of Korean War," *Boston Globe*, August 19, 1950, 1, 7.
- "The '8th Army's handsome, fair-headed boy'": KB, "War Zone Quiet," *Akron BJ*, August 24, 1950, 1, 2.
- "The enemy has only one regiment": KB, "Reds Said to Have Little in Reserve," *St. Louis Post-Dispatch*, August 12, 1950, 2.
- "which of the landing waves": Joseph W. Alsop, with Adam Platt, *I've Seen the Best of It: Memoirs* (New York: Norton, 1992), 319–20.

Night at the Chosun Hotel

- "the brooding face of a man of destiny": KB, "MacArthur's Greatest Feat," *Hon SB*, January 27, 1950, 11.
- "It was the most uneventful beachhead": KB, "Blazing Inchon 'So Awful,'" *Akron BJ*, September 16, 1950, 1.
- "Even as the Chosun moves": KB, "Reporter Going Back to Seoul," *Boston Globe*, September 18, 1950, 4.
- "it was good to be back": KB, "Herald Writer Leads Lost Marines," *Miami Herald*, September 19, 1950, 1.
- "That's the way I like to see them!": Toland, *In Mortal Combat*, 201–2.
- "well scrubbed and rosy-cheeked": KB, "Herald Writer Leads Lost Marines," 1.
- "We were out of our jeep": KB, *TAPE*, 161. "Seoul City Sue" was

the sobriquet given to the American-born woman who broadcast anti-American propaganda from North Korea during the war—the Korean War equivalent of Tokyo Rose.

- "One of us should go back and file": KB, *TAPE*, 172.
- "I died approximately one thousand times": KB, "Seoul Attack Delights Ex-Marine," *Nashville Banner*, September 21, 1950, 1, 4.
- "We came in here with a humanitarian viewpoint": KB, "Reporter's Laundry Missing," *Boston Globe*, September 28, 1950, 12.
- "Tonight in the gathering dusk": KB, *TAPE*, 174; KB, "Tolling Church Bells Mingle," *Fort Worth Star-Telegram*, September 25, 1950, 1. Without the snap of a leatherneck's quote, Higgins's lede was less punchy than Beech's: "A bell—the only thing left in a church stripped by Communist North Koreans—rang for American Marines Sunday afternoon after forward units of the Leathernecks for the first time pierced into Seoul proper." Marguerite Higgins, "Bell Tolls for Marines," *Morning Call* (Allentown, PA), September 26, 1950, 1, 17.
- "The marines fought their way": KB, "Fighting for City Vicious," *Akron BJ*, September 26, 1950, 1.
- "Civilians emerged from alleys": KB, "Tolling Church Bells Mingle," *Fort Worth Star-Telegram*, September 25, 1950, 1.
- "That night, Beech set out to retrieve his laundry": KB, *TAPE*, 175–76; KB, "Reporter's Laundry Missing," 12.
- Ray Murray, "whose nose still bears a mark": KB, "Emotion Fills Air," *Akron BJ*, September 29, 1950, 1, 2.
- "When the war began": KB, *TAPE*, 153.

Ray Murray Sheds a Tear

Background Sources

Billy C. Mossman, *Ebb and Flow: November 1950–July 1951* (Washington, DC: Center of Military History, United States Army, 1990), 84–103, 128–37. See also the unsigned pamphlet,

First Marine Division, Chosin Reservoir (Washington, DC: US Government Printing Office, 1951), which contains reports by Marine combat correspondents.

- "Riding in a jeep with Maggie": William Prochnau, *Once Upon a Distant War* (Westminster, MD: Times Books, 1995), 343.
- "Miss Higgins already has become a legend": Carl Mydans, "Girl War Correspondent," *Life*, October 2, 1950, 51–54.
- Beech's "best combat buddy": KB, *TAPE*, 183.
- "the best Christmas present of all": KB, "Early GI Withdrawal," *Akron BJ*, October 23, 1950, 1.
- "It was so cold . . . that men's feet froze": KB, *TAPE*, 196.
- "Remember . . . this was no retreat": KB, "No Retreat . . . We About-Faced," *Boston Globe*, December 11, 1950, 2.
- "Keyes! What the hell" and "Almond had to know": Toland, *In Mortal Combat*, 346–47; KB, "No Retreat . . . We About-Faced," 2; Zona Murray, *High Pockets: The Man, the Marine, the Legend* (Conneaut Lake, PA: Page, 2019), 212.
- "That's us, we never got the word": KB, *TAPE*, 201.
- "Evidently the general and I": KB, "War-Battered Seoul Shrouded in Gloom," *CDN*, December 13, 1950, 1.
- "He was the loneliest boy in the world," and the second fall of Seoul: KB, "Beech Sees Reds Take Over," *CDN*, January 4, 1951, 1, 4; KB, *TAPE*, 176–77. See also Toland, *In Mortal Combat*, 384.

CHAPTER 5: BETWEEN WARS II

The Pulitzer

- Russia-China basketball game: KB, "Russian Rules, Russia Wins!" *Akron BJ*, January 25, 1951, 1.
- "As soon as Homer kills off Maggie": Carl Mydans, "Girl War Correspondent," *Life*, October 2, 1950, 51–54.
- "No way can I make my behavior": Richard Kluger, *The Paper: The Life and Death of the* New York Herald Tribune (New York:

Knopf, 1986), 448.

- "To cover a war properly": KB, *TAPE*, 207–8.

Truce and Consequences

Background Sources

Wilfred Burchett, *At the Barricades* (London: Quartet, 1991). On the Communist promotion of germ warfare propaganda and the American reaction, see AP, "Red Charges U.N. Is Dropping Bugs on North Korea," *St. Louis Post-Dispatch*, February 22, 1952, 1; Ross Valentine, "Germ Warfare Soviet Style," *Richmond Times-Dispatch*, March 12, 1952, 14; Phillip Knightley, *The First Casualty: The War Correspondent as Hero Propagandist and Myth Maker from the Crimea to Vietnam* (London: André Deutsch, 1975), 351–52; AP, "Senators Claim G.I.s Untrained for Red Cruelty," *Boston Globe*, December 30, 1956, 4; Milton Leitenberg, letter to the editor, "No They Didn't," *New York Review of Books*, March 22, 2018, 45.

On the American pilots: KB, "U.N. Prisoners Grateful, Reds Violent and Rebellious," *Hon SB*, August 8, 1953, 12, and "POWs Give N. Koreans Big Edge in Brutality," August 13, 1953, 3. The account of the Mahurin and Evans interview is drawn from KB, "Yanks Tell How Mental Torture Forced Germ War Confessions," *St. Louis Post-Dispatch*, September 8, 1953, 2. See also KB, *TAPE*, 238–43.

On the acrimonious relationship between Warner and Burchett, see Denis Warner, *Call Me If There's Trouble* (Ringwood, Victoria, Australia: Penguin, 1995), 13–54, and *Not Always on Horseback* (St. Leonards, NSW, Australia: Allen & Unwin, 1997), 131–32. Gavan McCormack, "Korea: Wilfred Burchett's Thirty Years' War," in Ben Kiernan, ed., *Burchett Reporting the Other Side of the World* (London: Quartet, 1986), 162–211; Alex Carey, "The Bureaucratic Passport War: Wilfred Burchett and the Australian Government," also in Kiernan, 61–107; Jamie Miller, "Once Were Warriors: Wilfred

Burchett, Robert Manne, and the Forgotten History War," *New Critic* 8 (September 2008), http://www.ias.uwa.edu.au/new-critic.

- "Beech wrote about the confessions": KB, "Reds Cleverly Put Over Charge of U.S. Germ War," *Fort Worth Star-Telegram*, May 8, 1952, 32.
- "fleas, lice, bugs, ants": AP, "Red Charges U.N. Is Dropping Bugs on North Korea," *St. Louis Post-Dispatch*, February 22, 1952, 1.
- "thin to the point of emaciation": KB, "Yanks Tell How Mental Torture Forced Germ War Confessions," 2.
- "I only met him last night": KB, *TAPE*, 238–43.
- "always a competent craftsman": KB, "Australian Poor Boy," *Minneapolis Star*, October 27, 1953, 19.
- "like a snake staring at a mouse": Warner, *Not Always on Horseback*, 192.
- "Is this s.o.b. telling me the truth?": KB, "The CIA as a Source," in Harrison E. Salisbury, ed., *Vietnam Reconsidered: Lessons from a War* (New York: Harper Torchbooks, 1984), 129–30.

A Pretty Crummy War

Background Sources

Stanley Karnow, *Vietnam: A History* (London: Pimlico, 1994); John Mecklin, "The Revolt That Failed," *Time*, May 9, 1955, 18–19; John Prados, *Vietnam: The History of an Unwinnable War* (Lawrence: University Press of Kansas, 2009); William Prochnau, *Once Upon a Distant War: Young War Correspondents and the Early Vietnam Battles* (New York: Times Books, 1995); *Pentagon Papers*, vol. 1.

- "like Christians to await the lions": Warner, *Wake Me If There's Trouble*, 211.
- "a pretty crummy war": KB, *TAPE*, 252.
- "Do you like schematics?": KB, "Red Death Squeeze," *Boston Globe*, April 27, 1954, 1, 9.

- "Our altitude was a healthy 10,000 feet": KB, "Rebel Fire Outlines Besieged," *Boston Globe*, April 28, 1954, 1, 11.
- "they don't even have a logistics planning section"; "like an over-ripe melon": KB, "Indecent Luxury Flaunted," *Miami Herald*, April 29, 1954, 67.
- "I have no adjectives for today": KB, "Fort Counts Last Minutes," *CDN*, May 4, 1954, 2.
- "We're blowing up everything. Adieu": Bernard Fall, *Hell in a Very Small Place: The Siege of Dien Bien Phu* (Philadelphia: Lippincott, 1967), 408.
- "The United States position": KB, "You Can't Beat Something with Nothing," *Minneapolis Sunday Tribune*, July 25, 1954, 40.

Carpe Diem

Background Sources

Max Boot, *The Road Not Taken: Edward Lansdale and the American Tragedy in Vietnam* (New York: Liveright, 2018), 234–74; Cecil B. Currey, *Edward Lansdale: The Unquiet American* (Boston: Houghton Mifflin, 1988), 167–77; *PP*, vol. 1, 219–31; Warner, *Wake Me If There's Trouble*, 231–45.

- "The curse of French colonialism": KB, "Roulette Wheels Whir," *The Province* (Vancouver), October 22, 1954, 3.
- "A Time-Life journalist, John Mecklin": Warner, *Wake Me If There's Trouble*, 234–36.
- a "scene that compared with Seoul": KB, "Diem Looks Solid," *Minneapolis Star*, May 4, 1955, 1.
- "They . . . say Diem is stubborn, narrow-minded": KB, "Frightened French in Saigon," *St. Louis Post-Dispatch*, May 6, 1955, 21.
- "the country's 'weird assortment of racketeers, cutthroats'": KB, "Stubborn Premier Checks Reds," *Akron BJ*, May 30, 1955, 2.
- "the government had 'not only managed to survive'": KB, "South Vietnam with President," *Fort Worth Star-Telegram*, May

15, 1956, 45.

- "a 'beautiful doll of a woman'": KB, "She Redecorated the Palace," *Herald-News* (Passaic, NJ), May 23, 1956, 8.
- "The French don't want the U.S. in": KB, "The Truth About Indochina," *The Province* (Vancouver), April 23, 1954, 1, 3.
- "The French haven't won a war": Thomas Thayer, "Patterns of the French and American Experience in Vietnam," in W. Scott Thompson and Donaldson D. Frizzell, eds., *The Lessons of Vietnam* (New York: Crane, Russak, 1977), 36.

Revolution in Sumatra

- "How does it feel to be the husband": KB, "I Lost My Wife to Tokyo TV," *Saturday Evening Post*, April 25, 1959, 32–33, 89–92.
- "out of his depth when talking": George E. Taylor, "The Asia He Saw," *New York Times Book Review*, December 5, 1954, 18.
- KB, "lean, hard and handsome enough": "Indomitable Beech," *Newsweek*, November 29, 1954, 59.
- "I don't see anything here for the Duke": KB, "Hollywood's Oriental Fad," *Saturday Evening Post*, May 10, 1958, 28–29, 99–104.
- "opportunity to back rather than buck"; "the strangest revolution I have ever attended": KB, "Red Conquest Is Feared If Indonesia Rebels Lose," *Hon SB*, March 20, 1958, 4, and *NWTA*, 268, 273–75.
- "Warner and MacGregor had entered": Warner, *Wake Me If There's Trouble*, 266–75.
- "This TV business is taking up more time": KB, "I Lost My Wife to Japanese TV," 32–33, 89–92.

CHAPTER 6: THE AMERICAN WAR IN VIETNAM

Battle Lines

- "there better be three hundred bodies": Betsy Wade, ed., *Forward*

Positions: The War Correspondence of Homer Bigart (Fayetteville: University of Arkansas Press, 1992), 116–17.
- "we've got twenty Vietnams to deal with": Stanley Karnow, *Vietnam: A History*, rev. ed. (London: Pimlico, 1991), 265.

Vietnam's Churchill

- Johnson "drowned them in torrents of praise": KB, "Diem Hailed by Johnson," *Akron BJ*, May 13, 1961, 1, 2.
- Diem "is remote from the people": *PP*, vol. 2, 59.
- ARVN needed "to learn to live and fight like Communists": KB, "Vietnam Not Pushing Effort," *Akron BJ*, October 25, 1961, 1, 2.
- "I don't see nothing": Karnow, *Vietnam*, 271.
- "If they're dead, they're Viet Cong": KB, "We Aren't Losing," *Cincinnati Enquirer*, April 8, 1962, 16.

Ap Bac

- "Beware . . . of any information at all you get": Peter Arnett, *Live from the Battlefield: From Vietnam to Baghdad* (New York: Simon & Schuster, 1994), 77.
- "the strategic hamlets hold great promise": KB, "On South Vietnam," *Hon SB*, April 24, 1962, 7.
- "humorless, egotistical, incredibly stubborn": John Mecklin, *Mission in Torment: An Intimate Account of the U.S. Role in Vietnam* (Garden City, NY: Doubleday, 1965), 31, 62.
- "sink or swim with Ngo Dinh Diem": William Prochnau, *Once Upon a Distant War* (New York: Times Books, 1995), 49.
- "Neil Sheehan would make much of Ap Bac": Neil Sheehan, *A Bright Shining Lie: John Paul Vann and America in Vietnam* (New York: Random House, 1988), 203–65.
- "one of the stiffest fights of the war": KB, "Big Push Ready in New Phase," *CDN*, January 11, 1963, 4. See also Jack Shulimson, *The Joint Chiefs of Staff and the War in Vietnam, 1960–68, Part 1* (Washington, DC: Office of Joint History, 2011), 277–80.

- "It's entirely possible that American officials": KB, "Viet Nam Reds Reel," *CDN*, January 24, 1963, 2.

Caravelle Camaraderie

- "someone . . . would inadvertently create some type of disturbance": Interview with Daniel Boone Porter, March 29, 1982, LBJ Presidential Library, Oral History.
- "Everything was wrong": Horst Faas, Skype interview with author, March 5 and 9, 2012.
- Rusk "made a point of emphasizing the improvement": *New York Times*, August 17, 1963, 1.
- "On May 8, a Buddhist monk": see Denis Warner, "A Dynasty in Disorder," *The Reporter*, September 12, 1963, 34–35. Warner drew on sources in the intelligence community, probably including Lou Conein, to write a remarkably complete account of the riot and its consequences. Among other details, he identified the leaders of the coup that was to overthrow Diem two months before it happened.
- "If ever there was a man": KB, "Diem Driving Viet Nam to Chaos," *CDN*, June 14, 1963, 2.
- "normally pleasant capital": KB, "Nobody at All Might Be Better," *Detroit Free Press*, June 20, 1963, 6.
- "describing the street-corner immolation as a 'barbecue'" and "if she had her way the Buddhists": Mecklin, *Mission in Torment*, 170.
- Re: Diem's attack on the pagodas on August 20, see David Halberstam, *The Making of a Quagmire* (New York: Random House, 1965), 228–41.
- Diem had "won his battle with the Buddhists": KB, "Vietnamese Dragon Lady," *CDN*, August 22, 1963, 2.
- "In Washington, however, Kennedy's advisers": see John Prados, *Vietnam: The History of an Unwinnable War* (Lawrence: University Press of Kansas, 2009), 77–81.

- "Diem. . . must be given the chance": *PP*, vol. 2, 208–36.
- Kennedy: "With changes in policy and perhaps in personnel": *PP*, vol. 2, 241–42.
- Diem "is at war with his own people": KB, "U.S. Threatens Aid Cut," *Akron BJ*, August 26, 1963, 1.
- "no longer sleep in their homes": KB, "U.S. Threatens Aid Cut," *Akron BJ*, August 26, 1963, 1. See also Mecklin, *Mission in Torment*, 201–5; Prochnau, *Once Upon a Distant War*, 376; Denis Warner, "Agony in Saigon: The Lady and the Cadaver," *The Reporter*, October 10, 1963, 39–42.
- "It's getting so you don't amount to anything": KB, "Do Viets Have List," *Akron BJ*, September 10, 1963, 2.
- "You always look like the fucking company commander": Prochnau, *Once Upon a Distant War*, 260.
- "Browne had warned Arnett": Arnett, *Live from the Battlefield*, 76; Prochnau, *Once Upon a Distant War*, 306–7, 331, 375.
- "a fire-eating quote Commie-hater close quote": Prochnau, *Once Upon a Distant War*, 332.
- "Why don't you come on out and lose some weight?": KB, letter to MH, October 4, 1961, Marguerite Higgins Papers, Special Collections Research Center, Syracuse University Libraries, Higgins, box 1, folder: Beech, Keyes.
- "Viet Nam—Fact and Fiction": The series of articles by Higgins was published in the *New York Herald Tribune*, August 26 to September 1, 1963.
- On the Saigon reporters and Higgins: Prochnau, *Once Upon a Distant War*, 347–51.
- Fuerbringer, "'For all the light' they shed on the war": "Foreign Correspondents: The View from Saigon," *Time*, September 20, 1963, 52. See also W. A. Swanberg, *Luce and His Empire* (New York: Scribner's, 1972), 437–41.
- "a goddamned lie . . . and so is the rest of that crap": Prochnau, *Once Upon a Distant War*, 410.

- "In 16 years as a correspondent": KB, "Real Viet Story: Is It Being Told?" *CDN*, September 21, 1963, 1, 6.
- "nobody around here has a lust for power": KB, "U.S. a Bust at Busting Regimes," *Akron BJ*, September 27, 1963, 5.
- "Americans . . . aren't any good": KB, "U.S. a Bust at Busting Regimes," *CDN*, October 30, 1963, 2 (a different version of the article that appeared earlier in the *Akron BJ*).
- Beech article "a cautionary reminder": Malcolm Browne, *Muddy Boots and Red Socks* (New York: Times Books, 1993), 155.
- "the 'pleasant rustle of freedom'": KB, "Air of Freedom Flies," *CDN*, November 8, 1963, 3.
- "some thoughts how best to phrase": Higgins Papers, Higgins, box 10, folder: Ngo Dinh Nhu.
- "Where the hell do we go from here?": KB, *NWTA*, 104–5.

A Time for Warriors

- "something about Kennedy wounded in Dallas": Faas, interview with author, March 5 and 9, 2012.
- "I tell you, things are coming unstuck": KB, "South Viet Has Tools," *Akron BJ*, February 18, 1964, 2.
- Burchett on the Ho Chi Minh Trail: William G. Burchett, *Vietnam: Inside Story of the Guerrilla War*, 2nd ed. (New York: International Publishers, 1965).
- "a 'neutralist government'": KB, "Viet Reds Spreading Peace Talk," *Akron BJ*, November 14, 1964, 1, 2, and November 20, 1964, 1, 2.
- Re: the Gulf of Tonkin incident, see Edwin E. Moise, *Tonkin Gulf and the Escalation of the Vietnam War* (Chapel Hill: University of North Carolina Press, 1996); Daniel Ellsberg, *Secrets: A Memoir of Vietnam and the Pentagon Papers* (New York: Penguin, 2002), 7–20.
- "living in the hole of a doughnut": KB, "Americans Uneasy," *Pittsburgh Press*, August 12, 1964, 24.

- "Bundy blinked in the glare of the sunlight": KB, "Beech Takes the Bus," *CDN*, February 8, 1965, 1, 4.
- "Oh, they'll rattle their rockets, all right": KB, "Correspondents in Saigon Not Shocked," *Miami Herald*, June 18, 1974, 15A.
- "He said nothing of adding more later": see Daniel Ellsberg, *Secrets: A Memoir of Vietnam and the Pentagon Papers* (New York: Penguin, 1992), 88–95.
- "The 173rd is so security conscious": KB, "Search-and-Destroy Effort," *CDN*, August 2, 1965, 2.
- "That isn't the way I remember it": KB, "Heat and Heartbreak," *CDN*, August 11, 1965, 1, 2.
- "the dirtiest war Americans ever had to fight": KB, "The Dirty War in Vietnam," *CDN*, August 7, 1965, 2.
- Safer's account of the operation at Cam Ne: Morley Safer, *Flashbacks: On Returning to Vietnam* (New York: Random House, 1990), 88–92.
- "When Americans first 'swept' the village": KB, "Dirty War in Vietnam," 2.
- "More than 25,000 U.S. marines": KB, "Marines Fight Reds and Critics in the U.S.," *CDN*, August 12, 1965, 2.
- "smashing first-round victory": KB, "Young Marines Prove They Can Beat Reds," *CDN*, August 20, 1965, 2.
- "American military commanders have a load": KB, "Yanks' Viet Victory," *CDN*, August 21, 1965, 1, 2.
- On Arnett's story of the "lost column," see Peter Arnett, "Marine Supply Trip Runs into Disaster," *Evening Star* (Washington, DC), August 19, 1965, 1; AP, "Death Overtakes a U.S. Supply Unit," *New York Times*, August 20, 1965, 1; Arnett, *Live from the Battlefield*, 169–77; Marine Corps Command Center report on Operation Starlite, Vietnam Archive, Texas Tech University, acc. no. 1201063060.pdf: "Operation Starlite 18–24 Aug 1965," item 13, MCCC, HQS, USMC, 20 August 1965, Memo for the Record.

- "Sometimes reporters—good ones": "Who's News with Cobey Black," *Hon SB*, January 1, 1966, 26.
- "acres of PSP (perforated steel planking)": KB, "Screwy War to Lawmaker," *Cincinnati Enquirer*, November 22, 1965, 11.
- "we could save a lot of bloodshed": KB, "Peace in Viet More Remote," *Akron BJ*, November 18, 1965, 1.
- "It would be most agreeable": KB, "Both Sides Past Point of No Return," *Lincoln (NE) Journal Star*, November 26, 1965, 2.
- "a sort of confused honesty": KB, "Why We Fight," *Akron BJ*, February 2, 1966, 8.
- Ky "displayed an insatiable curiosity": KB, "Ky Plays Poker," *Akron BJ*, February 7, 1966, 2.
- "Boy . . . you speak just like an American": Nguyen Cao Ky, *How We Lost* (New York: Stein and Day, 1978), 81.
- Humphrey "so overcome by his own eloquence": KB, "Humphrey Beguiles," *Tampa Times*, February 19, 1966, 1.
- "Colonialism was their theme": KB, "Bandung Spirit," *Philadelphia Inquirer*, May 29, 1966, 65.
- "a small, hard-driving man"; "a funny way to fight a war": KB, "Cheerful GIs in Viet War Make General Choke Up," *Miami Herald*, June 10, 1966, 12.
- "now over 270,000 men": KB, "U.S. Buildup Speeds Tempo," *Philadelphia Inquirer*, July 3, 1966, 50.
- "By prolonging the war": KB, "Top Defector Tells," *Charlotte News*, December 3, 1966, 2.
- On Western visitors to Hanoi, see James Cameron, *Witness* (London: Victor Gollanz, 1966); Staughton Lynd and Thomas Hayden, *The Other Side* (New York: New American Library, 1966); Harrison Salisbury, *Behind the Lines* (New York: Harper & Row, 1967).
- "I don't see any fire down there": KB, "A Day in the Life," *Herald-News* (Passaic, NJ), January 24, 1967, 12.
- "no reason for the returning soldier"; "It took me back to the

days": KB, "Return of a Warrior," *Dayton Daily News*, April 18, 1967, 6.

- "North Vietnamese troops will filter": KB, "Vietnam—Answers," *Philadelphia Inquirer*, April 30, 1967, 132.
- "just 'the hippies and the teeny boppers'": KB, "Reporter Sees Peril," *Houston Chronicle*, May 7, 1967, 21.
- "I'm not going to say whether I will": President's Daily Diary, entry 5/13/1967, President's Daily Diary Collection, LBJ Presidential Library; KB, "Nixon's Risk," *Parsons (KS) Sun*, May 9, 1972, 2.

"War Isn't Fun Any More"

- "Anybody on the streets"; "Westmoreland keeps saying": KB, "Saigon: Anyone Out After 5," *CDN*, February 5, 1968, 1, 2.
- "well-laid plans . . . went afoul": Don Oberdorfer, *Tet!* (New York: Doubleday, 1971), 34.
- "Things are not so bad": KB, "Heavy Red Losses," *CDN*, February 8, 1968, 2.
- "They actually persuaded themselves": KB, "Big Red Push," *Boston Globe*, February 12, 1968, 8.
- "Commercial airline companies"; "I waited behind a sandbagged bunker": KB, "Nobody Walks in Khe Sanh," *CDN*, February 20, 1968, 2.
- "a remote patch of earth"; "Westmoreland's whole military future": KB, "Yanks at Khe Sanh," *CDN*, February 21, 1968, 2.
- "This used to be a right pretty town": KB, "Requiem for Proud City," *CDN*, February 26, 1968, 2.
- "Westmoreland's conduct of the war": KB, "Enemy's Strategy in Vietnam," *CDN*, February 29, 1968, 2.
- "War isn't fun any more": KB, "A General's Agony: 'Why Are We Here?'", *CDN*, March 11, 1968, 1, 2.
- "There has been more personal soul-searching"; "From the mist-shrouded northern highlands": KB, "From North to South,"

CDN, March 4, 1968, 2.

- "They speak of Ky and Thieu factions": KB, "Vietnam No. 2 Man," *Miami Herald*, August 4, 1968, 186.
- "But sir . . ."; "Stop shooting at the electricity": KB, "News Commentary," *York Dispatch* (PA), June 7, 1968, 4–5.
- "Both on the battlefield": KB, "Hanoi's Tactics Turn Fuzzy," *Philadelphia Inquirer*, September 25, 1968, 19.
- On the "often bitter, tension-packed negotiations" and Nixon's interference, see "News Media Coverage of Vietnam, Miscellaneous, April 1968–December 1968," LBJ National Security Files, 1963–1969, folder 002795-032-0122, LBJ Library (accessed through ProQuest History Vault); Ky, *How We Lost*, 166–67; John A. Farrell, *Richard Nixon: A Life* (New York: Doubleday, 2017), 342–44; KB, "U.S Gets Tough for Peace Plan," *Akron BJ*, October 18, 1968, 1; KB, "U.S. More Hard-Boiled," *Oklahoma City Times*, October 25, 1968, 42; KB, "Saigon Angered by Halt," *Des Moines Tribune*, November 1, 1968, 1, 6; KB, "U.S. Tried to Trick Us," *Akron BJ*, November 5, 1968, 1, 2; KB, "LBJ Becomes Most Hated Man," *Miami Herald*, November 5, 1968, 101.

We Learned Not to Run

- "frustrated by what he saw as a double standard": KB, "Communist Strategy Is Working," *Herald-News* (Passaic, NJ), April 15, 1959, 14.
- "In nearly all cases the pattern": KB, "Another Mass Grave," *Sunday Press* (Binghamton, NY), November 9, 1969, 64.
- "They were the only ones left to kill": KB, "Survivors' Stories Indicate 350–400 Died in Massacre," *Boston Globe*, December 1, 1969, 1, 3.
- "They [the Americans] were sweating": KB, "Survivor Tells of Son's Death at My Lai," *Port Chester (NY) Daily Item*, December 3, 1969, 28.

- "Before somebody proposes": KB, "The Other Side of the Calley Case," *Boston Globe*, April 6, 1971, 1, 21.

My Immunity Failed Me

- "the most heavily bombed piece": KB, "When B-52 Bombs Hit," *Akron BJ*, February 2, 1966, 74.
- On the "secret war" and Nixon's response, see John Osborne, *The Second Year of the Nixon Watch* (New York: Liveright, 1971), 41–45.
- "It looks like just another Laotian crisis": KB, "Struggle over Control," *Houston Chronicle*, March 6, 1970, 1, 2.
- "Pedicab boys tried to peddle": KB, "Sihanouk's Aim: Boot Reds," *Houston Chronicle*, March 15, 1970, 8.
- "If you attend enough wars": KB, "War Marks Cambodia," *Akron BJ*, June 30, 1970, 6.
- "huge columns of smoke": KB, "100,000-Man Provincial Guard," *Cleveland Press*, March 26, 1970, 11.
- "This lovely little town"; "The peasants . . . do not have": KB, *NWTA*, 289.
- "At least half a dozen times": KB, "Peasant Revolt Grows," *San Francisco Examiner*, March 30, 1970, 1, 6.
- "Casually, almost contemptuously": KB, "Viet Reds Swat Cambodians," *Miami Herald*, April 9, 1970, 3.
- "Nearly 100 Vietnamese civilians"; "But there were few"; "Half a dozen survivors": KB, "It's a Massacre," *Akron BJ*, April 11, 1970, 1.
- "The slaughter of Vietnamese civilians": KB, "50 Bodies Floated Past—Then I Gave Up Counting," *Toronto Star*, April 17, 1970, 39.
- "But what leaves the stomachs"; "This time the scene": KB, "Genocide in Cambodia?" *San Francisco Examiner*, April 18, 1970, 1, 2.
- "Half a dozen trucks": KB, "Phnom Penh Sees Growing Red Menace," *Des Moines Tribune*, April 22, 1970, 2.

- "So long as they don't bother me": KB, "Cambodia Struggle Shapes Up as Another Laos as Reds Recruit Peasants," *Buffalo News*, April 23, 1970, 5.
- "Before the Americans came": KB, "Cambodia Lived in Peace," *Des Moines Tribune*, May 6, 1970, 10.
- "furtive, un-American war": KB, "Asian Peace Prospects Poor," *Corpus Christi Times*, May 18, 1970, 1.
- "The 'melancholy lingers on'"; "I think all of us were aware": KB, "War Marks Cambodia," *Akron BJ*, June 30, 1970, 6.
- "It's as though they were saying": KB, "Little Black Puffs," *Charlotte Observer*, February 14, 1971, 2.
- "After a decade of bitter fighting": KB, "Tribal Chieftans Run Out of Sons," *Parsons (KS) Sun*, February 22, 1971, 7.
- "Our intelligence was lousy": KB, "Hill 31 Survivors Critical of U.S. Air Support," *Evening Press* (Binghamton, NY), March 3, 1971, 1, 9.
- "Buildings are blown up": KB and Georgie Ann Geyer, "Pick Any Bombing," *Miami Herald*, October 13, 1970, 1, 18.
- "Casual, sometimes cynical" and "To be without illusions": Maj. Harry G. Summers Jr., "Putting Vietnam in Perspective," *Kansas City Times*, February 17, 1971, 34; John P. Roche, "Keyes Beech Has Put His Finger on Asian Situation," *Journal & Courier* (Lafayette, IN), March 30, 1971, 4.
- "We had not won the war": KB, *NWTA*, 321.
- "in order to make the election": KB, "Bunker Knew Thieu Rigged Vietnam Election," *Boston Globe*, August 25, 1971, 2; KB, "Did U.S. Envoy Attempt," *Miami Herald*, August 29, 1971, 3A, 123; Ky, *How We Lost*, 194–95; KB, "Thieu Triumphs," *Billings Gazette*, October 4, 1971, 1.
- On leaving Saigon: "I don't want to talk to anybody": KB, "One Man's Farewell," *Parsons (KS) Sun*, October 30, 1971, 6.

GI Go Bye-Bye

- "act of an angry and desperate man": KB, "Nixon's Risk: Bigger War," *Parsons (KS) Sun*, May 9, 1972, 2.
- "the most savage bombing": KB, "Did Nixon Overplay Hand on Bombing," *Parsons (KS) Sun*, December 26, 1972, 4.
- "It was a most unhappy war": KB, "Vietnam—1949–1973," *Boston Globe*, January 24, 1973, 3.
- "GI go bye-bye": KB, "Now, GI-Pure Saigon," *Des Moines Tribune*, May 1, 1973, 11.
- On the return of American POWs: KB, "Reporter Compares Operations," *Mercury* (Manhattan, KS), February 9, 1973, 20; and KB, "POW Bitterness," *Charleston Daily Mail*, February 13, 1973, 1.
- "so thick with anti-aircraft weapons": KB, "Communist Strength in South Viet Is Highest Ever," *Miami Herald*, December 26, 1973, 92.
- "sacrificing blood for lack of ammunition": KB, "Aid Cut Alarms Saigon," *Corpus Christi Times*, August 22, 1974, 28.
- "So much for peace with honor": KB, "Shabby End," *Corpus Christi Times*, April 1, 1975, 14.
- "There ought to have been a less shabby end": KB, "Shabby End," *Corpus Christi Times,* April 1, 1975, 14.
- "Thus began the exodus": KB, "No Poor Soldiers, Only Poor Leaders," *Commercial Appeal* (Memphis, TN), April 6, 1975, 2.
- "Some obviously would have been better off": KB, "Survival of the Fittest," *Commercial Appeal* (Memphis, TN), April 12, 1975, 11.
- "Beech 'liked to be where the action was'": Denis Warner, *Not Always on Horseback* (St. Leonards, NSW, Australia: Allen & Unwin, 1997), 217–18.
- "North Vietnamese forces were tightening": KB, "Xuan Loc Falls," *Des Moines Tribune*, April 18, 1975, 1, 2.
- "The final American bugout": KB, "Final American Bugout,"

Lincoln (NE) Journal Star, April 23, 1975, 16.

- "If the airlift continues long enough": KB, "Refugees Reflect High, Low Life of Vietnam," *Commercial Appeal* (Memphis, TN), April 29, 1975, 2.
- "Nobody on the bus will ever forget": KB, "A Desperate, Chaotic Exodus," *Des Moines Tribune*, May 2, 1975, 4. See also Milton J. Bates et al., eds., *Reporting Vietnam Part Two: American Journalism 1969–1975* (New York: Library of America/Penguin, 1998), 531–36.
- "I was on your side": David Butler, *The Fall of Saigon* (New York: Simon & Schuster, 1985), 478.

CHAPTER 7: AFTER THE WAR

- "War . . . has been part of the Asian scene": Beech, *NWTA*, 3.
- "Well, if that was the case": KB, *TAPE*, 163.
- "Technical Sergeant Beech continued to expose himself": Marine Citation, courtesy of Walter Beech.
- "The French don't want the U.S. in": KB, "The Truth About Indochina," *The Province* (Vancouver), April 23, 1954, 1, 3.
- "The reporting from Saigon": KB, "Why We Fight," *Akron BJ*, February 2, 1966, 8.
- On the number of journalists in Saigon: William M. Hammond, "Who Were the Saigon Correspondents and Does It Matter?," Joan Shorenstein Center, Working Paper Series (Harvard University, 2000), https://shorensteincenter.org/wp-content/uploads/2012/03/2000_08_hammond.pdf.
- "who often were less sympathetic": William M. Hammond, *Reporting Vietnam: Media and Military at War* (Lawrence: University Press of Kansas, 1998), 126–27.
- "that Beech became angry": Prochnau, *Once Upon a Distant War*, 268n.
- "the only war ever lost": Denis Warner, *Certain Victory: How Hanoi Won the War* (Kansas City: Sheed Andrews and McMeel,

1978), 182–86, 205.

- "For the first time in modern history": Robert Elegant, "How to Lose a War," *Encounter* 57, no. 2 (1981): 73–90.
- "I don't think I'd go quite that far": KB, "Elegant's Viet Nam," letter to the editor, *Encounter* 60, no. 1 (1983): 94.
- "one of that new breed": Prochnau, *Once Upon a Distant War*, 268.
- "took a 'neo-colonialist' turn": Tim Page, "Reliving the Fight," *The Independent* (London), November 25, 1986, 6.
- "to all the Asians who died in the war": "Vietnam War Reporters Reminisce at Reunion," *New York Times*, November 23, 1986, 37.

Index

Note: Page numbers in italics refer to figures.

About the Author

Jonathan Webb is the author of half a dozen books in almost as many genres, including a prize-winning adult novel and a number of books for young readers. Much of his career has been as editor and publisher with Canadian publishing houses. He attended Queen's University and the University of Toronto, where he earned a master's degree in history. He lives with his wife, Vivian, in Guelph, Ontario.

www.ingramcontent.com/pod-product-compliance
Lightning Source LLC
LaVergne TN
LVHW091300250826
846436LV00026B/188
9781682833193